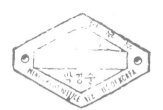

REPUBLIC OF KENYA
IMMIGRATION OFFICER
110
10 NOV 1998
NAIROBI AIRPORT

DEPARTMENT OF IMMIGRATION
PERMITTED TO ENTER
AUSTRALIA
on 24 APR 1986
For stay of 12 Month
SYDNEY AIRPORT 54

IMMIGRATION DIVISION BANGKOK THA.
A
72
DEPARTED
SIGNED

D1120720

IMMIGRATION & ETHNIC AFFAIRS
...........Person
30 OCT 1989
DEPARTED
AUSTRALIA
SYDNEY 32

T R A V E L E R'S
KENYA
C O M P A N I O N

上陸許可
ADMITTED
15. FEB. 1986
Status: 4-1-4
Duration: 90 days
NARITA(N)
Immigration Inspector
日本国

ADMITTED
20 OCT. 1988
Status: 4-1-16
Duration 180 day
Port: HANEDA
Signature

№ 011278

THE UNITED STATES
OF AMERICA
NONIMMIGRANT VISA
ISSUED AT

PASSED
Air Port

U.S. IMMIGRATION
170 HHW 1710
JUL 2 0 1983

HONG KONG
(1038)
- 7 JUN 1987
IMMIGRATION
OFFICER

The 1998–1999 Traveler's Companions

ARGENTINA • AUSTRALIA • BALI • CALIFORNIA • CANADA • CHINA • COSTA RICA • CUBA •
EASTERN CANADA • ECUADOR • FLORIDA • HAWAII • HONG KONG • INDIA • INDONESIA • JAPAN •
KENYA • MALAYSIA & SINGAPORE • MEDITERRANEAN FRANCE • MEXICO • NEPAL • NEW ENGLAND •
NEW ZEALAND • PERU • PHILIPPINES • PORTUGAL • RUSSIA • SPAIN • THAILAND • TURKEY •
VENEZUELA • VIETNAM, LAOS AND CAMBODIA • WESTERN CANADA

Traveler's KENYA Companion
First Published 1999
The Globe Pequot Press
6 Business Park Road, P.O. Box 833
Old Saybrook, CT 06475-0833
www.globe.pequot.com

ISBN: 0-7627-0359-8

By arrangement with Kümmerly+Frey AG, Switzerland
© 1999 Kümmerly+Frey AG, Switzerland

Created, edited and produced by
Allan Amsel Publishing, 53, rue Beaudouin
27700 Les Andelys, France.
E-mail: Allan.Amsel@wanadoo.fr
Editor in Chief: Allan Amsel
Editor: Anne Trager
Original design concept: Hon Bing-wah
Picture editor and designer: Laura Purdom and David Henry

All rights reserved. No part of this publication may be reproduced, stored in
a retrieval system, or transmitted in any form or by any means, electronic,
mechanical or otherwise without the prior permission of the publisher.
Requests for permission should be addressed to Allan Amsel Publishing,
53 rue Beaudouin, 27700 Les Andelys France outside North America;
or to The Globe Pequot Press, 6 Business Park Road, P.O. Box 833,
Old Saybrook, CT 06475-0833 in North America.

Printed by Samhwa Printing Co. Ltd., Seoul, Korea

TRAVELER'S KENYA COMPANION

by Jack Barker, Peggy Bond and Michael Bond

photographs by Storm Stanley

Kümmerly+Frey

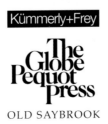

The
Globe
Pequot
Press

OLD SAYBROOK

Contents

TRAVELER'S
KENYA
COMPANION

Kimili
Peris

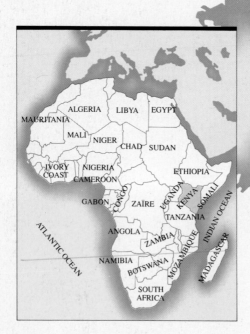

100 miles

160 km

TOP SPOTS

Ride the Lunatic Line

UNTIL THE LAST CENTURY KENYA'S CAPITAL WAS MOMBASA, AND NAIROBI WAS JUST A SWAMP. What opened up the country's interior was the "Lunatic Line," the railway track laid across the country even before the colonial forces had explored the interior and well before there were any settlers to actually use the railway. In 1896 the first stretches were laid, and for the next three years the track made laborious progress through forest and swamp, across river and mountain. Twenty-eight workers were eaten by lions and countless more died of disease, and laborers imported from India were to permanently change the demography of Kenya. By the time the track reached Nairobi, in 1899, sheer exhaustion might have dictated a permanent settlement;

while the railway tracked on to the shores of Lake Victoria and would eventually split off to reach Uganda, the city that is now capital of Kenya took shape.

The story is vividly told in Nairobi's Railway Museum, on Station Road but best reached by taxi, complete with the first trains and carriages that opened up the continent.

However if the museum experience isn't enough, the railway line itself still provides one of the great train journeys of the world. While road traffic founders in the washed-out surface of the road to the coast, the train runs from Nairobi to Mombasa, every night, in a white-gloved atmosphere of ultimate luxury. For 12 hours — admittedly, sometimes it takes longer — the train makes stately progress along the meter-gauge track, passing through Tsavo and down to the steaming flatlands of the coast. Three-course meals prelude nights spent rocked to sleep by the unhurried motion of the ancient train, turned-back linen sheets recreating a golden age of colonial luxury. Dining is on crisp white tablecloths using crockery left over from the colonial era. Sometimes it seems as though the cuisine dates back from the same period. Don't expect haute: hope for wholesome.

OPPOSITE: The Kenya Railway, once nicknamed the Lunatic Express, winds up and down near-vertical Rift Valley escarpments TOP and dashes straight across the flat Tsavo plains BOTTOM. The locomotive used in *Out of Africa* is on display at the Nairobi Railway Museum ABOVE.

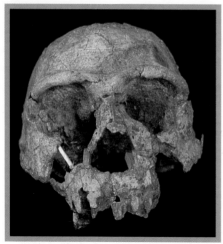

crosses one of the few international borders still with neither electricity nor telephone: the journey takes 24 hours and although the same luxuries are available on board, many travelers find this is just too slow a way of completing a journey that takes eight hours by *matatu*, the packed local minibuses, and one by air. The track east of Nairobi is sometimes washed out and the service doesn't always take passengers.

Reservations are essential for traveling first or second class: reserve the day before, although two or three days in advance is safer, to secure a berth. Without a reservation you'll end up traveling on the benches in third. Reservations can be made in person at Nairobi Station, one and a half kilometers (one mile) from the city center on Station Road, or at Mombasa Station, on Haile Selassie Avenue near the junction with Moi Avenue. Reservations are apparently taken by telephone, **Nairobi** ((02) 221211, **Mombasa** ((011) 312221, or perhaps easiest through a travel agent such as **Let's Go Travel** ((02) 340331 FAX (02) 336890 E-MAIL info@letsgosafari.com, Box 60342, Nairobi.

In first-class compartments just two passengers share a cabin fitted with washbowl and served by an attentive drinks waiter: linking two cabins together is possible for families on the move. Second-class travel puts four to a cabin but is also perfectly acceptable. Third — crammed wooden seats with chickens in the aisles — might be cheap but is not recommended for overnight journeys. And in Kenya almost all rail trips take place at night. First-class tickets cost 3,000 KSh and include all meals. The perfectly adequate second-class fares are 2,100 KSh per person. Third-class travel does not include food, a reserved seat, or even a seat of any kind, but only costs 300 KSh.

The journey from Nairobi to Kampala in Uganda is significantly longer and

Meet the Past

THE PREHISTORY OF MAN IS WRITTEN IN THE STONES OF THE RIFT VALLEY, and for anyone interested in the birth of mankind, Kenya has archaeological sites and sights galore.

Much of the pioneering excavation that mapped out man's early years was performed by Louis and Mary Leakey. The Rift Valley, which stretches from Ethiopia in the north to Mozambique far to the south, passes down through the length of Kenya, and cradles most of the country's most spectacular lakes. The Leakeys discovered that although the Rift Valley was one of the world's oldest geological structures, comparatively recent volcanic activity had entombed a treasure-house of prehistoric remains and fossils, only now being laid bare by the actions of wind and rain. In many cases, the fossils literally lie on the earth's surface, just waiting to be picked up and identified.

Some of the Leakeys' most important discoveries were made in Olduvai Gorge in northern Tanzania. However there are plenty of important sites in Kenya, often discovered even more recently and even now still not fully researched. One of the world's densest collections of surface fossils is found in the north of the country, at the Koobi Flora fossil site in Sibiloi National Park on the shores of Lake Turkana: get there by flying or driving to Ferguson's Gulf, and then hire a boat or plane (see EAST OF THE JADE SEA, page 191, for further access details). Other sites of interest include Hyrax Hill south of Nakuru, three hours drive north of Nairobi, home to some of Kenya's earliest inhabitants and still bearing clear traces of their waterside camp and final tomb.

Even closer to Nairobi to the south, within range for a long day-trip or an overnight camping visit, is Olorgasailie, threaded with catwalks, pathways and informative signs, inhabited by human beings half a million years ago. Countless hand-axes and animal remains have been found at this site, but so far no human remains. Archaeologists continue their painstaking search.

For the subsequent 500 millennia, pastoral Kenyans trod lightly on the earth and left little trace of their tranquil way of life. Exceptions to this include the coast, where Swahili settlers left stone mosques and villages. Perhaps the best of these are Gedi Ruins at Watamu (see GEDI MONUMENT, page 276). This almost complete Swahili village dates back to the fourteenth century, bigger and better than Jumba la Mtwana near Mombasa. Gateway to Kenya's colonial past, Mombasa's most atmospheric sight is Fort Jesus, symbol of the quite justified paranoia of the first years of colonial occupation, finally stormed by Omani forces from the Middle East.

But sometimes it seems the past is still there, an integral part of everyday life. Sail-powered wooden dhows trade up and down the coast, while inland, wandering spear-carrying tribesmen track across vast plains. In Africa the far past is a timeless part of the present.

OPPOSITE: A million-and-a-half-year old skull TOP of *Homo erectus* is displayed at the archaeological site of Koobi Fora on the shores of Lake Turkana. Fort Jesus, Portugal's toehold BOTTOM on the coast of East Africa. ABOVE: The Chuka dancers of the Meru area.

Take to the Skies

IN THE COOL MORNING HALF-LIGHT, THE ROAR OF THE BURNERS HEATED THE AIR AND DROVE COLOR INTO THE BILLOWING FOLDS OF THE BALLOON'S SPREADING CANOPY. Soon it rose, half-willing and wobbling, into the still air and caught the first rays of the sun on it's upper crescent. Gradually the basket lost weight on the ground and, trembling, strained against the restraining ropes, before smoothly and silently taking to the air.

As the yellow light of dawn lit up the tips of low brush, the balloon glided over peaceful herds of grazing game, wildebeest and zebra, gangling giraffes and purposeful, padding lions. A blast on the burner and a family of elephants scattered, suddenly scared, trumpeting and kicking dust-trails far below. In silence we glided on, over the endless plains of the Maasai Mara, sheltered by the distant shades of the mountains of the Rift Valley. Binoculars brought the ground up close as the sun warmed the morning air and bled color into the tranquil scene. Whether dropping low for a closer view or drifting high for

Africa's full panorama, the views were magical and the experience serene. Watched by a cautious herd of buffalo we touched gently on the ground and the balloon sagged gracefully to the earth. In the heart of the bush we watched the dust-trail of the support vehicle tracking close through the broken ground. Within minutes tables were unfolded and laid out, gas braziers lit for breakfast, and we were sipping at the day's first glass of bubbly.

Kenya's climate is ideally suited to ballooning, at least in the timeless savannas of the Maasai Mara. Unlike Europe, where fickle weather often means flights have to be canceled at short notice, in the Maasai Mara mornings are almost invariably calm and cool, perfect for raising these fragile airships. And there is no better way to appreciate the full beauty of the African bush than from the still platform of a viewing basket, suspended high over the heads of some of the world's most exotic animals.

Ballooning in Kenya isn't cheap. It costs about US$380 per person for seats in a 12-seater basket, although this might be less expensive if reserved in advance

14

through an overseas operator. Three companies offer ballooning in the Maasai Mara. **Adventures Aloft** ((02) 221439 FAX (02) 332170, Box 40683, Nairobi, offers flights from Fig Tree Camp; **Balloon Safaris Ltd.** ((02) 502850 FAX (02) 501424, Box 43747, Nairobi, takes off from Keekerok Lodge; and **Mara Balloon Safaris Ltd.** ((02) 331871 FAX (02) 726427, Box 48217, Nairobi, flies from Governors' Camp.

Although ballooning has been tried in other areas, it has never been quite as successful. In Samburu, thorns ripped the canopies to pieces and the only place to land the balloon safely turned out to be in the river which irritated passengers, hippos and crocodiles. For travelers based on the coast, the Maasai Mara would require two flights or several days on the road: the Hilton runs ballooning safaris from **Salt Lick Lodge** in the Taita Hills, which is much more convenient and even a few dollars cheaper. Contact their reservations department in Nairobi ((02) 334000 FAX (02) 339462: they can take reservations although they don't always realize this immediately.

Take a Hike

KENYA HAS GREAT HIKING COUNTRY. Although in many national parks walking is not permitted, the same animals regularly stray just outside the borders into areas where walking most emphatically is allowed. At the same time, in most of Kenya there are too many wild animals — and sometimes bandits — to make walking alone completely relaxing. Best take an organized hike with a guide who will, if necessary, be armed.

Some of the best walking country is a six-hour drive southeast of Nairobi, in the Chyulu Hills near Tsavo West, or the Galana River near Tsavo East. On foot, game tends to avoid human contact, so you won't see as many animals as from the top of a game viewing vehicle, but the experience will be far more intense.

If it's a lone buffalo, possibly too intense. Alternative areas for hiking include the Nandi and Cherangani Hills to the east of the country, the foothills of Mount Kenya a four-hour drive north of Nairobi, the eastern slopes of Mount Elgon with its famous caves on the border with Uganda (see ELGON AND VICTORIA, page 216), or the rugged slopes and plains of the northern Rift Valley.

Several specialist operators offer hiking tours and informed advice: the two most consistently recommended companies are **Tropical Ice Ltd.** ((02) 740811, Suite 8, Muthaiga Shopping Center, Muthaiga Road, Box 57341 Nairobi; and **Bushbuck Adventures** ((02) 212975 FAX (02) 218735, Third Floor, Gilfillan House, Kenyatta Avenue, Box 67449, Nairobi. Other Nairobi operators include **Naturetrek Adventure Safaris** ((02) 220491 FAX (02) 242563, Box 70933, and **Hiking and Cycling Kenya** ((02) 218336 FAX (02) 224212, Box 39439. From the coast, hiking tours around the Galana River, bordering Tsavo East, can be arranged through **Hemingways** ((0122) 32624 FAX (0122) 32256 WEB SITE www.hemingways.com/, Box 267, Watamu; or **Ocean Sports** ((0122) 32008, FAX (0122) 32266, Box 100, Watamu.

OPPOSITE: By balloon is the best way to see the Maasai Mara. ABOVE: Walkways bring the Gura Falls into view in the Aberdares.

Take a Camel Safari

IF HIKING IS TOO STRENUOUS, LET A CAMEL TAKE THE STRAIN. Ships of the desert are ideally suited as companions over a long journey through the bush. First, they are very strong, and a single camel can carry a load that will keep the average hiker living in luxury. They don't need to spend most of their days eating and drinking, and can keep going as long — or rather longer — than their human keepers. And finally, they form a comfortable steed — with a refreshingly high viewpoint — whenever you feel like taking a break. Ride sidesaddle for maximum comfort.

A camel's long range means that it is perhaps the best way of getting far from roads and civilization. Generally a camel safari will only be slightly more expensive than the equivalent lodge-based trip, with comforts varying according to your exact requirements.

ABOVE: Samburu *morans* are great camel handlers. OPPOSITE: Three zebra TOP watch as camels BOTTOM drink.

Simple safaris get close to nature with simple fly-camps and meals around the flames of a campfire. Vehicle assistance is needed if you want to arrive each evening to a pre-erected luxury camp with East African walk-in tents and en suite bucket showers.

One of the advantages of a camel safari is that it is a real chance to get to know the local people. Most camel handlers are Samburu warriors (*morans*) and know the land like the back of their hands. It's always useful to have a *moran* along, not least because they don't get lost; and lions are scared of these braided men in red. They also act as guides, knowing most of the people along the way, from insignificant children too small to acknowledge, busy attending to father's cattle, young warriors striding through the bush looking for something to kill, or elderly women, leaning on sticks, tracing lonely tracks across vast spreading plains.

On my first day out on a camel safari, I met a newly-circumcised brave, dressed in black, plastered with ash and with a dead bird tied round his head. At night, after putting up my complex and cumbersome tent, my Samburu *moran*, called Tched, simply rolled up his ochered braid of hair, folded himself flat on his back, pulled his red blanket up over his eyes, and went immediately to sleep, straight as a pole. By the end of a week, I too had begun to share his timeless familiarity with life in the bush.

There are specialist companies that offer camel safaris, almost invariably in the arid north of the country. Probably the cheapest is **Yare Safaris Ltd.** (/FAX (02) 214099 E-MAIL travelkenya @iconnect.co.ke, Box 63006, Nairobi, based two kilometers (slightly over a mile) south of Maralal on the Nyahururu-Nairobi Road, with prices starting at around US$500 per person for seven days; longer trips are possible. More upmarket operators include **Desert Rose Camel Safaris** ((02) 228936 FAX (02) 212160, Box 44801, Nairobi, who operate eight-day safaris around the Lake Turkana area from

their beautiful lodge in the northern Rift Valley, and Simon Evans, who runs safaris around the Ewaso Ngiro River in Samburu district: make reservations with **Let's Go Travel** ((02) 340331 FAX (02) 336890 E-MAIL info@ letsgosafari.com, Box 60342, Nairobi. More casual safari experiences can also be undertaken at any small town in the north: the cheapest safari experience I've ever been offered was a US$10-a-day proposition from an unemployed Turkana graduate trailing three borrowed donkeys around the village of Baragoi, north of Maralal.

Ride the Rapids

ONE MAN HAS DONE MORE THAN ANY OTHER TO OPEN UP INLAND KENYA TO THE WORLD OF WHITEWATER RAFTING, AND THAT IS MARK SAVAGE, who — between taking expeditions scaling the peaks of Kenya's mountains — has run his zodiacs along the lengths of every navigable river in Kenya — and a few that aren't.

Regular clients include the British Army, for whom he trains instructors, but trips are usually tailored to the requirements of first-time rafters or experienced oarsmen. One-day trips take place on the Tana River, starting from Nairobi. One option is to start with three kilometers (two miles) of class II and III whitewater, followed by six kilometers (four miles) of calm scenic river (paddling) before completing the day with an exhilarating six kilometers (four miles) of fast class IV and V rapids. Alternatively, a quieter day has been tailored to the requirements of ornithologists: a scenic, bird-filled float of three to four hours on eight kilometers (five miles) of river within easy reach of Nairobi. At least 100 species of bird have been regularly spotted by the guides on this stretch of the Tana, and they're fully trained to identify fast flitting rarities. Also possible as a one-day trip is running the length of the Muthoya North River, with a runable distance of 22 km

(nearly 14 miles) and a drop of over 450 m (1,450 ft). The water is not very big — the river is narrow and low-volume — but technically very difficult: lunch and drinks are carried on board the zodiac inflatables so everybody prays that it won't capsize, at least until the afternoon.

For whitewater enthusiasts, or anyone wanting a different "take" on Kenya, longer trips are also available. The Athi River is raftable from near Nairobi all the way to the coast — a distance of 450 km (280 miles) that takes 21 days, and can be combined with walking and caving in the Chyulu Hills. However it is the first 80-km (50-mile) stretch of the Athi River that is most popular: three days combining medium-grade whitewater with the sights and sounds of a scenic stretch of the river. Much of the time the launches run along the borders of Tsavo East, and wildlife abounds: bushbuck, giraffes, buffalo and elephants are frequently seen, while crocodiles and prolific birdlife are constant companions.

Talk to Mark Savage though and it's clear he has one particular favorite: the three-day trip rafting the Ewaso Ngiro River. This starts west of Barsalinga with a roller-coaster 35 km (22 miles) over almost continuous rapids. Extensions to this trip can continue east for a further 100 km (62 miles), through Samburu National Reserve and up to Chandler Falls in Shaba National Reserve. All along the way game abounds: even lions have been spotted during rushed glances from the bucking platform of the paddling zodiac. For safety reasons, two boats are the minimum to run this route, with four people on each, but often Mark Savage is able to combine two or more groups to make this experience possible for smaller groups.

The lower age limit for whitewater rafting is 14, with parental consent, but there's no upper limit: it just depends on individual health. Old 40-year-olds have found it hard, while a 72-year-old grandmother new to the sport was a complete convert and

booked again. Full safety equipment, including lifejackets and crash helmets, are supplied and must be worn. Camp is on scenic points along the river, with two-person dome tents, air beds and sleeping bags provided. Perishables are carried in a freezer trailer, along with soft drinks and beer, and while lunch is cold and casual, dinner has five courses, all cooked over a wood fire. May, June, July and November, December, and January are the best months, as rafting is dependent on water levels, but there can be too much water for some routes. In any case, rafting trips run year-round on one river or another. Rates start at US$95 for a full day's rafting from Nairobi, including meals, beer and transport. Contact **Savage Wilderness Safaris Ltd.** (/FAX (02) 521590 WEB SITE www.kilimanjaro.com, Thigiri Road, Box 44827, Nairobi.

OPPOSITE: Lions in Samburu National Reserve establish a licking order. BELOW: Brownwater rafting on the Ewaso Ngiro River.

Game Fishing

SUDDENLY THE TWIN CATERPILLAR ENGINES CUT AND THE TUBBY BOAT WALLOWED TO A HALT. In the silence, the racing of the reel, letting line out into the ocean, was loud. One of the rods was taut and trembling. We had a bite. The air filled with shouts and activity. As I lurched up from the bench, a crewman pushed me towards the rod, the 36-kg (80-lb) line spinning out from the Shimano reel. While I pulled at the rod to strike the fish, two deckhands feverishly reeled in a kilometer of line from the other eight rods, as well as the two lines of teasers that streamed from outriggers, clearing the way for me to play the fish. My rod, friction reel whirring out line, jumped and fought my arms as I was ushered into the "fighting seat," a racked wooden chair built out of rough-cut planks and sturdy metal fitments. It looked rather like an early dentist's homemade treatment chair.

A sailfish, blue and glittering graceful, broke the surface of the ocean 275 m (900 ft) behind our slackening boat with a sun-glinting splash. In a desperate attempt to break free of the one-inch hook, the sailfish had flipped into the air to try to void its stomach. The fish was getting tired. I started to haul in, taking the strain by pumping the rod, reeling in as I dipped the tense, bowed tip.

The sailfish crescented above the surface again, sail flashing lower and tired, and I kept reeling in. In the final moments the silver-sided form could be seen weaving exhausted below the stern of the boat, and then deckhands were pulling at the line, maneuvering the sailfish into position so they could grab its bony bill with thick protective gloves, remove the hook from its mouth and insert a tag. It wasn't a record-breaker — about 35 kg (77 lbs) — but it was my first game-fish and a lot taller than me. As my moment of glory faded, the deckhand took over an even more important job: sluicing water through the exhausted fish, waving its bony snout in the warm oxygenated surface layers to get the fish's powerful tail muscles working again and the energy to swim weakly clear. Once revived, it was pushed free and I watched the silvery-blue shape snake off at a tangent to the safety of the deep.

Most of Kenya's better operators have caught up with environmental considerations, and now feature the tag-and-release program, where instead of being killed and weighed the fish are fitted with a small identifying tag and released back into the wild. Game fishing, though, will never be a sport

for the softhearted. The trauma of being towed around the ocean on the end of a hook will always prove fatal to some fish. On the day I was fishing, one of the three sailfish caught had been hooked in the gills and had no chance of survival. Meanwhile a 16-kg (35-lb) Wahoo was destined for the pot. Swordfish, famous fighters now being caught at night in Kenya by boats trailing diving-light lures, often die of exhaustion in their struggle.

But you don't have to catch a big game-fish to experience the thrill of fishing. And the best outing I had was where I caught least: spinning. "In America they'd laugh at you for going fishing in a boat like this," Ken Adcock,

son of Mombasa fishing legend James Adcock, told me as we set off in a seven-meter (20-ft) canoe built from mango wood in a timeless narrow, deep design. Rolling on the swell a couple of miles offshore, we powered after horizon specks of flocked feeding birds, slowing to approach as they dive-bombed, speckling the water with white plashes as they hunted bite-sized shoals of fry. Their feeding frenzy showed us that hunting below the water would be the ocean carnivores: tuna and snapper, chased in turn perhaps by sailfish and shark. Stressed by their position halfway up a

Lake Victoria's Nile perch can take some landing. It can be useful to have some local help.

food-chain, any of these fish might be panicked into mistaking our lures for an exotic snack.

Each shoal would drop away as our boat shadowed close. So there was only time for one cast, maybe two, before fish dropped away to the deep and birds wheeled off to another bit of ocean. Standing insecure on the rocking canoe we flicked our rods to send crazy-colored rubber squid across the water, winding in, frantic and fast, to send the hooks skimming and splashing across the choppy waves. For the first time I could feel the excitement of the chase, as we added our hooks to the game of eat or be eaten being played out below the ocean's swell. And a bite: my line went tight and I started to reel in. My red rubber octopus had caught a myopic Dorado. As the birds wheeled off towards their next meal, I played the fish in and lifted it over the side. Three kilos (seven pounds) only, but this time, I felt, caught with skill. And anyone who seriously considers tagging and releasing a Dorado has never worked up a decent appetite.

Fishermen in Kenya are spoiled for choice. Bad times for offshore fishing are May, June and (in the north) July, when rough sea conditions mean the boats can't clear the fringing reef and many operators close their doors. Even at this time of year there's still fly-fishing in the rivers streaming off Mount Kenya, especially for browns and rainbows in the Burguret and Nanyuki Rivers; you can rent fly tackle at the Naro Moru River Lodge (see MOUNT KENYA, page 159). For lake fishing, upmarket lodges at Mfangano and Rusinga Islands in Lake Victoria offer full equipment to hunt down Nile Perch. And you can always go native. Local boats might lack sophisticated tackle, but plenty of Kenyans live on the waters of Lakes Turkana, Naivasha and Baringo. It's a great way to settle in to the Kenyan pace: just make sure the boat you hire isn't likely to sink. See SPORTING SPREE, page 38, for listings of the most reliable game fishing operators.

Brush up Your Birding

FEW COUNTRIES ARE AS REWARDING AS KENYA FOR BIRD WATCHING. Perhaps the best place to settle down with binoculars is at Lake Baringo. Flat waters, dotted with floating cabbage, are home to countless species, including Humprick's hornbill. On my last visit, I caught sight of a group of colorful Madagascan bee-eaters. Hyrax clamber round the Baringo Cliffs while Kingfishers dip into the waters of the lake. Boats paddle carefully in shallow waters, constant haunt of hidden hippos, who seem to get annoyed at the beat of engines. Resident ornithologist at **Lake Baringo Lodge** (reservations through Block Hotels ((02) 540780 FAX (02) 543810), Stephen Heparsa-Laach, told me not to be concerned. "The hippos at Naivasha are far more aggressive."

A pity and a worry. Naivasha might not be as quiet and remote as Baringo, but the birdlife is just as prolific, as at all the flamingo-pinked lakes that glow blue along the floor of the Rift Valley. And there are plenty of different habitats. The enthusiastic birder will find different species on the hot humid coast, on the open savannas, in the inland forest and swamps and around tall mountain peaks. Whether predator or prey, all Kenya's birds share exceptional beauty and aerial grace.

And for the determinedly red-blooded, there's one further sport these birds can provide. In the Galana River area, just outside the borders of Tsavo East National Park, you can make reservations for vacations with **Hemingways** ((0122) 32624 FAX (0122) 32256 WEB SITE www .hemingways.com/, Box 267, Watamu, and go out to their tented camp. In the bright light of dawn, you can walk out from your luxury camp into the bush, admire the thrilling sound of these beautiful birds' morning song, wonder at the flash of their feathers, lift your rented gun, and blast them from the sky.

A Goliath heron feeds on a shoreline in Nairobi National Park.

Meet the Animals

IT'S ALL VERY WELL SEEING KENYA'S GAME, BUT SOMETIMES IT'S TEMPTING TO MAKE CONTACT THAT MUCH CLOSER. There are a couple of opportunities to get close to Kenya's wildlife. In Nairobi's **Giraffe Sanctuary** ((02) 891658, endangered Rothschild's giraffe lean over to extend long gray tongues to slurp up afternoon tea: cattle nuts, held out on flat palms. Travel north to Nanyuki and Laikipia, where **Sweetwaters** camp is home to a

PREVIOUS PAGES: Feeding time for orphan rhinos. ABOVE: An elephant meets an Olive baboon at Amboseli National Park. OPPOSITE: Panning for gold in Kakamega.

tame rhinoceros. Once orphaned by poachers, he now thinks he's a pet, and trundles around after guests like a big — very big — dog, and likes having his stomach tickled. Book Sweetwaters through **Lonhro** ((02) 216940 FAX (02) 216796, Box 58581, Nairobi (US$205 per double, full board): it's just about close enough for an overnight visit. At a more modest outlay of time and money, Nairobi's **Maasai Ostrich Farm** (0150 22505/6 lets you get close to these ungainly birds, and on Sunday afternoons you can ride them. A ride on an ostrich might give you an appetite: if so you can always tuck into an ostrich steak at the **Carnivore Restaurant** ((02) 501775, around the corner on Langata Road.

TOP SPOTS

Go for Gold

AS I SWIRLED THE MURKY RIVER WATERS AROUND IN THE PLASTIC PAN, ONE SIDE RIDGED TO CATCH FOUR CRESCENTS OF GRITTY ORE IN SERRIED RANKS, I CAUGHT MY FIRST GLINT OF GOLD. I was hooked. But these weren't perhaps the best circumstances to strike the precious metal. For a start, I was being watched by a crowd of about 12 ragged local children, so the chances of keeping this important discovery secret were small. Not that it was specially secret. This area of western Kenya hosted the country's only gold rush. The first strike was made in the 1930s, but only the local subsistence farmers still find it worth the search.

Still, it was gold. And it was mine. I panned on, flushing out light yellow sand, then dark metallic sand, until I had isolated the elusive metal. It was more a flake than a nugget, probably worth quite a lot less than a dollar. I put it in a medical specimen bottle. It was coming home with me.

It hadn't even come from prime river silt. Coming late in the evening to the river, I'd hacked at the first bit of bank I could easily reach and loaded an arbitrary collection of sand and boulders into a bucket. As a village-worth of children stared on, I loaded up a hopefully more silty panful and started to wash off the lighter sand. I was no longer shy about onlookers. My nervous glances were at the sky. Which had gone black. Minutes before I'd been panning in the clear light of a tropical afternoon, cooled by about 1,800 m (6,000 ft) of altitude. But suddenly, heavy pads of rain started to confuse my technique and everyone ran. Chucking my panful of precious silt back into the river, I grabbed my socks and struggled through a maize-field after my fleet admirers. Then the heavens opened as if someone upstairs had pulled out a plug, and a local farmer waved us in to her thatched shack.

Much underrated are the thatched shacks of the Kakamega area: totally waterproof, for a start; floored with cow-dung for a second. I asked why and was told that this was because this was proof against the local worms who infested the ground outside, waiting for soft bare soles to hatch in your feet. Imagining festering nests of weevils, I emptied the rain from my shoes and put them on to wait out the storm.

I'd already learned rather more about the sharp end of gold mining than I'd expected that day, a chance to find out more about the daily life of most Kenyans that usually stays a blur in the side windows of a speeding safari vehicle. I had stopped off to see a Swedish couple, Bertil and Gunilla Fagerholm, who'd abandoned careers in computing for a hobby in gold-rushing, bought themselves a field in the middle of western Kenya, and built a hotel.

What had finally convinced them hadn't been the gold. Their decision was ultimately swayed when they discovered Kiminga, a local mining village, had school uniforms which matched the colors of the Swedish flag, blue scattering across rolling highland landscapes, and within minutes of meeting several hundred grinning adverts for their homeland, a charity was born.

In the west of Kenya, getting fed isn't the problem. Plant a fence and it will grow, and probably produce two crops of fencelets every year. Getting cash, on the other hand, is difficult. Long after the area's local gold rush, the locals are still trying to dig a living out of the ground, and seemed anxious to show me the problems they faced.

This involved showing me their mine; I stood in a bucket attached to a handwoven sisal rope and was lowered 80 m (260 ft) down by a couple of fit-looking Africans on hand-welded handles. As the outside world receded to a small lit circle high overhead, my eyes adapted to the dark and I started to get scared.

Not that the mine was badly built. It wasn't. But the steep seam-chasing passages were small, too small to turn round, and the air musty. Worse, the mines were flooding. With the richest seams already underwater. In the candle light, miners' faces glistening my way, expectant, waiting for me to tell them how to drain the water from their mine.

All I could do was leave a cash tip. The 200 miners who run Kiminga mine as a cooperative are pleased to show how gold mining works in Kenya. But what they really want is someone to tell them how to stop their mine turning into a well. Bertil Lindstrom and Gunilla Fagerholm can be contacted at **Rivendell Lodge** ((0331) 41316 E-MAIL gb@net2000ke.com. Accommodation costs 3,000 KSh per double.

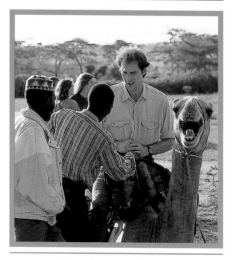

Race to Victory

MY CAMEL LAY LIKE A LARGE DESERT ICEBERG, LEGS CONCERTINA'D IN THE DUST. "Hello, Charlie," I said and wondered if I should pat him on the head. Languidly Charlie turned around and gave me a camel's gaze of indifferent contempt, chewing slowly. I wondered if he'd spit. Or maybe bite. He shook his head and I jumped back.

Then Tched, the camel handler, pulled on the ropes attaching the loose bundle of sticks and foam rubber laughingly called a saddle. Charlie brayed in irritation, giving me a grandstand view of enough teeth to scalp a hairdresser and an insight into his diet. "Don't annoy him," I advised Tched, who smiled shyly. He was an ochered Samburu warrior who hardly spoke Swahili let alone English and acted as though I'd told him the opposite. He planted his foot against Charlie's flank, pulled harder, and this time I was sure I could detect an edge of serious irritation in Charlie's anguished shout. Tched stood back, indicating I should climb on. It was time to race.

I had signed up to ride in the Camel Derby at Maralal in northern Kenya, which takes place every year in July. Originally started to educate the locals about the environmental advantages of camels in this harsh land, it is nothing like the competitive Middle Eastern races or professional eleven-year-old jockeys and

pedigree steeds. In Maralal, the name of the game is endurance and anyone can play. I had entered the 10-km (six-mile) amateur category. The night before, I'd ridden a camel for the first time.

Reluctantly I scrambled aboard and began a slow lurching ascent. Against a background of shouted orders and flicking switches, Charlie unfolded long joints, heaving up at the front, and then high at the back. I was tipped forward in my seat, perched insecurely looking down on an audience of Samburu tribesmen who scattered clear in case I fell off on them. More shouts and a final heave: Charlie straightened his front legs and my seat flattened out, leaving me two and a half meters (eight feet) in the air. It seemed much more and the ground a long way down.

For a minute Charlie appeared to be reconsidering his original decision to stand. Fortunately Tched spoke some camel, shouting orders and applying a stick until Charlie lurched off. I jammed my feet into the crooked sticks that made up the saddle and hung on tight.

With a certain ungainly grace, Charlie strolled up to the starting line and a thousand spectators: groups of tribesmen looked on from under shady trees while women and children, festooned in beads, hung onto the fences that kept spectators and racers apart. Charlie jostled in with the other competitors at the starting line in a loose crowd of high flaring nostrils from the camels and nervous downward glances from the riders. Charlie's stomach rumbled; the camel next door farted.

Less than half the racers in the amateur race were white, and they included a ten-year-old boy, an American woman in her seventies, an Australian television journalist, and a couple of overlanders.

A brief countdown was lost in the background noise and the race was underway. One camel set off in the wrong direction, and a few others, including Charlie, showed no particular urge to go anywhere, but in a minute or two we all thundered down the track between cheering (or were they laughing?) spectators.

The race was along the dirt road from Yare Safari Camp, down and through the town of Maralal, a wild-west scene of clapboard houses and shady verandahs, and back. Charlie was clearly aware he was in for a long haul and shambled off at a gentle trot.

From watching other riders, I had noticed rising to the movement seemed to be the way ahead, but Charlie's rhythm was hard to catch. Rather like dancing to an unfamiliar African jazz band, periodically I'd find myself out of phase. Charlie would quickly pick up my confusion and take this as an opportunity to get away with a walk.

OPPOSITE BOTTOM: Mining for gold in Kiminga. ABOVE: Saddling up LEFT for the Camel Derby. The start line CENTER and trouble at the finish RIGHT.

Camel psychology is still a closed book to me. Camels only need food or drink every few days, and Charlie showed none of a horse's enthusiasm for the road home. I muttered encouragement, endearments, and threats, but he didn't seem to speak English. I watched the camel in front, shuffling along on feet the size of dinner plates, running like two tired knock-kneed men jammed into a pantomime suit. It was getting further away. I looked over my shoulder. The competition was falling back too. Psychology was cast to the wind as the race became a battle of wills, my acacia whip flailing against his tough hide, my voice wearing hoarse with continual threats and entreaties which fell on large, indifferent ears. I kept him trotting — barely.

Fifty minutes after I'd started, Charlie lollopped over the finishing line, to rapturous applause from the crowd whose enthusiasm didn't seem to have been diminished by eleven camels before me. Charlie sank to the ground and I tottered about on rubber legs, while occasional bursts of applause indicated the arrival of another racer. The ten-year-old boy had come third and I thought I'd done quite well to finish. Out of 25 starters, 19 made it across the finishing line. Despite the fact no riders wore protective helmets — Kenya, after all, is a land of adventure — there had been no casualties.

There was drama off course, too. The Camel Derby brings together half the country's tourist industry in a convivial, off-duty mood. A tented town makes the camp look rather like a luxury refugee camp, humming with life and a great place to make contacts.

In the aftermath on Monday, the overland trucks threaded off in various directions and the tents were dismantled, packed and dispatched to Nairobi and beyond. Once more birdsong could be heard in the Safari Camp and herds of zebra grazed closer. A small group of travelers set off on a camel trek lasting days or maybe weeks. For another year the Camel Derby was over.

Maralal is 350 km (217 miles) north of Nairobi, the road paved for much of the

way. Allow five hours by fast car, or a day by *matatu*, changing at Nyahururu. To get the dates of the next Camel Derby, call **Yare Safaris Ltd.** ℂ/FAX (2) 214099 E-MAIL travelkenya@iconnect.co.ke, Box 63006, Nairobi.

Track the Migration of the Wildebeest

EVERY YEAR, BY SOME MASS INSTINCT, THE MAASAI MARA SETS THE SCENE FOR ONE OF NATURE'S GREATEST WONDERS: THE MIGRATION OF THE WILDEBEEST. By some unspoken signal, many millions of these animals, broad-shouldered and slim-hipped, crowned with powerful horns, start off

on a long and hazardous trek between Kenya's Maasai Mara and Tanzania's adjoining Serengeti Plains. In endless lines they flood through the bush, trailed by lions, following instincts that have driven their movements since time immemorial.

Although at any time of year the Maasai Mara is one of the only places in Africa to see the dense herds of game that once covered Africa before the arrival of man, every year when the migration happens concentrations build up to inconceivable levels. The exact timing depends on the weather, and sometime between July and September over a million wildebeest and hundreds of thousands of zebra arc through the Maasai Mara National Reserve in uncountable crowds on their circuit around the plains of the Serengeti, following the rains in search of fresh pastures. Some predators trail, others lie in wait. The wildebeest add up to nine million kilos (20 million pounds) of meat to the park's predators through their long trek. Perhaps the most overwhelming image is of the panicked crossing of the Mara River, crocodiles snapping at their heels hungry for their annual feast: an unforgettable sight.

The Maasai Mara is best reached by air from Nairobi, although if traveling on a budget there are plenty of operators who arrange transport by road. Contact **Let's Go Travel (** (02) 340331 FAX (02)

Crossing time for wildebeest on their annual migration in the Maasai Mara.

336890 E-MAIL info@letsgosafari.com, Box 60342, Nairobi, or choose any of the operators listed in TAKING A TOUR, page 76, to arrange your visit. See MAASAI MARA, page 237, for details on the Mara camps and lodges.

Rave It Up at Lake Turkana

I STARED AT THE SUNSET. ON EITHER SIDE, RED, BUT THE CENTER WAS DYED A BRILLIANT JADE. It was the Jade Sea, Lake Turkana, reflected in the sky. I'd never seen anything like it. I'd been dragged from the high-street restaurant where a sign painted on the wall said "We give you the best service no matter how long it takes" and out on the street. But my new friends had no interest in waiting for service, however good, nor in looking at the sky.

"Come on. We'll miss the film." My companions were impatient. "It's *Demetrius the Greek.*" By way of encouragement they recited whole scenes from memory, filled me in on the plot. They pulled me away from the sunset. "How tall are you?"

The Catholic mission has the television. Every Sunday they fire up the generator, plug in the video, and point the screen out through a doorway. A sea of 150 little faces, cross-legged, gazed up into the cathode glare: adolescents, strictly ranked by height, had a more distant view, and I worked out why I'd been asked my height as I squinted at the dated colors of a very old movie. Gasps followed every blow, giggles every kiss. Well, not so much followed. Often a voice from the crowd would beat the actor to their lines, and everyone knew each twist of the simple plot. Heroic Christians wow dissolute Romans. Then Chartlon Heston froze as the video broke down. The audience, chattering excitedly, didn't seem disappointed or surprised. Without hanging around in the hope of any repair they flooded out of the mission compound and split into countless paths that traced the stony ground, home to their clustered *manyattas*, reed or mud dwellings.

Soon the sounds of chanting echoed across the desolate landscape from clusters of round Turkana huts. There wasn't much moon, but the stars gave plenty of light. I followed faint trails, silver threading through the piled boulders of a barren land, and I discovered the locals don't mind spectators. In circles they chanted out traditional songs, while the men danced, pogoing across a charmed circle of spectators, in competitive groups or taking huge solo leaps, men singing and bare-breasted girls helping the chorus. Shyly the girls clapped and assisted, subordinate but interested, especially in the highest jumpers. I asked a spectator to translate the lyrics, expecting tales of romance and love. Far from it. All the songs were about cattle, cows with large humps, bulls with nice horns.

Which was rather sad. Because in the desolate rocky wasteland that was home to these Turkana, the land isn't rich enough to support many animals. A few goats were the limit of most people's wealth and the constant complaint amongst the young is that the cost of a new bride is far beyond their means. But dancing the night away costs nothing, and until Turkana girls get married they're free to flirt as much as they like. I slipped away at about ten in the evening. Early. From all directions the sound of private parties continued well into the night.

This scene was at Loyangalani on the shores of Lake Turkana, a stiff 12-hour drive or charter flight north of Nairobi. See EAST OF THE JADE SEA, page 191, for access information. However every weekend is a celebration in Kenya. Where there's electricity, there are concerts of local music and thumping discos held by overloaded speakers. And beyond the reach of electricity, where a white face is a novelty, they are pleased to welcome visitors to far more elemental festivities, the very different traditional dances of very traditional societies. Don't take a camera. With such cultures it is easy to give offense and the easiest way to do this is by taking a photograph.

The sun sets over Lake Turkana, the Jade Sea.

YOUR CHOICE

The Great Outdoors

For many visitors, Kenya *is* the great outdoors. Sun-baked bush stretching as far as the eye can see, mountains glowing blue on the far horizon. Exotic animals grazing on thorny bushes, predators waiting to pounce... and that's the problem. Hungry wild animals keep many visitors to Kenya confined to their four-wheel drives, nervously watching the drama of the bush through the safe hatch in the roof of their vehicle. Unlike some other African countries, walking is not permitted in most of Kenya's national parks for the simple reason that there's too much game. But Kenya has plenty of fine hiking country where you can escape from the car.

Some of these are areas where subsistence farmers have long displaced animals. The slopes of Mount Elgon on Kenya's western Ugandan border are threaded with paths and trails where wildlife poses little threat. Humans can be more of a problem: check the security situation by asking around, since border areas are often sensitive. Weeks can be spent on extended treks along the intervillage trails in the Nandi and Cherangani Hills in Western Kenya (see ELGON AND VICTORIA, page 218) which is a memorable way to meet Kenya's welcoming people, even if on a tight budget. Camping out in these populous districts is not wise: better to come to an arrangement with a villager to stay with their family or use one of the mountain huts. You won't be short of offers and you will generally get the family bed. Bear in mind that medical facilities are few and communications can be poor. Falling off mountains is not advised.

Hiking is possible independently around Mount Elgon, but the most popular area for hikers is Mount Kenya, where a guide is almost always advisable. Mountaineers definitely need a guide: many climbs are technical and demanding. Contact the **Mountain Club of Kenya** ((02) 501747, Box 45741,

OPPOSITE: Shaba National Reserve is one of Kenya's least visited. ABOVE: Normally placid, this elephant is starting to get twitchy.

Nairobi, or **Savage Wilderness Safaris Ltd.** (/FAX (02) 521590 WEB SITE www.kilimanjaro.com, Thigiri Road, Box 44827, Nairobi, or if in the Mount Kenya region, **Joseph Muthui** ((02) 242627 FAX (02) 250734, Box 391, Naro Moro, offers friendly and flexible guide services.

Those with just a day to spare can head out of Nairobi to the Ngong Hills, but not alone: over the past few years it has acquired an unsavory reputation for robbers.

Other areas are safe simply because the countryside is too inhospitable to support enough wildlife to be dangerous. Usually the problem is lack of water: most of northern Kenya is classed as desert, a rugged world of exceptional beauty and piled dried boulders where dramatic color-shifts mean even the same view constantly changes. Dotted by the red robes of nomadic hunters, trekking in the drylands takes planning, and preferably a camel. Once more, camping out here is only advisable in groups.

Some areas of Kenya can be explored on foot simply because that's the only way to travel. The forests of Arabuko-Sokoke near Watamu Bay on the northern coast (see ARABUKO-SOKOKE FOREST, page 276, for details of how to get there and accommodation options) or of Kakamega in the west (see KAKAMEGA, page 218) are threaded with narrow game trails. No danger of getting eaten here: big predators would have no chance of hunting as they crash through the undergrowth, although buffalo can make faster progress than fleeing humans. Grab a stone or climb a tree if you meet an angry one. In such forests the greatest risk is getting lost: underneath the jungle canopy it would be easy to lose your bearings. In practice it's not such a problem, as both these forests have friendly and informative guides just waiting to show you around.

Overlooking the Leno Valley from the Tot Escarpment.

To walk amongst wildlife takes more than nerve and a total lack of imagination: in fact it takes an armed ranger, a watchful eye and thorough respect for Nature's killing machines. In general, animals steer well clear: although they're well used to cars and safari vehicles, predators and prey alike tend to take flight at the first whiff of a human on foot. Notable exceptions include hippos and buffalo: easily the most dangerous of all Kenya's wildlife and always to be treated with the greatest respect. If traveling with an experienced guide, the risks are small, and there are some private game reserves, often bordering national parks, where walking safaris are a specialty. The best of these include **Sweetwaters**, reserved with **Lonhro** ((02) 216940 FAX (02) 216796, Box 58581, Nairobi (US$205 per double, full board); and **Lewa Downs**, bookable through **Bush Homes of East Africa** ((02) 571661 FAX (02) 571665 E-MAIL Bushhome@africaonline.co.ke, Box 56923, Nairobi (US$325 per night, full board).

Many visitors, especially those who've been on safari before, find there's no better way to get a feel for the bush, and it is undeniable that seeing an elephant on foot is a very different experience to spotting one from the high viewpoint of a car. Especially if it's coming your way.

Sporting Spree

For the sportsman, Kenya offers a special welcome. Kenyan gold medals, especially for track events, have over the years shown the country's attributes of speed and endurance. On every flat patch of land goalposts seem to have been put up for soccer matches, and Rugby too is very popular. But few travelers arrive in Kenya with a whole team at their disposal, so for most visitors it's the individual activities, such as fishing, golfing, diving, mountaineering and horseback riding, that provide the sporting high points of their stay in the country.

Golfers in Kenya have the pick of some of the world's finest greens, often enlivened by crocodiles and hippos adding their own special frisson to water hazards. In Nairobi there are a range of golf clubs, most of which offer special guest membership rates to patrons of the city's most famous hotels. There are six high-quality 18-hole golf courses in the Nairobi area, with the best being the **Windsor Golf and Country Club** ((02) 802206 FAX (02) 802188, 13 km (eight miles) from the city center off Garden Estate Road. Another ten 18-hole courses are spread within easy reach of Nairobi around the Rift Valley and Central Highlands. Golfing safaris can be arranged by **UTC** (short and long travels, golf safaris, nanny services) ((02) 331960 FAX (02) 331422 WEB SITE www.unitedtour.com, Box 42196, Nairobi; or **Let's Go Travel** ((02) 340331 FAX (02) 336890 E-MAIL info@letsgosafari .com, Box 60342, Nairobi. Malindi, Diani and Mombasa have good courses while most other major towns have the facilities to play nine holes at least. In Kenya, the clubhouses are often cozy time-warp zones that retain the atmosphere of colonial days, quietly set and overlooked by the rush of the twentieth century. A game of golf is a great way to unwind as a change from the excitement of life on safari. For

further information, contact the **Kenya Golf Union** ((02) 763898, Box 49609, Nairobi.

Riding and **horseracing** are big in Nairobi. Throughout the year the Nairobi Racecourse on Ngong Road holds horseracing, with events taking place almost every other weekend. This can be a great day out, and although it is never quite going to match the famous races of Europe for sheer scale and pageantry, it makes up for it with a cheerful and convivial atmosphere in the stands. Bar, restaurant and the chance to place some really small bets (20 KSh or 30 cents is the minimum) make this an ideal way to pass a Saturday or a Sunday afternoon. Everyone says the races are fixed, but then who cares? Look in the sporting pages of the *Nation* newspaper to see if there's a race on or call the **East African Jockey's Club** ((02) 561002.

If you want to ride yourself, it's a great way to experience the country. Lessons and horse rental are available in Nairobi from **Arifa Riding School** ((02) 882937, Marula Lane, Karen, Nairobi, while the **Kitengela Polo Club** ((02) 882782 also offers picnic rides and polo. For long-distance horseback safaris and

up-country operators contact **Let's Go Travel** ((02) 340331 FAX (02) 336890, Box 60342, Nairobi. One United Kingdom operator who specializes in offbeat farmhouse and horseback safaris is **Art of Travel** ((0171) 783 2038 FAX (0171) 738 1893, 21 The Bakehouse, Bakery Place, 119 Altenburg Gardens, London SW11 1JQ.

Mountain biking is relatively new to Kenya, where ancient bone-shaking bicycles are nothing but transport to impoverished farm workers. It can — for the fit — be a great way to see the country, perfect for exploring the footpaths and game tracks of Kenya. A new operator opening up this field of African travel is **Bike Treks** ((02) 446371 FAX (02) 442439, or reserved with **Let's Go Travel**.

Deep-sea fishing has been popular since Hemingway's day. All along the coast of Kenya operators offer fishing from charter boats with a new specialty of night-fishing with diving-light lures for swordfish. The north is best known

OPPOSITE: Sheldrick's Falls in Shimba Hills National Park. ABOVE: A diver explores coral on Kenya's fragile coral reef.

for sailfish while the south prides itself on marlin catches.

North to south, every major town is home to at least one reliable operator who operates the tag-and-release scheme, where fish are re-released live into the wild. In Malindi it is **Kingfisher** ((0123) 21168 FAX (0123) 30261, E-MAIL kingfisher @swiftmombasa.com, Box 29, Malindi. Ten kilometers (seven miles) to the south, Watamu Bay is home to **Hemingways** ((0122) 32624 FAX (0122) 32256, WEB SITE www.hemingways.com/; and **Ocean Sports** ((0122) 32008 FAX (0122) 32268, Box 100, Watamu. Just to the north of Mombasa, **Hallmark Charters Ltd.** ((011) 485680 FAX (011) 475217 are at Mtwapa Creek. Head south to Diani beach, and **Grand Slam Charters** can be reserved through the Safari Beach Hotel ((0127) 2726 FAX (0127) 2357. Towards Kenya's southern border with Tanzania, Shimoni is base for **Sea Adventures Ltd.** FAX (011) 227675 and the famous **Pemba Channel Fishing Club** ((011) 313749 FAX (011) 316875.

Lakeland game fishing is also possible on Lake Victoria. **Mfangano Island Camp** is booked through **Governors' Camps** ((02) 331871 FAX (02) 726427 (US$250 per night per double, full board) and **Rusinga Island Club** ((02) 447224 FAX (02) 447268 (US$460 per double, full board including all excursions).

Scuba diving attracts enthusiasts from all over the world. Diving off the

Kenya coast is notable for pelagic sightings and countless shoals of smaller fish. The Indian Ocean here has twice as many fish species as the Red Sea and rewards snorkelers and divers alike. Reputable operators, from north to south along the coast, start in Malindi, and can be reserved through the **Driftwood Beach Club** ((0123) 20155 FAX (0123) 30712. A good school in Watamu is **Aqua Ventures** ((0122) 32008 FAX (0122) 32266. In Mombasa, the top operator is **Buccaneer Diving**, based at the **Whitesands Hotel** ((011) 485926 FAX (011) 485652. At Diani the largest operator is **Dive the Crab**, which can be booked through **Safari Beach Hotel** ((0127) 2726 FAX (0127) 2357. To explore the spectacular waters of the southerly Kisite Marine Park, diving is operated by the **Wasini Island Restaurant** ((0127) 2331 FAX (0127) 3154 or **Pemba Diving Ltd.** ((0127) 2331 FAX (0127) 3151.

Whitewater rafting is a increasingly popular way to explore Kenya, although not many of the seven major rivers are suitable. Just one operator exploits Kenya's raftable rivers, which include the Athi, the Tana, the Muthoya, or the Ewaso-Ng'iro. Day-long excursions or longer river-based safaris out of Nairobi are offered by **Savage Wilderness Safaris Ltd.** (/FAX (02) 521590 WEB SITE www .kilimanjaro.com, Thigiri Road, Box 44827, Nairobi (see RIDE THE RAPIDS, page 18, in TOP SPOTS).

The Open Road

At first sight, driving in Kenya would seem to be the action of the terminally insane. I prefer to see it as an adventure. By Western standards, the roads in Kenya are poor. Even the best-surfaced ones have sudden jarring potholes, and the worst tarmac often entails a laborious, snaking slalom which leads some drivers to take to new tracks on either side. Many roads are still *murram*, or surfaced with local clay: if not regularly maintained these turn into rutted and unforgiving channels and however well prepared, any rain will transform the surface into mud more slippery than ice. This is even more of a problem if the surface is deeply rutted: the effect on the car is to make it, as the locals say, "dance." At any point roads can be blocked by trucks or cars that break down or simply get bogged.

Car rental is expensive, especially for a four-wheel-drive. Traffic is heavy, with slow trucks crawling up the steeper hills. Constant passing in the face of oncoming traffic can be wearing. Driving at night is not recommended, as other vehicles often drive without lights, and if they have them, rarely turn down the brights. Blind corners are littered with unlit broken-down trucks, and a growing incidence of banditry and car-jacking make daylight hours the safest option. At any given time some of the roads in the country will be unsafe due to cattle rustling or tribal disputes, and the only way of finding out where it is safe to travel is to ask locally and place your trust in the answer.

Each Easter the East African Safari Rally takes place on public roads: for much of March it seems that half the population is practicing speed-driving, often in heavy rain. Long distances irresistibly increase speed: watch out for speed bumps, often unmarked, that are frequent hazards near every school and settlement. Sometimes they are mere rumble strips, but often very serious mounds of tarmac that can bump the unwary driver hard against the roof and cause you to lose control. Off the beaten track road bumps are less of a problem than finding gasoline: sometimes it's necessary to phone ahead and ensure supplies are available at key lodges on your route. In any event, keep the tank well topped up: it is easy to run dry in Kenya. Street signs are limited: even major junctions are frequently unmarked. It's not even easy to get an accurate map: the authorities regard these as classified information and seem to believe the average visitor is planning an invasion rather than a vacation.

OPPOSITE: Horseracing TOP at Nairobi Racecourse. Windsurfing BOTTOM on Diani beach. ABOVE: Driving in the Maasai Mara LEFT. On track RIGHT in Samburu.

Put off? Don't be. The freedom of having your own vehicle can transform your experience, and a self-driver in Kenya is also rewarded with a considerable sense of achievement. All Kenya's roads have aspects of beauty: however, for the driver, this is often dependent on the road surface. Roads subject to heavy traffic are usually the worst. The main road artery between Nairobi and Mombasa, for instance, is a bore: bad surface and slow trucks mean the view palls even for passengers. Many of the same trucks continue through towards Uganda and Africa's interior, taking their toll on routes across the Rift Valley, but better views compensate. Main roads not used by heavy traffic, dead-ending up towards Lake Baringo, Eldoret and Kitale are usually far better, with light traffic and the only hazards are occasional potholes and stray animals.

Minor roads can deteriorate quickly over the wet season, and their condition depends whether they have been graded. The little-used western route down from Kericho into the Maasai Mara is one of the country's most scenic, but the dreadful *murram* surface means that pleasure is tinged with concern: will you make it? In the wet season the answer is often no, although a little maintenance would make a great difference. The only way of finding out if this has taken place is to ask locally. See GRAND SAFARI, page 81, which covers most of Kenya's major roads and the state of the road is described in the text. However the situation can change from mile to mile.

There are special considerations that apply to renting cars in Kenya. The first pitfall for the unwary is the excess charged by the rental company in case of accident or theft. In some cases this is set as high as 100,000 KSh: this converts into US$16,000, and this is after you've paid the optional collision damage waiver (CDW). Everyone hopes accidents won't happen, but this level of excess means even a minor traffic bungle could represent a major financial disaster. Avoid firms which charge such punitive

excesses — you certainly won't find them recommended here. Also beware of low daily rental charges balanced by high per-kilometer mileage fees: if touring it's usually cheaper to go for unlimited mileage. Even so, their idea of unlimited is not always the dictionary version: usually there is a limit after which per-kilometer charges click in anyway. It takes careful calculation to work out if their limits will be sufficient.

Another important consideration is that the condition of the vehicle is all-important. It is not always easy to find competent mechanics up-country, and there are plenty of situations where your life depends on the car's correct mechanical function. In general, the driver is responsible for minor repairs that become necessary along the way and just to complicate matters there are unscrupulous mechanics — especially around Kenya's third city, Nakuru — who specialize in tricking motorists into shelling out substantial amounts of money on unnecessary repairs. The favorite trick is to pour oil under your car when it's parked and then persuade you to visit their local garage. Don't let anyone take a wrench to your rented car without checking first with your rental agency. Travelers visiting Nakuru with a car and driver are faced with the same problem: often the driver will disappear for half an hour and come back with a mechanical fault. Nine times out of ten your vehicle has been sabotaged.

When choosing a car rental company, our best recommendation, in terms of vehicle reliability, price, and overall helpfulness, is **Central Rent-a-Car** ((02) 222888 FAX (02) 339666, Standard Street, Box 4939, Nairobi, while other reputable operators — with offices in Nairobi and Mombasa — include **Avis** ((02) 334317 FAX (02) 215421, Box 49795, Nairobi; and **Hertz** ((02) 214456 FAX (02) 216871, Box 42196, Nairobi; and **Europcar** ((02) 334722, Bruce House, Standard Street, Box 40433, Nairobi.

The Talek River in the Maasai Mara Reserve: a dry-season magnet for game.

The best map of the country for motorists is Freytag and Berndt's 1:1,500,000, which also includes reasonable city-maps of Mombasa and Nairobi as well as a useful 1:700,000 inset of the Kenyan coast.

Courtesy on the road takes a slightly different form in Kenya. Whereas in the United Kingdom flashing highbeams means "Go ahead," in Kenya it is more likely to mean "I am going ahead — keep clear" and often it just means "hello." Although in principle cattle, bicycles, ox-carts and pedestrians should get out of the way of trucks and cars, in practice frequent use of the horn serves as a useful reminder to people who might have forgotten that they are sharing the road with faster vehicles, and constant beeping that would seem rude and assertive in the West is perfectly acceptable in Kenya. Although it might seem harsh, it is no longer recommended to stop for broken-down vehicles or hitchhikers waving desperately by the side of the road: there have been too many cases of ambush or hijack.

In case of breakdown, pile branches or trees fifty yards downstream on the road. It's a local equivalent to a warning triangle and will warn oncoming traffic, which might or might not have functioning lights. Get flat tires repaired as soon as possible: there are plenty of cheap puncture repair places (agree on the price first) in every village and you never

reasonable supply of these small blue notes, worth about 30 cents, as the alternative might be to part with a larger note, encouraging inflation as well as increasing the cost of traveling.

Drivers who are prepared to face these challenges will be rewarded with some of the finest views in the world, the chance to spot exotic game by the side of the road, and the unbeatable sense of satisfaction inherent in independent exploration.

Drive on. In the end, perhaps all you need to know is that driving is on the left. There are a number of truly spectacular drives. The newly-surfaced and little-used C51 from Marigat to Eldoret passes through the Tugen Hills in an endless succession of switchbacks and turns, combining ease and beauty; but many of the country's greatest drives match beautiful landscapes with quite demanding conditions. The C71 heading north to the eastern shores of Lake Turkana is an adventurous epic journey that few visitors — or even Kenyans — ever manage. Dropping down to the Maasai Mara from the west or north, over the Soit Ololol or Mau Escarpments provide vivid memories no amount of time can erase. The coast road breezes through the lowland heat with patches of jungle and farmland, strips developed for tourism, and other communities where life goes on at the speed of the seasons. And whenever the sun gets too tempting, the sheltered waters of Kenya's Indian Ocean shore are never more than five minutes away. And if you can cope with the slow belching traffic heading north out of Nairobi, the view on cresting the African Rift Valley stretches further than you knew existed.

Wherever you drive in Kenya, the journey is spiced by the beauty of the landscape and the details of everyday life, the roadside shacks and shops, colorful costumes and gentle smiling people, and glimpsed game feeding by the side of the road or racing, flustered, away from your car.

know when it might happen again. Keep the doors locked when driving through cities, and be ready to step on the gas if approached. In the event of an accident involving a pedestrian or casualty, it is recommended to drive to the nearest police station rather than stopping to assist. Emotions can run high and the situation can spiral out of control to no one's benefit. It is wise to sacrifice common humanity and play things safe.

It is usual, when parking in towns or cities, to pay a small parking fee to private security guards or official parking boys: they will also, to a considerable extent, look after your car and its contents. A 20-KSh note is useful here: motorists should make sure they keep a

Conditions are harsh in the Northern Frontier District, but the views superb.

Backpacking

Backpacking in Kenya is easy, cheap, and recommended, although travelers should be ready for a completely different experience of the country than their more moneyed counterparts will find in lodges and game-parks.

Whatever the style, on a budget the travel experience is going to be crowded. Clunky ancient buses, packed minivan *matatus*, or fast station-wagon expresses hurtling between cities all have one thing in common: they're always packed to capacity and beyond. Don't carry too much luggage: often it will stay on your lap, and bulky backpacks, especially with an external frame, will be a constant burden. It will be the lucky backpacker who avoids any experience of breaking down on Kenya's broken roads. When and if this happens is important to be flexible: if your *matatu* is clearly not about to be fixed by nightfall, flag down any passing vehicle. Whether truck or motorcar, your chances of getting a lift are better as a backpacker than a local Kenyan, not least because you are most likely to be able to pay for your onward lift.

If the light is failing in a patch of country haunted by either buffalo, lion or bandit, getting to the nearest town should be your first objective and

there will be other times to fret about your special status and the eventual fate of your fellow passengers. Generally they arrive, tired and dusty, a few hours later. In normal circumstances hitchhiking is no longer safe between the major cities but can be the only way to travel around rural areas. All passengers are expected to pay for their rides, and in any case be ready for it to take some time. I once spent eight days hitching to Lake Turkana, a distance that took me as many hours returning in a fast car. Near urban areas transport is so plentiful — and cheap — that few people try to hitch, and in any case it is not safe. Bear in mind that the poorest backpacker will be far richer than most Kenyans, and will be assumed to have valuable baggage. The first car to stop might not be a Samaritan.

Accommodation in Kenya can be very cheap, in small B&Ls ("Boarding and Lodgings") that range in comfort from clean-sheeted double beds with en-suite bathrooms gushing hot water

to small, insect-ridden sheds with a long-drop toilet, half a candle for lighting, a rag of a towel and a bucket in case you demand a shower. Rates as low as 50 cents allow travelers on any budget to visit Kenya for extended periods, but it won't always be comfortable. Don't get too hopeful when you see a sign saying "Hotel": often this just means restaurant and doesn't necessarily mean they provide accommodation. Small restaurants serving local food are almost always cheap and welcoming: there's a sink to wash your hands before and after eating, as cutlery is a luxury. In any case, the local staple, *ugali* (maize) is best eaten with the fingers and mashed into the rest of the meal: eaten with a fork it's completely tasteless.

Seeing Kenya's game is where backpackers might lose out. Going into a national park involves choosing between blowing your hard-kept budget or just giving it a miss. Park entry fees vary down from US$27 a day: enough to keep public transportation well clear. Ostrich, zebra and buffalo glimpsed from a crowded *matatu* is the most that can be expected from public transportation. Unless you strike it lucky and find someone — by hitching or starting up a conversation in a bar or hotel — who has a car and can give you a lift to a national park, the only way of ticking the "Big Five" — elephant, lion, buffalo, rhino and leopard — off your list is to reserve a quick camping safari through a budget operator. Good companies in this field include **Gametrackers Ltd.** ((02) 338927 FAX (02) 330903, Box 62042, Nairobi; and **Safari Camp Services** ((02) 228936 FAX (02) 212160, Box 44801, Nairobi (operators of the famed Turkana Bus). Even cheaper companies direct-sell on the streets of Nairobi. Three that have been around for long enough to acquire a veneer of respectability include **Savuka** ((02) 225108; **Kenia** ((02)

OPPOSITE: Campfire cuisine tastes even better in the bush. ABOVE: Local guides are best in the remote Shaba Reserve.

444572 WEB SITE www.gorp.com/kenia/;
and **Come to Africa Safaris** ((02)
213186. However, these are just the
most established of a rather risky end
of the industry. Providing the safari
experience for as little as US$50 a day,
they don't venture far from the beaten
trail or offer much in the way of
backup, service or information, but for
many young travelers they offer the
only affordable way to meet Africa's
wildlife. Industry insiders suspect that
they can only maintain their prices by
cheating the national parks out of
much-needed revenue on entry fees.

One example of what can go wrong
on these cheap safaris happened to me
in the city of Nakuru. Our driver/guide
interrupted our dinner to tell us the
morning game-drive would have to
be delayed. Our vehicle had broken
down. He suggested that we spend the
morning while he got the car fixed.
The infamous mechanics of Nakuru
had struck again. In this case our safari
vehicle had been sabotaged in the hope
of stopping our morning visit to the
national park. Each client had prepaid
park entry fees of US$27, but two of
us also had night flights to catch in
Nairobi. A few hours detained by a
back-street garage would mean racing
direct to the airport, releasing the park
entry tickets for sale on the black
market. I looked at the engine. Exhaust
was leaking from the joint between
manifold and muffler. Could be simple
to fix: but with a couple of stripped
threads and a few inventive mechanics
it was easy to see how the job could
be stretched. It was a bit difficult.
I wanted him to go and fix the problem
immediately while we finished our
meal. But for him to do this would
have gone too far to admitting the
con. I insisted that we take the game
drive, at least, the next morning. Even
though it wasn't ideal having a noisy
car it removed the motive to stretch
the repair.

This wasn't the only problem I found
on a recent trip investigating cheap
safaris. Others included breaking down

in the Maasai Mara — not so funny
next to five angry lions — and being
abandoned by the side of the road
for half a day. This meant that instead
of providing the evening game drive,
our vehicle could slip into the national
park on a minor track under the cover
of dusk.

In most cases, making reservations
locally doesn't even save money. Kenya's
cheapest safaris rely on subcontracted
minivans with no history of maintenance
and drivers who don't speak English and
would never be featured by international
tour operators. Move up a notch to
the middle of the market and service
improves dramatically: savings evaporate
as bulk reservations cut out the benefits

of tracking down safaris privately. Even backpackers are better advised to keep off the absolute baseline: beyond a certain point economies can only be made at your expense.

When safaris go wrong, there's more than convenience at risk: in isolated national parks, untrained guides or mechanical problems with subcontracted vehicles both spell danger. International tour operators choose reputable ground operators, and if difficulties arise are an easy target for complaints or legal action. Make reservations in Nairobi and any dispute will be resolved in a place where Africa's wildlife can really charge: a Kenyan courtroom.

Backpackers in Kenya can have the best time of all. They are more likely to meet the local people and find out about local culture first hand. Backpacker centers in Kenya include Lamu Island off the northern coast, where many visitors stay for months, and the distinctly untouristy center of Maralal town to the north of Nyahururu. Don't let shortage of funds stop your visit: just leave the game viewing until you're older. And richer.

Diani Beach is a favorite with travelers and also popular with European tour operators. OVERLEAF: Buffalo drink at Mountain Lodge's waterhole on the slopes of Mount Kenya.

Living It Up

The Kenyan high life is not
something you usually have to get
dressed up for. The country's most
luxurious establishments are generally
also the simplest, and the idea of total
paradise for most Kenyans — and
visitors — is to take a private tented
safari. Only in Africa are the most
exclusive places to stay campsites!

They are not campsites as we
know them. The tents are made from
heavy canvas, are large enough to
walk around and almost always offer
en-suite facilities, even if the shower
comes from a bucket swinging from
an overhanging tree. Dining is often
under the stars, with silver service,
linen tablecloths and cut glass, lit
by the flickering light of hurricane
lamps and the dancing shadows
of a campfire. Instead of the grand
buildings of the great European
hotels, in Africa the magnificent
landscapes and prolific game take
center stage: accommodation is
modest and practical, with the
luxuries being the view from the
wooden deck of your tent or lodge,
and the sophistication provided by
the company of fellow travelers and
the insights of your hosts around a
communal dining table.

Some of the smartest establishments
are operated by luxury chains, as these
are the only organizations with the nerve
to charge nightly rates that match many
Kenyans' annual income. Thus the
Mount Kenya Safari Club, the **Aberdare
Country Club**, and **Sweetwaters Tented
Camp**, all north of Nairobi, and the
luxurious **Mara Safari Club** in Kenya's
southwest are all operated by **Lonhro**
((02) 216940 FAX (02) 216796, Box 58581,
Nairobi. **Kichwa Tembo** in the Maasai
Mara is operated by the **Conservation
Corporation** ((02) 441001 FAX (02) 750512
E-MAIL conscorp@users.africaonline.co.ke,

Camping in Kenya doesn't always mean roughing it.

Box 74957, Nairobi (see MAASAI MARA, page 237). In Amboseli, **Tortilis Camp** ((02) 748307/27 FAX (0154) 22553 or (02) 740721 E-MAIL chelipeacock@attmail.com WEB SITE www.chelipeacock.com, Box 39806, Nairobi, is an outpost of luxury. In the north, the Samburu National Reserve is home to one of Kenya's most traditional tented camps, **Larsens** ((02) 540780 FAX (02) 543810, Box 40075, Nairobi.

Only in towns and cities do travelers have much choice of entertainment options. In cities, Kenya's nightlife is the stuff of legend. If, that is, you like drinking and dancing. The one thing that sets the country apart from almost anywhere else in the world is the open and friendly welcome that foreign visitors almost invariably receive. Poorly-lit streets are unsafe at night, and travel is best by taxi, but once inside almost any bar, the visitor seems to enter a charmed circle. Even the most boisterous bars seem to accept a single white face in a sea of Kenyans.

Every city maintains an independent nightlife that reflects its special personality. In Nairobi, the scene is divided into two separate parts. In the city center, the evenings start with drinks *al fresco* at the Norfolk's quietly-set **Delamere Terrace** with a clientele of visiting businessmen and war-seeking correspondents, or the **Thorn Tree Café** at the New Stanley, a haven of waiter-patrolled grace with low glass walls keeping at bay floods of returning office workers streaming from the city. Meanwhile at the **Jockey Club** in the Hilton the occasional Asian yuppie will try to drink a yard of ale in the hope of getting a night's free drinking, while what seems to be the city's entire criminal underclass gathers at the **Green Bar**, proud of being open day and night since 1919, in hope of catching a confused tourist early in the evening.

At this point it would be only sensible to do some fancy eating. To spend some serious money head for the larger hotels. The food's unlikely to be great but the prices will be reassuring. It's far better to try one of Nairobi's smaller restaurants, where the clientele are Kenyan and the prices are more realistic. The best French cuisine, a fraction of the cost in Europe, is **Allan Bobbe's Bistro** ((02) 336952, Cianda House, Koinange Street. Call ahead for reservations. For Japanese, try **Restaurant Akasaka Ltd.** ((02) 220299, 680 Hotel, Kenyatta Avenue, Box 47153; for Indian, **Haandi** ((02) 448294, in Westlands' Shopping Mall; while to sample all of Africa's wildlife take a 600-KSh taxi out to traditional favorite, the **Carnivore Restaurant** ((02) 501775, Langata Road, conveniently close to the national park, which serves a range of grilled game. None of these will break the bank, but all provide some of the finest food in Kenya (see WHERE TO EAT, page 129 in NAIROBI).

Back to the bars and the smart money, by this time, will have moved out of the city center. This late at night most of the local dives will be infested with at least one too many drunks, but if you don't fancy catching a taxi you can gatecrash the **Tanager Bar** in Rehema House to join senior civil servants wearing suit and tie, or **Invitation Bar** for office workers on the way up: they have a disco if the electricity is working, but it is often candlelit. The *wazungus* (white people) will have moved on to the suburbs: either to the mock-Tudor **Horseman** in Karen, or to Westlands where two bars close together form a focus. **Gypsies'** serves seafood *tapas* and drinkers spill out onto the street, while **Papa Loca** is a Tex-Mex joint with a shady courtyard. Depending on the crowd, both these bars are quite capable of serving through until four in the morning, but after about midnight serious party animals head on out: the **Simba Disco**, a part of the Carnivore Restaurant, offers disco at least and often live music, while the **Cantina Club**, on Wilson Airport Road, features African music, dancers and acrobats. Meanwhile, every night is crowded at both the **Florida nightclubs** in the city

A swimming pool is an ideal refuge from the midday sun.

center, where you can be sure of a live dance display and the opportunity to meet more prostitutes than you ever knew existed.

For a more restrained but potentially even more expensive finale to the evening, Nairobi has a choice of casinos: largest is the original **International Casino** on Chiromo Road, but this area is unsafe at night, even in a taxi: better to go the extra mile to the rather more civilized casino attached to the **Mayfair Court Hotel** in Westlands.

Family Fun

The excitement of watching the world's wildlife walk from the pages of books and onto the savanna by your safari vehicle will bring a smile to the face of any child. The sheer size of some of nature's wonders can't fail to impress, and the experience sets the groundwork for a lasting interest in wildlife and conservation in almost every child.

Under the age of five or so, they probably won't appreciate some of the more wonderful sights, and might remember instead long hours spent in vehicles, the company of strangers and the break of their routine. Renting a car is one option as this will give you the freedom to stop where necessary and alter plans to suit changing requirements. Bear in mind that you probably won't find a child seat in Kenya and should bring your own. Bring any light collapsible stroller as many hotels have long paths between rooms and public areas.

Children aged six or above are usually transformed by the experience of nature and also the excitement of camping out and eating around a bonfire. Flat spots can occur driving along dusty roads in the middle of the day: bring plenty of things to entertain them. One thing that does help are excellent children's toys on sale locally. Handcrafted from wood or wire, these can often provide hours of entertainment for the imaginative child, but then hours of entertainment might actually be needed.

At the same time parents will also want to bear in mind that in the wild, infants of all species are generally prey. Some of the unfenced game lodges don't accept children simply because they don't want to see their guests eaten, and their cut-off ages can vary: some lodges aren't prepared to take children under seven while for others, 12 is their lower limit. Check ahead with your selected lodges to see if they have any special restrictions.

Fenced lodges are generally far more accepting of small children. And for warm, loving childcare, there is no better place than Kenya. With one of the world's highest birthrates they get plenty of practice: the majority of the population is under 15 years of age. There aren't that many facilities especially for children: normally they're just included in adult activities from a very early age, and for most Kenyans this generally means work.

Kenya is an exotic destination at all levels and the average child will be absolutely fascinated by its surroundings. This can be dangerous, as they will have no clear understanding of the possible risks and hazards. It will take time to persuade them not to eat the local insects or drink the water. Nairobi's **Snake Farm** might be a good early stop if children are unaware of the dangers of venomous snakes, as they will get the chance to see a selection in relative safety.

Most resort hotels have babysitting and nanny services that are staffed by well-trained and practiced professionals, but it is well worth considering hiring a nanny for the duration of your stay, to ensure continuity of attention and consistency of care. The rate should not be too expensive. **Let's Go Travel ℂ** (02) 340331 FAX (02) 336890 E-MAIL info@ letsgosafari.com, Box 60342, Nairobi, should be able to assist in this.

Health is of course the major problem. To ensure clean toilet facilities stay in mid-range hotels and lodges. Most good

Children love Kenya but constant supervision is essential. There are crocs out there!

Malaria is a special problem. Even if young children can be persuaded to swallow malaria medicine — not always easy — it's still important to minimize their exposure to mosquitoes morning and evening. Which means nets: not every child's favorite way to go to sleep. Risks of malaria are much lower in the cool up-country air rather than the steamy climate of the coast — a fact that, with young children, might end up dictating much of your travel itinerary.

In rural areas, it's accepted to view the whole country as a playground. This indeed is what the local children do if they haven't been taken out to work the fields. But there are few establishments set up specifically to cater to children. There are two waterslide centers that should be top of the list for parents: in Nairobi, there is **Splash**, next door to the Carnivore Restaurant, and in Mombasa there is **Pirates** on Nyali Beach, where waterslides through the day will keep children entertained, at least until 6 PM when both are turned back over to the adults. In Nairobi there are several opportunities for children to get right up close to animals, but this should not be attempted if they are young or naturally nervous: at Nairobi's **Giraffe Sanctuary** a raised platform allows kids to feed endangered Rothschild's giraffes, but any child younger than eight might find the animals just a little big. Although Nairobi's **Maasai Ostrich Farm** gives a unique opportunity to can get close to the world's largest birds, it is important to remember that ostrich don't hide their heads in the sand: when scared they kick.

hotels have links with reliable and well-qualified doctors and most mainstream western drugs are available to those who are able to pay for them, but bear in mind that in case of injury or serious illness good medical facilities are generally limited to the major cities.

For general child maintenance you can buy all the basics, including sterilizer, diapers and baby food in the supermarkets of any major town but your favorite brands might only be available — if at all — in the boutiques of the better hotels. Disposable diapers, preferred brands of baby food and motion sickness pills should all be brought along in case they are unavailable: hats, sandals and sun screen are also wise supplies to carry.

In the coastal resort hotels, most of the swimming pools are surveyed by alert lifeguards, but don't leave children unattended, especially on the beach. Occasional strong currents can be a danger and the tropical waters contain unexpected hazards from hard-to-spot stonefish to fluffy-looking sea urchins.

And whatever older children may claim, discos in Kenya are rarely suitable for teenagers.

Cultural Kicks

Kenya has a lively theatrical scene, based in Nairobi, and the self-censorship of the 1970s is starting to fade in the more overtly malcontented 1990s. The best theater is generally thought to be Nairobi's small **Professional Center** ((02) 225506, Parliament Road, that puts on modern works from Africa and classics from the West — usually with fast-talking ad-libs reflecting the concerns of the local audience. It's a small theater where the audience feels directly involved, and some of their musicals are sometimes well worth catching: contact them to find out what they're showing. The **National Theater** ((02) 220536, Moi Avenue, just opposite the Norfolk Hotel, also puts on good performances, with the focus clearly on African drama and Kenyan writers. Sometimes this means that you won't understand a word! Ask what's on and don't forget to ask which language will be used. More live performances are put on at the adjacent **French Cultural Center** ((02) 336263, Loita Avenue, and the **Goethe Institute** ((02) 224640, also on Loita Avenue near Uhuru Highway in the

city center: although primarily intended to present the French and German cultures (respectively) to a Kenyan audience, they also showcase Kenyan art and dance. Call for their schedules.

Tracking down good art can take rather longer. Most commercial art in the city center tends to be aimed squarely at the tourist market with an unrelenting focus on wildlife scenes: allright in itself, but too much can wear thin. To see good contemporary Kenyan art, check out the upper floor of the National Archives, in the old Bank of India building on Moi Avenue, at the **National Gallery** and, of the private galleries in the town center, the **Gallery Watatu** on Standard Street can usually be relied upon to show some works by new artists of interest, at least until they are sold.

Much of Kenya's cultural heritage is not based in theater or flat, representative paintings, but in vivid and organic sculptures in wood or stone. There's a fast tradition of copying quality though,

OPPOSITE: At Nairobi's Giraffe Sanctuary TOP these magnificent creatures eat from your hand. But in the Maasai Mara BOTTOM it's safer to stay on the roof. ABOVE: Entertainment by Kamba dancers from the Machakos region.

and it can be hard at first sight to distinguish real originality and flair from cheaply-produced products made on industrial scale. All it takes to get your eye in is to take a look at some quality sculpture. Some of this can be found, as you'd expect, at Nairobi's **National Museum** on Museum Road, while still more is jumbled on the floor of the **National Archives** on Moi Avenue. The **African Heritage** off Kenyatta Avenue is a combination shop/museum/restaurant where some of the finest handicrafts and sculptures from Kenya and Ethiopia can be found and, if required, bought. As an added attraction, live African music is played on Saturday and Sunday afternoons. Some high-quality modern sculpture — often at high prices — is on display at the **Africa Cultural Gallery** on Mama Ngina Street in the Jubilee Insurance Building.

More of Kenya's culture is encapsulated in dance and costume. Once more, your first stop should be the National Museum. However more dramatic displays are on offer in the capital. The **Bomas of Kenya** on Forest Edge Road, just past the national park main gate, offers daily displays of traditional dancing every afternoon between 2:30 PM and 4 PM. Somewhat disconcertingly, these are performed by a professional dance troupe who quickly change between Kenya's tribal cultures, which might maintain standards of dancing but detracts from the authenticity.

A rather better experience of potted culture awaits visitors to Mombasa in the **Bombolulu Center**, just south of Nyali Bridge, which also has tribal *manyattas* (reed or mud) dwellings, and costumes. Other ways of experiencing local dance styles are more haphazard: many lodges persuade their local communities to show off the local dances, while travelers getting off the beaten trail will find it quite easy to gatecrash local dances that take the place of television in outlying communities: just follow the noise after nightfall and find fireside hop-alongs where the music is by voice and drum, and the lyrics mainly focused on cattle, their horns and overall condition.

To track down the rich musical traditions of the present day, it helps to find a Kenyan guide: it's quite hard to find live local music venues in Nairobi, as most turn to the more moneyed tastes of White and Asian communities. Regularly worthwhile venues that specialize in African music include the **Ngong Hills Hotel** on Ngong Road, the **Makuti Park Club** in Nairobi South B Shopping Center and the nearby **Peacock Inn**. These regularly provide local music with the big nights being Wednesday, Friday and Saturday. At Mombasa local bands lured by foreign dollars line the hotel waterfronts along the lively beach on Bamburi Beach to the north of Mombasa Island. In general, authentic local music is easier to find in the less cosmopolitan provincial cities, especially on weekends. Just ask at your hotel, but specify that it's live African music you're after (mime a guitar) or you'll get directions for the nearest disco if you're lucky, and brothel if you're not.

ABOVE: Mombasa's Jain Temple is a vibrant blast of Hindu culture. RIGHT: The colorful dress of Kenya's rural pastoralists.

Shop till You Drop

First-time visitors to Kenya are likely to be overwhelmed by the first onslaught of the souvenir sellers. Prices start high, especially for visitors with the characteristic pallor of a new arrival, and an American accent is a real drawback in negotiations.

But persist and there are real bargains on offer. Craftsmanship can be high although you'll have to expect this to be reflected in the price. It is worth paying more for something that will persist as a thing of value than buying cheaply something you'll be embarrassed to give away on your return. Whatever you're buying, the more you know about what is available and the quality to expect will help you gain the upper hand in the long and convoluted bargaining process.

Bargaining is almost always necessary, apart from a few fixed-price shops and hotel boutiques. Even then it's always worth pointing out flaws or trying for a reduction. Some people find it a frustrating waste of time while the vendors invariably regard it as an endlessly interesting duel of wits. Their opening price depends on any number of factors, one of which will be how much money they think you have. The first secret of successful bargaining is to avoid getting bounced into making an offer higher than what you think the product is actually worth. If in doubt keep quiet, and don't let a big opening price persuade you to revise your initial estimate of value upwards. Once you've named a price you will be expected, if not to shift upwards, at least to stick to it. An offer once made cannot be retracted without causing real offence. An occasional and rather dishonorable way of getting the keenest deal can be to bargain on the basis that you're buying five — or ten — of whatever object is being discussed, and then, at the last minute, decide just to buy one.

Wood carvings can represent exceptional value. Napkin rings, salad servers, elegant hardwood bowls and coasters, if well-made, are always useful: stylized stick sculptures, masks festooned with matted hair, and herds of miniature carved rhinos can travel less well. "Makonde statues," usually of people and with a high ebony gloss, are often just lighter wood dyed with shoe-polish: check the quality by the weight. Best, in general, to buy blackened lightwood: there are more souvenir vendors around than surviving ebony trees and it is illegal to carve Kenyan ebony.

Basketry is an art form in Kenya, and prices often very low indeed. Craft-shops invariably have a stock of handmade place mats, fruit bowls and laundry baskets, painstakingly crafted and often using natural dyes. For more substantial products like sofas, dog kennels or carports, head out to the Racecourse Road. Sisal handbags are strong and hard-wearing, but check how much they cost, imported, back home: essential information for the bargaining process.

Soapstone sculpture is found in almost every Kenyan souvenir stall, and all originate from mines near the village of Tabaka near Kisii in the west of the country. Often beautifully carved and painted, it is also very cheap, considering the hours of work that go into carving and polishing. Once more, bowls and plates are most likely to be useful, but bear in mind that soapstone is heavy: think ahead to how far you'll have to carry it.

Tribal beads characterize many goods fashioned by the Maa tribes, which include the Maasai, the Samburu and Turkana. From key-rings to necklaces, these are often exceptionally beautiful and easy to carry, and also provide a lifesaving income to traditional women working from their home *manyattas*. Price should depend on quality: watch carefully to make sure it does. In the same category shields, spears and tribal regalia are more expensive if actually used rather than purpose-made for the tourist industry. These can be cheaper bought in their region of origin but if

TOP: Watch painters at work in Nairobi's art galleries. BOTTOM: Cowrie-shell necklaces are very much part of Kenyan culture.

that isn't possible and you're in Nairobi on any Tuesday, check out the **Maasai Market** that takes place on waste ground off Muranga'a Road one day a week. Quality is often very high and the prices low.

The single most underrated product available in Kenya are the batiks and weavings produced for the — highly critical — local market. *Kangas*, designed for women, are sold in pairs with one half used as a papoose for the inevitable child. In thin cotton and delicate patterns, they also generally have a proverb included in the design. Ask the vendor to translate the message: my favorite read "Don't sleep with fleas." *Kikois* derive from the coast: generally striped, they have their origins in Islamic Lamu, are made in thicker cotton and are designed to be worn by men. Other fabrics on offer include batiks, often designed to be stretched and hung, with prices totally dependent on the quality of workmanship and the textile used. Pay a lot for a lot.

One of the best places to buy handicrafts in general is Nairobi, which attracts some of the best produce from all over the country. Shop at the **Central Market**, however, and expect to pay dearly for the privilege. Around a small core of vegetable sellers are poised ranks of sharp salesman selling products, usually, of indifferent quality. Better is the **Kariakor Market** (named after the First World War "Carrier Corps" in which many Kenyans "decided" to help the British war effort), off Racecourse Road east of the city center, where you'll be rubbing shoulders with local shoppers rather than other tourists. Or let your money go to a good cause: some of the best outlets are run by charities or have a proportion of their revenue going to a good cause. Two of these in Nairobi include the **Undugu Shop** in Woodvale Grove, Westlands, with a wide range of handicrafts benefiting charities around Nairobi, or the **Utamaduni Crafts Center**, Bogani Road, Langata, where 18 specialist shops trade on behalf of the Kenyan Wildlife Service.

Short Breaks

Kenya might seem a long way to go for just a short time. But there are plenty of short breaks that can give a vivid feel of the country in just a few days.

If it's your first visit to Kenya and you have little time, there's really no contest. Kenya's main international attraction lies in its wildlife. As such the Maasai Mara, the country's most game-filled national park, is the obvious choice. Fly-in safaris can quickly reach most of the main lodges, meaning that within hours of leaving your desk it is possible to be immersed in the famous migration of wildebeest. You won't be the first — or indeed the only — person with more money than time, so most of the mainstream travel companies are used to arranging short breaks in the Mara and many have daily departures — by air or road — at prices far lower than you would be able to arrange independently.

Whether to drive or fly depends on how much time you have available. A jet-lagged drive from Nairobi will knock much of the pleasure out of a short stay. Even two nights in the Mara will seem rushed after six to eight hours on a poor road with the same prospect again on the way home. Flights are a little more expensive, but the Maasai Mara is popular enough to support a full scheduled service and to fly is usually more convenient. Domestic flights go from Wilson Airport, five kilometers (three miles) south of the city center on Langata Road: passengers from the International Airport therefore do not need to travel in to the city center to transit for their domestic flight. Don't cut things too fine on the way back though: internal flights in Kenya are liable to delay and a missed international link can stop a short break being short.

But if the Maasai Mara epitomizes classic scenes of African wildlife, many

Africa's giant baobab trees can live for more than 1,500 years.

visitors will want to take a more individual look at a different aspect of Kenya. Charter flights and many small, dirt airstrips open up the most remote parts of Kenya as realistic destinations for increasingly busy travelers to pack the African experience into just a few days.

And at this point you realize the sky's the limit. Most of Kenya's more expensive lodges are well used to collecting clients from the local airport and just as capable of arranging short game-spotting breaks, as well as being valuable parts of longer tours. Choose one that combines several immediate activities such as riding, as well as tame — or at least reliable — game since there's not going to be time to tune in thoroughly to the wild. Although a town with an airport is ideal, most of the more expensive lodges have access to private airstrips.

A short break is probably not the best time to experiment with complicated travel arrangements within Kenya. Internal flights are subject to overbooking and schedules change. Although individual lodges are described in detail later in this book and contact details are given, in the context of a short break

it is probably wise to use a major Kenyan operator accustomed to making travel arrangements on the ground such as **Let's Go Travel** ((02) 340331 FAX (02) 336890, Box 60342, Nairobi, or **UTC** ((02) 331960 FAX (02) 331422 WEB SITE www.unitedtour.com, Box 42196, Nairobi.

If restricted to travel by car it is best not to aim too far from Nairobi. The main safari operators are well able to supply vehicles and drivers to explore further, or you can rent a car of your own. Don't be too ambitious on brief itineraries if traveling overland: heavy traffic and poor roads can make distances feel longer than they look on the map. You will see a lot of Kenya, but on a long jet-lagged drive, are unlikely to enjoy it. Sensible objectives for short breaks starting in Nairobi generally head north up the spectacular Rift Valley and include Lake Naivasha. Not only beautiful in itself, it is good for bird watching, spotting hippos and relaxing, and is only a two-hour drive north of Nairobi. There is a good range of accommodation options, but it's popular with city weekenders too: reserve ahead. In town, **La Belle Inn** ((0311) 21007 FAX (0311) 21119, Moi Avenue, Naivasha, is one of the oldest hotels in Kenya; the rate is 1,900 KSh for a double, bed and breakfast. On the lake shore, best is the **Lake Naivasha Country Club** ((02) 540780 FAX (02) 543810, Block Hotels,

ABOVE: Three-horned chameleons blend in with the leaves. OPPOSITE: Bird watching TOP on Lake Naivasha. Zebra in Samburu BOTTOM take no notice of safari vehicles.

Box 40075, Nairobi (US$162 per double, full board); alternatively **Elasmere** ((0311) 21055 FAX (0311) 21074, Box 1497, Naivasha, where Joy Adamson lived and worked with lions, is an atmospheric place to stay (see LAKE NAIVASHA, page 139).

Lake Nakuru is a two-hour drive further north from Naivasha and contains an underrated park surrounding a flamingo-filled lake and is a good place to spot game of all kinds including black rhinoceros. Around Lake Nakuru, the best dwellings are the **Sarova Lion Hill** ((02) 713333 FAX (02) 715566, Box 72493, Nairobi (US$120 to US$180 for a double, full board); and **Lake Nakuru Lodge** ((02) 226778, Box 561, Nairobi (US$100 to US$160 for a double, full board). There is camping (US$15 per person) inside the park (see LAKE NAKURU, page 142).

Beyond the Rift Valley lakes are the Aberdare Mountains, a drive of five hours north from the capital. These cloud-kissed mountains are unspoiled and little visited: partly because the roads are so bad within the park. It's easy to get stuck and this is not an excuse accepted by many airlines for missed flights. So it's safest to stay instead at the **Aberdares Country Club**, where the greatest danger is a low-flying golf ball; and if time permits reserve a night spotting game at the **Ark**. See THE ABERDARES, page 159, for further details. Reservations for both the Country Club and the Ark are available through **Lonhro** ((02) 216940 FAX (02) 216796, Box 58581, Nairobi.

An alternative destination, a five-hour drive from Nairobi, is **Sweetwaters Reserve**. This private sanctuary is near Nanyuki and is home to a tame rhinoceros called Morani who likes to have his stomach scratched, but also houses Kenya's largest chimp sanctuary. Night drives in search of leopard are a specialty. Reserve through **Lonhro**.

If time is really short, a matter of a few hours between connecting flights, there's the chance to spot almost all the "Big Five" — elephant, lion, buffalo, rhino and leopard — within half an hour of the airport in Nairobi National Park. Even a taxi driver can be persuaded to drive through, although you're likely to see a lot more from the higher position of a safari vehicle, and a qualified driver/guide, possibly linked by radio with other vehicles and park rangers, is much more likely to find you good sightings. Within hearing distance of the hum of Nairobi's traffic, the 120-sq-km (46-square-miles) of the national park contains everything from rhinoceros to cheetah: only elephants are banned as they knock over too many trees.

OPPOSITE: Five out of Kenya's seven rivers start from the Aberdares Mountains. ABOVE: Hippos yawn through the day. RIGHT: Lamu Island is perfect for a beach break.

The best way to see this is on a half-day tour: minivans and drivers are available at reasonable rates through **Let's Go Travel**, or with other operators such as **UTC**.

Fly into Mombasa's international airport and a whole range of different opportunities open up along the coast. If time permits best to make the three-hour drive to Watamu. If splashing out, check straight into **Hemingways** ((0122) 32624 FAX (0122) 32256, www.hemingways.com/, Box 267, Watamu; live rather more cheaply at **Ocean Sports** ((0122) 32008 FAX (0122) 32266, right next door, or go all-inclusive at **Turtle Bay** ((0122) 32003 FAX (0122) 32268, Box 10, Watamu. All these can plug you in to a quick dive with Aqua Ventures, and both Hemingways and Ocean Sports are fully involved with the area's other specialty, game fishing, while Turtle Bay leads the way on conventional water sports. Not a bad way to fill the decompressing hours, as 24 hours are needed after scuba diving before any flight. If time is really short there are plenty of worthwhile dives and beaches even nearer Mombasa: **Bamburi Beach** is barely 20 minutes by car from the airport. If only the best is good enough, check in to **Whitesands** ((011) 485926 FAX 485652 E-MAIL whitesands@form-net.com, Box 90173, Mombasa.

Your beach hotel will, in any case, be surrounded by exotic plants and animals: look closely and however luxurious the facilities, there'll never be any doubt you're deep in Africa. Watamu is backed by the Arabuko-Sokoke Forest while in Mombasa itself, the resident hippopotamuses are just part of the attraction of the **Bamburi Quarry Nature Trail**. For a short-break safari experience from a coastal base, ideal for overnight stays, head back inland from Mombasa to the **Shimba Hills Forest Lodge** or **Kwale Elephant Sanctuary**, both within two hours of Mombasa and with transportation readily arranged from Mombasa's hotels or through **UTC**.

Festive Flings

With a per capita income of US$320 a year, most Kenyans need quite a lot of encouragement to come out and party. The many religions of the country provide the vital spark.

For the majority Christian population, the biggest public celebration is Easter, with Christmas, as in the West, being a quieter, more low-key display. And it is the Christian calendar that dictates Kenya's national holidays. However Muslims make up 30% — and rising — of the population so their big festivals are also observed, especially on the coast. The beginning and end of Ramadan and the Muslim New Year are the cause for major celebrations, but exact dates will vary from year to year. The biggest parties happen at Eid, the end of Ramadan, now around Christmas but steadily shifting earlier in the year. Maulidi, the Prophet's birthday, is celebrated most in Lamu, with processions.

Meanwhile a significant minority of Hindus celebrate the colorful festivals of their own religion, especially inland.

Once more, the exact dates vary and predicting them even a year ahead is a matter for an astrologer familiar with the lunar calendar. Further festivals particular to specific tribal groups are also observed but rarely advertised. It's a question of asking around.

Some of the biggest festivities are entirely secular, grouped around government-run agricultural shows. These tour the provincial cities and can provide fascinating insights into Kenya's rural way of life.

For most "Kenyan Cowboys," the endangered, hard-drinking white Africans, the last weekend in May is their party time. To attend you'll need initiative and probably camping equipment, as their precise location moves about. From the coast, they converge on Diani for an anything-goes sporting extravaganza called "**Diani Rules**," the secret being that there are no rules. To track down this year's Diani Rules, a good starting point is the **Safari Beach Hotel (** (0127) 2726 FAX (0127) 2357, Box 90690, Mombasa. Meanwhile on the same weekend the Nairobi population decamp in their green Range-Rovers and baggy shorts to a secret location in the heart of the bush for an unique rally called the Rhino Charge. The aim is to cover ten checkpoints over the course of a day while clocking up the minimum mileage: many cars don't make it, but the weekend in the bush has become a Kenya tradition. One operator who can help you find this event, and can even arrange for you to enter if you give plenty of notice, is **Rafiki Africa Ltd. (** (02) 884238 FAX 710310 E-MAIL safarico@arcc.or.ke WEB SITE kilimanjaro.com/safaris/rafiki, Box 76400, Nairobi.

Public holidays follow the Christian calendar, with New Year's Day, Good Friday and Easter Monday, Christmas Day and Boxing Day. June 1 is Madaraka Day, celebrating the granting of self-government; October 10 is Moi Day (with crowds paid to celebrate this one at the moment); October 20 is Kenyatta Day and December 12 is Independence Day.

Galloping Gourmets

East Africa is not known as a gastronomic paradise. So Kenya comes as a pleasant surprise. The best chefs are the subject of hot competition amongst Kenya's top restaurants and lodges and standards are often extremely high. They are helped by one great factor: Kenya's range of climates that run from the snow-capped peaks of Kilimanjaro, through the temperate highlands and down to the steamy tropics of the coastal belts. Great cooks can pick and choose from the finest ingredients, be they lobster from the sea or Aberdeen Angus from the fields. Meanwhile, a thriving agricultural sector produces every type of fruit: strawberries and apples rival the finest of Europe, while mangos and papayas are just some of the tropical specialties. In every case, everything is locally grown, glistening fresh and tasting of rich Kenyan soil. As a result, the best restaurants and hotels are free to specialize in every type of world cuisine, working with the best ingredients.

These advantages do not apply so readily to the local cooks at traditional restaurants, whose aim is generally to provide cheap, filling dishes at minimal cost. Often the cooking equipment is

LEFT: Kenya's Muslims celebrate the holy days of Islam according to the lunar calendar. ABOVE: Cooks in Kenya lack sophisticated kitchens but cuisine can be superb.

limited to a saucepan and a small clay oven filled with firewood. However the local Kenyan cuisine should be a feature of every visitor's experience of the country, and can often be delicious, especially at the better restaurants. The cheaper versions are likely to be a central feature for travelers on a budget.

In the mornings, the standard diet at local establishments are *mandazi*, home-cooked doughnuts washed down with a mug — or two — of hot, sweet tea. Local restaurants are often open only at lunchtime, and serve a limited menu that comprises maize (*ugali*) with beans and a tough stew made from whatever meat was available that morning, often goat, and perhaps a plate called spinach but usually kale. *Matoke* is something of a luxury: this Ugandan specialty is made from mashed green plantains. *Githeri* is a vegetable stew with everything put in, sometimes meat. Thanks to the Asian influence, a common side-dish is chopped *chapatis*.

Generally Kenyan food is eaten with the hands, partly because knives and forks are a comparatively recent sophistication, but also because many of the dishes, especially *ugali*, need to be kneaded with the fingers to become at all palatable.

Almost every hotel will advertise "Nyama Choma," the classic Kenyan dish of roast meat, usually goat. Perhaps surprisingly in view of the primitive conditions in which they are prepared, meals are often absolutely delicious. Even the meanest shack can sometimes surprise. However most good hotels will put on Kenyan dishes, prepared to the highest standards, for their guests to experience local styles of cooking.

On the coast, the long maritime tradition has made coconut milk and the spices of Asia integral ingredients in meals that reflect the cosmopolitan influence of many cultures. The basis is invariably fish from the ocean. Meanwhile the pastoral tribes, such as the Maasai and Samburu, live entirely on blood, "milked" from the necks of their cattle, and milk.

Only in the cities, Mombasa and Nairobi, will visitors to Kenya have the chance to experience a true variety of cuisines. Kenya's widespread Asian influence means that there is a wide range of — often excellent — Indian restaurants. Urban Kenya has some world-class restaurants specializing in French, Japanese, and Chinese cuisine. Tourist lodges and hotels offer a range of classic recipes and small establishments specialize in Ethiopian or West African traditional menus. If just seeing Kenya's wildlife isn't enough, restaurants such as Nairobi's **Carnivore Restaurant** on Langata Road, or the restaurant at the **Safari Park Hotel**, 14 km (nine miles) north of the city center, offer special all-you-can-eat selections where the animals of your choice are grilled and carved onto your plate. Zebra steaks hover between the flavors of cow and horse, giraffe has a gamey edge, while crocodile, despite tasting rather of lobster, invariably manages to turn my stomach with its reptilian texture.

For drink, the choice reflects an enthusiasm which leads many visitors to assume that this is Kenya's elusive national sport. Although there is a full range of soft drinks available, my favorite is Stoney, the local ginger beer. As for real beer, countless versions are produced, all tasting much the same, sold in half-liter bottles and all of about the same strength — four to five percent alcohol. Kenyans take their choice of brands very seriously, and will often refuse a drink if the label's wrong. Tusker is the market leader, White Cap favored by more mature drinkers, Export for the upwardly mobile (if you believe the advertising which most Kenyans do), and Malt (sold in smaller bottles) for epicures. Cans of Castle Beer, from South Africa, are a relatively new arrival and tourist lodges and hotels will sell a range of imported beers. Sometimes, to justify

TOP: The wildlife's on your plate at Nairobi's Carnivore Restaurant. BOTTOM: Kenya's farms provide a steady supply of fresh fruit.

high prices, they only serve imported beers. Beer in tourist lodges will be sold chilled, but most of the drinks handed through security cages in local bars will be warm. Specify *"baridi"* if you'd like your drink chilled and hope they have a working refrigerator.

For wine, some drinkable brews are produced in the Naivasha area, but nothing that would have serious tasters reaching for their wallets. Papaya wine is an interesting experience — worth one try at least — while most good wines in Kenya have been imported from South Africa.

Most rural Kenyans have never tasted wine, and can't afford beer. They rely on *changa'a*, distilled from maize in huts and *manyattas* all over the country. Fiery and potent, newspaper stories often report drinking binges that end in sickness, blindness and death, but old ladies sipping and stirring their homemade spirits in the privacy of their own huts insist this is an evil rumor put about the mainstream brewers to try to sell more beer. Better stick to the local spirits, vodka, whiskey or rum, sold in bottles or 30-ml (one-fl-oz) sachets (called mini-packs) by small bars and shops throughout the country. Tear the mini-pack open with your teeth and mix the contents with anything that will mask the taste.

Special Interests

Kenya has a wide range of special interest operators, often focused on specific sports and so listed in SPORTING SPREE, page 38. But not everything in Kenya has to do with sport. The following specialists cater to focused travelers.

BUSH HOMESTAYS

One of the best ways to experience Kenya is by staying in private houses. Meet highly knowledgeable farmers and ranchers on their home turf. This is not the cheapest way of seeing the country — Kenya's landed gentry value their privacy and charge for it — but it can be extremely rewarding. Many of the best private farms and rural manor houses can be centrally booked in Nairobi by **Bush Homes of East Africa** ((02) 571661 FAX (02) 571665 E-MAIL Bushhome@africaonline.co.ke, Box 56923, Nairobi.

BIRDWATCHERS

Kenya is a paradise for birdwatchers. A range of habitats is available: the arid north, the Rift Valley lakes, forests at Kakamega in the west and Arabuko–Sokoke on the hothouse lowlands, swamps at Saiwa and the different habitats of the famous national parks mean that every species of East African bird and European migrant are represented. Specialist safaris for ornithologists are offered by **Bataleur Safaris** ((02) 227048 FAX (02) 891007, Mezzanine Floor, Hilton Building, Mama Ngina Street, Box 42562, Nairobi.

LITERARY TOURS

Kenya's great literary traditions are reflected in a number of special attractions. Remember *Out of Africa*? Isak Dinesen's house in Nairobi has been lovingly preserved as a recreation of the pioneer years where Happy Valley was a larger-than-life world at the frontier of civilization. The modest grace of her plantation house puts the experience in perspective, and even the shortest visit will bring her novels to vivid life. Much of the film was shot in the grounds, although interior shots were in studio. But the ghosts of the past are so stained in the wood that after visiting the house one question remains: how much was fiction?

Kuki Goldman, author of *I dreamed of Africa* and other books, is also still resident in Kenya, and has a stunning home to the north of the country northeast of Lake Baringo called Mukutan Retreat. Chalets built in the style of African Rondavels are built into the rock of Mukutan Gorge and

Water is the lifeline in the arid north of Kenya.

are run as an exclusive homestay where Africa takes center stage. The main person doing the retreating, however, is Kuki herself and guests she hasn't met are positively discouraged. Only the determined should make the pilgrimage!

Joy Adamson's famous house, Elasmere, set on the Naivasha Lake shore towards Kongoni Game Valley, is a pleasant and very quiet place to stay and soak up the atmosphere of a private ranch. This was where her life with lions brought Africa to life for millions and thrust conservation issues onto the world stage. Less a hotel experience and more like staying in a private house, the friendly staff are happiest when they find guests are familiar with Joy Adamson's life and work, and committed to conservation. Reservations can be made directly from **Elasmere** ((0311) 21055 FAX (0311) 21074, Box 1497, Naivasha (7,000 KSh per double, full board).

Taking a Tour

Although many travelers prefer the freedom and flexibility of making their own travel arrangements, in Kenya this won't always save money. Some of the larger companies are able to negotiate special rates and discounts and whether for a safari or a beach break, reserving with a tour operator often works out cheaper than going it alone. Tour operators based in Nairobi can sometimes offer more up-to-date knowledge about the local situation while larger international companies have the advantage that travelers enjoy the protection of their domestic consumer laws. Listed below are some of the more respected operators in Kenya with overseas contact details where appropriate.

Let's Go Travel ((02) 340331 FAX (02) 336890 E-MAIL info@letsgosafari.com, Box 60342, Nairobi, has been

The cliffs around Lake Baringo teem with life, a paradise for birdwatchers.

consistently recommended by travelers over the years for being knowledgeable, efficient,
and helpful without being pushy. They specialize in coming up with travel plans for independent travelers and are based in Caxton House, Standard Street, Nairobi.

UTC (United Touring Company) ((02) 331960 FAX (02) 331422 WEB SITE www.unitedtour.com, Box 42196, Nairobi, is one of the largest operators of scheduled tours and tailor-made travel in Kenya and supply the ground arrangements to many tour operators who, after adding their markup, feature set itineraries in their overseas brochures.

SOMAK Travel specializes in packaged safaris to suit a range of budgets, from cheap and cheerful *matatus* to high-gloss beach breaks, and have offices in the United Kingdom, Nairobi and Mombasa: in the United Kingdom ((0181) 423 3000 FAX (0181) 423 7700, Harrovian Village, Bessborough Road, Harrow on the Hill, Middlesex HA1 3EX; in Nairobi ((02) 337333 FAX (02) 218954, Eighth Floor, Corner House, Mama Ngina Street, Box 48495, Nairobi; in Mombasa ((011) 313871/2 FAX (011) 315514, Somak House, Mikindani Road, Box 90738, Mombasa.

Abercrombie & Kent are a leading operator at the top end of the market with 30 years of experience arranging travel in Africa. They have offices in the United States ((708) 954-2944 US TOLL-FREE (800) 323-7308, 1520 Kensington Road, Oak Brook, IL 60521; in Australia ((03)9699 9766, 90 Bridgeport Street, Albert Park, Melbourne, Victoria 3206; in the United Kingdom ((0171) 730 9600 FAX (0171) 730 9376, Sloane Square House, Holbein Place, London SW1 8NS; and in Nairobi ((02) 334995 FAX (02) 228700, Bruce House, Standard Street, Box 59749.

For specialist wildlife expeditions in search of gorillas in Zaire and longer private tented safaris way off the beaten track, one Kenyan operator who has received particular praise from film companies and private parties for personal service at reasonable cost is **Rafiki Africa Ltd.** ((02) 884238 FAX (02) 710310 E-MAIL safarico@arcc.or.ke WEB SITE www.kilimanjaro.com/safaris/rafiki, Box 76400, Nairobi.

The **African Adventure Company** ((954) 781-3933 US TOLL-FREE (800) 882-WILD, 1600 Federal Highway, Pompano Beach, FL 33062, offers a range of African programs and safari choices to the United States market.

Mountain Travel Sobek ((510) 527-8100 US TOLL-FREE (800) 227-2384, 6420 Fairmount Avenue, El Cerrito, CA 94530, specializes in hiking, rafting and adventure travel for travelers based in the United States.

Africa Travel Centers are specialist safari outlets, and have offices in Australia, America and New Zealand, all sister companies to the London-based Africa Travel Shop. Contact details are: in the United Kingdom ((0171) 387 1211 FAX (0171) 383 7512, 4 Medway Court, Leigh Street, London WC1H 9QX; in the United States, ((908) 870-0223, FAX (908) 870-0278, 197 Wall Street, West Long Branch, NJ 07764; in Australia ((02) 9267 3048, Level 12, 456 Kent Street, Sydney NSW 2000; in New Zealand ((09) 520 2000, 21 Remuera Road, Box 9365, Newmarket, Auckland.

For imaginative tours that combine riding, walking and stays in bush homes, contact London-based **Art of Travel** ((0171) 738 2038, FAX (0171) 738 1893, 21 The Bakehouse, Bakery Place, 119 Altenburg Gardens, London SW11 1JQ, UK, who are opening up an increasingly imaginative set of options.

In rural Kenya, life is still lived according to ancient traditions and ceremonies.

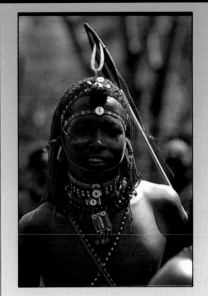

The
Grand
Safari

"The hump of Africa
  Soaring skywards amid the clouds
  Like a covenant knot upon th'equator
  A sentry among the clouds
  Forever pointing us to God,
  For us soliciting the rain
  The blessed milk of Africa.
  In whose northern desert land
  Sand dunes roll over eternal silence…"

— John Mbiti, *Kenya our Motherland*

In everyone's heart is a longing for adventure. The open savanna, the lions, cheetahs, antelope, elephants, and giraffes, the setting sun, the color of coal and blood, the dry desert air, the warriors leaning on their spears as they watch their herds, the grass-roof huts clustered behind thornscrub fences, the miraculous stars of clear African nights: all these images haunt our ancestral memories and the reveries of our childhood. But it is not a vanished world.

Modern, exciting, cosmopolitan Kenya, "the pride of Africa," has incomparable parks and reserves that resurrect this vanished world. Here, with excellent accommodations at more than reasonable prices, you can still see the earth in its pristine beauty. And because the Kenyan people have an ethic, a tribal philosophy if you will, of welcoming strangers and sharing with them, it is a uniquely warm and friendly place to travel.

Thus, we say, if you ever travel anywhere in your life, let it first be to Kenya. No other destination will repay you with such lasting memories of the most diverse experiences and adventures. If you can afford to rent a four-wheel drive vehicle, and depart on safari for a month or more, you are guaranteed the trip of your life. But even if you only have two weeks, or must travel on cheap public transportation, Kenya's sure to leave you with a treasure trove of memories.

But be warned. There is no "final reality" to Kenya. It is a land of too many places, far too many cultures, too long a history, and too many different viewpoints to be captured in one book. Thousands of photographs cannot capture it, nor a multitude of words.

For the same reason, it cannot be known in one trip. But if you have the time, two weeks to a month at least, more if you can afford it, you can scratch the surface of this mysterious, multicolored land, meet its peoples and share a trace of their cultures, and watch and learn from its marvelous animals.

THE GRAND SAFARI

Kenya's geography and climate — its vegetation, wildlife, and cultures — are so diverse that only a complete tour can begin to encompass it. This we did as a family, on our most recent visit, an itinerary that we called the Grand Safari. The Grand Safari requires transportation of your own — either with a driver or self-drive — and a minimum of six weeks to be able to savor places of special interest.

Urban Kenya can be seen more cheaply: careening buses and overloaded *matatus* link towns and villages, are cheap, sometimes exhilarating and a good way to meet the people. However they do not traverse the national parks and reserves, so you must find other means of transportation to get there, and they don't stop to look at the views: they only stop when they break down.

LIONS UNDER THE STARS

The costs of safari groups and tours vary depending on the type of vehicle, duration, accommodation, and number of fellow travelers. Generally, the individual's interests have to take a back seat to the group's. There's little "self-determination" — you can't stay watching cheetahs if the driver or the other passengers want to move on — and you are usually well-insulated from the local people and their way of life, except for occasional fake tribal ceremonies. For individualists, top on the list of requirements are a private vehicle and a driver/guide; some Kenya travelers begin this way, then give up the driver/guide after a week or so, and carry on in a rented car, once they've learned a bit about the roads, customs, and parks.

Our family chose to go on our own because we like to follow our own path, and camp under the stars, serenaded by lions. Vehicle rentals are expensive in Kenya, but

PREVIOUS PAGES: Lean, sleek and menacing, the cheetah is found throughout Kenya. Parental bonds are strong: cubs mature in a year but will stay with their mother far longer. OPPOSITE AND PREVIOUS PAGE RIGHT: Maasai and Samburu warriors.

savings in accommodations (tent camping) and food (cook your own) recoup some of these costs. Being a family of five, we found the overall cost per person to be less than the equivalent rate on some package tours. Bear in mind, however, that large four-wheel drive vehicles often cost twice the rent for two-wheel ones, but Kenya's pot-holed roads and the effect of rain on dirt tracks make four-wheel drive almost essential.

Our most recent two-month tour of Kenya by four-wheel drive, excluding air-fare, cost a total of about US$20,000 (or about

less), and US$2,000 for miscellaneous expenses, biggest of these being park entry fees.

Naturally, the more people sharing a rented vehicle, the lower the individual cost. Two persons renting a smaller vehicle than the Trooper, for example, a Suzuki Sierra, would pay less per month (US$2,430 to US$2,913 per month compared to US$5,000 for a larger and more comfortable Mitsubishi Pajero), and would pay proportionately the same for food and lodging.

In and around national parks and reserves, tented camps and lodges are com-

1,250,000 KSh) for a group of two to three adults (depending on whether our college-age son was with us), and two younger sons (who were usually charged half-price each at restaurants and hotels). The per-person cost was around US$5,000 for a 63-day trip through what is probably the most magnificent natural place left on earth.

This total amount included US$8,000 for our rented Isuzu Trooper, US$9,000 for food and lodging (about US$150 per day), US$1,000 for gas (we drove 10,000 km or 6,200 miles, but you'd probably drive far

paratively expensive. In general, the smaller the camp the greater the cost, but rates vary considerably according to season, and anyone who can convincingly claim to be a Kenya resident is likely to get a discount. They range from US$120 to all the way up to US$500 per day for a double and full board, often including picnic lunches and sometimes game drives. This can be quite a bargain for luxurious accommodations, invariably superb service, and usually excellent food.

Our most common practice was to camp two or three nights in a row, then spend a night in a lodge or a tented camp. We often camped in our tent near a hotel, and ate dinner and breakfast there rather than over our campfire. When possible, we stayed at

A balloon safari PREVIOUS PAGES provides breathtaking panoramas on a grand scale; but ground transportation ABOVE is the only way to get to know the wildlife.

moderately-priced "Kenyan" hotels (also frequented by tourists) rather than in the more expensive tourist establishments. Every major town will have one or more hotels that used to be grand in colonial times and are still open for business, charmingly starting to become rundown. Rates priced in Kenya Shillings are almost always lower than those rated in dollars and often you'll find a great atmosphere: such places are almost always family-run. A double, with a good dinner and breakfast, at a "Kenyan" hotel, can run as low as US$30 for a comfortable, clean room with a private toilet and bath. We have kept this distinction when we quote prices in this book: those places quoted in Kenya Shillings are invariably looking more to a resident market and, as we said, are invariably cheaper. The service is more off-hand, the food more African. Those quoted in dollars are after the tourist market, are slicker but sometimes lack the Kenyan feel.

THE BUGS ARE FREE

Those who are willing to rough it can find board and lodging at very inexpensive rates in all Kenyan towns and some back-country areas, anywhere from US$1 a night upwards. Hitchhiking is not generally recommended and is most unwise near large towns and cities, but *matatus* and buses are cheap: travelers in Kenya can survive on US$10 a day, or even less if they travel slowly. This manner of seeing Kenya, however, might prevent the tourist from seeing any animals but the bugs in his bed, as park fees alone for the best national reserves are US$27 a day. Shelling out more money often makes for a more worthwhile experience.

Thus, there are many ways and means to travel in Kenya. The following Grand Safari includes travel information for travelers on all budgets and covers just about all of Kenya's accessible sites and areas of great interest, which are known for their wildlife, people, prehistory and history, landscape, vegetation, and geography. Nearly all of Kenya is visually magnificent: it's easier to list the few places which are better missed, as we've noted in the text.

Depending on your time and other constraints, portions of the Grand Safari can be taken alone. The best and most inclusive of these are included in the six shorter itineraries we recommend for those who do not have a full two months to devote to Kenya.

But if you can beg, borrow, or steal two months, do it. Kenya is so vast, so diverse, so unique — tiresome adjectives but *true* — that a longer trip is never a waste of time or money. It is similar to investing in a fine jewel: it will stay with you all your life. We've traveled a good part of the world, often for years at a time, yet in looking back, nothing can compare to Kenya. Nor has any other place sunk into our memories and hearts as has this beautiful place.

OUTFITTING THE GRAND SAFARI

If you choose to explore Kenya on your own, as opposed to having a safari company bounce you from place to place in a minibus or stretch Land Cruiser, you'll have more responsibilities and hassles, but infinitely more fun. We've seen literally hundreds of these minibuses banging around the landscape, full of folks from Decatur, Stockholm, and Milan, all having a good time, to be sure, but also suffering some of the same hardships Montgomery's troops endured in North Africa. Locals jokingly call safari company tours "the roads of Kenya," because in their mad rush to drag you from place to place — for instance, to Meru, the Aberdares, Mount Kenya, and the Maasai Mara in a week — they ensure that you spend more time on Kenya's often abysmal roads than in the parks themselves.

If you intend to wander the back country and the wilder game parks, or do any dirt-road driving during or just after the rainy season, bite the bullet and rent a four-wheel drive. We found that Central Rent-a-Car in Nairobi often had the best deals, and they rented us an excellent Isuzu Trooper at the most reasonable price, although the stronger Mitsubishi Pajero is also a popular choice. Hertz and Avis are also represented and reputable. With any car rental pay special attention to the small print on the contract — often the excess on the insurance is excessive — and the condition of the vehicle. Check with them and the others listed in TRAVELERS' TIPS, page 294.

Before you leave, make sure your vehicle is roadworthy, that it has good tires and a good spare (two spares, and extra tubes and patches if you intend to attempt East Turkana and the Chalbi Desert), a functional jack, and at least one extra jerry can for gas. Check that your vehicle is in tip-top condition, doesn't overheat, or burn too much oil. Any troubles you may have near Nairobi will be multiplied tenfold in the desert. If your vehicle isn't equipped with a five-gallon jerry can for radiator water, ask at gas stations — you should be able to pick up a used plastic one for 100 to 200 KSh.

Read the sections of this book pertinent to the areas you want to visit (especially the Northern Frontier District) before venturing into them. In the desert of the Northern Frontier District, for example, gasoline is even rarer than water; and it's *very important* to call ahead and reserve gas at the few places listed, which may have some.

Camping is enjoyable throughout Kenya, but you'll need to bring or rent a tent if you are going to the Northern Frontier District or other remote areas. Your tent should be large and comfortable, with mosquito netting on *all* the windows and doors, and should zip tight at night. It should have a sewn-in groundsheet to keep out scorpions, snakes, and other undesirables. It's also essential to rent mosquito netting — either single or double, depending on how close you are with your companion(s), if you plan to sleep out under the stars. The nets hang from trees, or you can rig them between a tree and your car.

We always make it a point to bring camp beds — fold-down cots that stow easily with the tent in the back of the car, and which keep you off the ground and away from crawling creatures. Scorpions are infrequent, but they love to sleep in shoes, so always shake yours out in the morning before putting them on; it can save a very nasty bite. They are more common in the dry country and live under rocks and in brush and piled wood — snakes live in such places, too — therefore, a general rule in Kenya is to avoid putting your hand or any part of your body where it shouldn't be!

Up close the sheer size of an African elephant is suddenly clear.

Don't let the considerations mentioned above intimidate you, though. Take the necessary precautions, then relax and have fun.

THE ULTIMATE ITINERARY

Like a grand prix circuit, the Grand Safari can begin and stop at any point, but it most logically starts in Nairobi. If you wish to rent a four-wheel drive, and provision yourself for the trip, Nairobi's the best place to do it. The ultimate itinerary for nine weeks (63 days) might be devised as follows:

Days Destination

1–2	Nairobi: museum, other sites, National Park
3–4	Lake Naivasha and Hell's Gate National Park
5–7	Aberdare National Park
8–11	Mount Kenya National Park
12–13	Meru National Park
14–16	Samburu/Buffalo Springs/Shaba National Reserves
17–22	Hiking in the Matthews Range
23–24	Marsabit National Park
25–29	Chalbi Desert, east shore Lake Turkana and Sibiloi National Park*
30	To Maralal
31–35	Camel safari on the Ewaso Ngiro
36	To Lake Baringo, or to Nyahururu and Lake Nakuru National Park
37–39	West shore Lake Turkana*
40–42	Saiwa Swamp and Mount Elgon National Parks
43–44	Kakamega Forest Reserve
45	Kisumu and Lake Victoria
46	Ruma National Park, or Kericho and the Mau Escarpment
47–49	Maasai Mara National Reserve
50–51	Nairobi
52–53	Amboseli National Park
54–55	Tsavo National Parks
56–63	Watamu Marine National Park, Mombasa and the coast

*You may not wish to visit both sides of Lake Turkana, especially in view of the shortage of accommodation on the western side, although they are quite different experiences.

SHORTER TRIPS

If you don't have nine weeks, there are shorter alternatives. The following itineraries provide the greatest range of experience possible for the time allowed, while avoiding as much as possible "the roads of Kenya."

Two Weeks — Predators and Peaks

1–2	Nairobi and Lake Naivasha
3–5	Maasai Mara National Reserve
6	Kericho, Lake Nakuru National Park
7–8	Aberdare National Park
9–11	Mount Kenya National Park
12–13	Meru National Park
14	Nairobi

Two Weeks — Predators and Beach

1–2	Nairobi
3–4	Amboseli National Park
5–6	Tsavo National Parks
7–13	Watamu Marine National Park, Mombasa and the coast
14	Nairobi

Three Weeks — Predators, Peaks, and the Jade Sea

1–2	Nairobi
3–5	Mount Kenya National Park
6–7	Aberdare National Park
8	Lake Baringo
9–11	West shore Lake Turkana
12–13	Mount Elgon National Park
14–15	Kakamega Forest Reserve

16 Ruma National Park, or Kericho
    and the Mau Escarpment
17–20 Maasai Mara National Reserve
21 Nairobi

**Three Weeks — Peaks, Predators,
and Beach**
1 Nairobi
2 Amboseli National Park
3–5 Tsavo National Parks
6–10 Watamu Marine National Park,
      Mombasa and the coast
11 Nairobi

18 Lake Nakuru National Park
19–21 Maasai Mara National Reserve
22 Lake Naivasha or Nairobi
23 Amboseli National Park
24–27 Mombasa, Watamu Marine
      National Park and the coast
28 Nairobi

**Four Weeks — Beach, Predators,
and Peaks**
1–2 Nairobi
3–4 Amboseli National Park
5–7 Tsavo National Parks

12–14 Mount Kenya National Park
15–16 Aberdare National Park
17 Lake Naivasha
18–20 Maasai Mara National Reserve
21 Nairobi

**Four Weeks — Predators, Peaks, Beach,
Chalbi Desert, and the Jade Sea**
1–2 Nairobi
3–6 Mount Kenya National Park
7–8 Aberdare National Park
9–10 Samburu, Buffalo Springs, Shaba
      National Reserves
11–12 Marsabit National Park
13–16 Chalbi Desert and east shore Lake
      Turkana (Sibiloi National Park)
17 Maralal

8–12 Watamu Marine National Park,
      Mombasa, and the coast
13 Nairobi
14–16 Maasai Mara National Reserve
17 Ruma National Park or Kericho
18 Lake Victoria and Kakamega
    Forest Reserve
19–21 Mount Elgon National Park
22 Lake Baringo
23–24 Aberdare National Park
25–27 Mount Kenya National Park
28 Nairobi

OPPOSITE: Two of the black rhinos to be seen in
Kenya's game reserves. ABOVE: Lions in the Maasai
Mara National Reserve have come to accept man
and his vehicles as part of everyday life.

Out of the Jade Sea

TWENTY MILLION YEARS AGO, Kenya extended from the Congo to the Indian Ocean as a vast equatorial plain on the island continent of Africa. A carpet of thick tropical forest and woodland covered the flat and rolling plains. Animals of all stripes and colors inhabited the ground, branches, and treetops, among them a variety of forest-dwelling, slender, muscular, and apelike primates we now call *dryopithecines*.

But Africa collided with Eurasia in the next few million years, creating the Mediterranean. This imperceptible but implacable grinding of the continents gave rise, literally, to Kenya as it is now. Over the land bridges from Africa to Eurasia crossed numerous species; the climate underwent drastic changes, and the drying habitat of the *dryopithecines* was invaded by the *ramapithecines*, whose teeth were more adapted to the harsh diet found in the woodlands and open country.

The collision of the continents, though spanning millions of years, was catastrophic in its impact: Africa was split centrally north to south by a vast, sheer fracture. The molten lava underlying the continental plates escaped from volcanoes and poured across the land, over endless millennia, pushing up the earth's crust more than 1,093 m (3,586 ft), even as the shifting tectonic plates pulled it apart. In 15 million or so years, it deepened what we members of the subspecies *Homo sapiens* now call the Rift Valley, and created the great volcanoes of Mount Kenya, Mount Elgon, and Mount Kilimanjaro.

In the north, the Rift extended into what is now Ethiopia, creating the enormous and landlocked Lake Turkana, former source of the Nile, and often called the Jade Sea because of its marvelous green color. As the southern extension of the Rift Valley deepened, it cut off segments of earlier tropical rain forest. Its varied altitudes and climates preserved or gave rise to a diversity of ecosystems, including semiarid desert areas, grasslands, woodlands, and alpine meadows, habitats that offered new biological niches for the emerging *ramapithecines*. As the lava flowed and the volcanoes spread, they pushed the earth's crust down, widened the Rift Valley floor, and filled extinct craters with lakes, until the Valley walls soared a vertiginous 914.4 m (3,000 ft).

FROM JUNGLE TO SAVANNA

As the valley walls rose, they cut into the clouds that, for millions of years, had carried the continent's wind drift from West to East Africa. Over long stretches of time, they blocked the rain's passage to the east, over what is now the majority of Kenya.

The lands changed in response: instead of unending tropical forest, the drier climate produced woodlands and savanna (treeless plain or a tropical grassland of seasonal rains and scattered trees). Like regiments cut off from retreat, patches of lingering tropical forest endured, preserving vegetation and animal species like those still found in West Africa, and antedating Kenya's rise from equatorial plain. Such vestigial tropical areas, with their unusual vegetation, birds, and insects, include the Arabuko-Sokoke coastal forest south of Malindi, the Kakamega Forest north of Lake Victoria, and smaller areas along the lower reaches of the Tana River.

As the climate and vegetation altered on the East African plains, so did the animals that lived there. The drier climate, the seasonal rains, and the sparser forest gave rise to great herds of ungulates protected by the open spaces. Like many apes of today, *ramapithecus* were omnivorous, eating leaves, stalks, berries, fruits, insects, eggs, and meat. At some point, perhaps because its prey moved out to the expanding savanna, *ramapithecus* left the jungle and the woodland to follow.

Such excursions favored upright locomotion, which, although it requires more energy per distance traveled, has many other benefits. It gave a higher range of vision, freed the hands, and stimulated the brain.

TELLING THE FIRST STORIES

Because of the thinner forest shelter in the woodland and savanna, *ramapithecus* and its peers may have tended to band together; at some point they learned to feed not only themselves and their offspring but also others. Thus began communal sharing of food from whence developed language.

The circumcision ceremony is a complicated ritual: this Samburu adolescent is preparing for the operation that will turn him into a warrior.

About three million years ago, *ramapithecus* began to walk habitually upright. Hunter-gatherers, Kenya's world-renowned paleontologist Richard Leakey called them. They dug roots and berries, harvested nuts, shoots, eggs, insects, and fruits, hunted live animals, and feasted on dead ones when the opportunity arose.

With communal existence came the need for a broader language to convey such matters as the location of foodstuffs, or to argue the division of spoils or the tactics used to achieve them. These issues all became part of the story that enlarged their experience — the way we humans have of sharing and building on each other's experience. And as the need for language expanded, so did the brains of these animals.

Fossil remains of *ramapithecus* show up in Africa, southern Europe, and Asia. But traces of its descendants have, so far, turned up only in Africa. They constitute three distinct *hominid* types (including our direct ancestor, *Homo habilis* — able man — and two separate *australopithecines*), and are five to two million years old. It's possible that man's ancestors existed in Asia and Europe during this time, but their remains have not been found, or that for climatic or other reasons, they ceased to exist except in Africa.

HOMELAND OF OUR ANCESTORS

On the shores of Kenya's Lake Turkana, in Tanzania's Olduvai Gorge, and at the juncture of southern Ethiopia's Omo River with Turkana's northern shore, the Leakeys and other scientists have discovered tools and fossilized bones of several different hominids. They include the complete skull of a human ancestor who lived by Lake Turkana a little over two million years ago, and younger skulls of up to a million and a half years old.

Traces of *hominids* and the two *australopithecines* from a million and a half to a million years ago have been found outside Africa, but after that point, none have appeared in Africa or anywhere except man's ancestor, *Homo habilis*. Again on the shores of Lake Turkana, at Koobi Fora, a team of paleon-

Tribal dwellings as sketched by a mid-eighteenth-century traveler to Kenya.

tologists, led by Richard Leakey, found remains of a more recent human ancestor, *Homo erectus* (standing man). It is a million and a half years old, predating others of its species that lived in many parts of Asia (Peking man) and Europe up to a half million years ago.

From *Homo erectus* evolved *Homo sapiens* (thinking man), and 50,000 years ago came modern human beings, anatomically unrecognizable from ourselves. But it is the find of *Homo erectus* skulls at Lake Turkana which proved for the first time that man's ancestor evolved in Africa.

the ungulates they formerly stalked, farm the land, and set up property. These advances led to even greater warfare and dissension, but also to building cities, roads, universities, industry, and now the rockets which take them into space, perhaps soon to new worlds far from the ancient plains of Kenya.

NATURE UNPOSSESSED

"…they walked about their country without appearing to possess it… they had not aspired to recreate or change or tame the

About the time of *Homo erectus*, the shape and precision of stone tools became finer than was necessary for their immediate purpose. Anthropologists think this resulted from growing language skills. Through changing climates, the advance and retreat of northern glaciers, new shifts in continental drift, and the narrowing and widening of the Mediterranean, *Homo erectus* and his peers populated Africa, Eurasia, Asia, and Europe. Their descendants learned to paint cave interiors, fashion sculpture, and celebrate the burial of their dead (sometimes by partaking of the corpse, from which descends the modern religious custom of communion).

They improved the arts of habitation and war, literature and music, and learned to herd

country and to bring it under their control… had accepted what God, or nature, had given them without apparently wishing to improve upon it in any significant way. If water flowed down a valley they fetched what they wanted in a large hollow gourd; they did not push it into pipes or flumes, or harass it with pumps. Consequently when they left a piece of land and abandoned their huts, the bush and vegetation grew up again and obliterated every trace of them, just as the sea at each high tide wipes out footprints and children's sand-castles, and leaves the beach once more smooth and glistening." (Elspeth Huxley, *The Flame Trees of Thika*.)

Because the ancient residents of inland Kenya built no castles, roads, or cities, few clues exist as to their recent history. Through archaeology, we know that approximately eight to nine thousand years ago, Kenya became the home of primitive hunters, probably related to the Bushmen and Hottentots of southern Africa. About 2000 BC, pastoral Cushitic tribes from Ethiopia moved into western Kenya in search of new grazing land. Some two thousand years ago, other pastoral and agricultural migrants settled the Rift Valley, and by AD 100, there may have been 1,400 pastoral communities living among what are now agricultural populations on both sides of the western Rift Valley.

These tribes migrated along the Valley, interacting with other tribes from what are now Uganda, Ethiopia, Sudan, and Tanzania. They exchanged and developed cultures that are identifiable in present-day tribes, such as the Kambas in central Kenya, the Kikuyu on the slopes of Mount Kenya, the Luo along the shores of Lake Victoria, and the Kalenjins on the high slopes of the western Highlands.

When trade routes were established in the seventeenth century, the Europeans found four basic population groups: the Hamitic, Nilotic, Nilo-Hamitic, and Bantu. The National Museum in Nairobi has superb ethnological displays of numerous tribes within these groups. Today, many of them still keep their social structure and traditions, though their lifestyles and dress have not completely escaped the influence of the West. It is not uncommon to see some exchange their traditional clothes for Western garb.

The Hamitic tribes (Galla, Somali, and Rendille) came originally from the north, settling in the Tana Valley and northern Kenya between 1300 and 1500. The Nilotic people (Luo) migrated from Sudan along the Nile River to settle along the shores of Lake Victoria. According to Luo tradition, they were led to Kenya by two brothers, Adhola and Owiny. Near Mount Elgon, they quarreled and the tribe split. Adhola and his followers stayed around Mount Elgon; Owiny with his supporters settled the area south of Kisumu.

The Nilo-Hamitic tribes, which originated in Sudan, inhabit most regions of Kenya: the Turkana are found near Lake Turkana in the north, the Suk south of the lake, the Kalenjin tribes (Nandi, Kipsigis, Marakwet, Tugen, etc.) in west-central Kenya, and the Maasai in the south.

The fourth group consists of Bantu-speaking peoples who are spread throughout southern Africa. In Kenya, the Bantu tribes (Kikuyu, Meru, Embu, Chuka, Tharaka, Kamba, and other smaller tribes) live around and to the south of Mount Kenya. The Luhya to the northwest of Lake Victoria, and the Nyika along the coast are also Bantu.

The ancestors of the coastal Bantu came to the Tana and Juba river valleys from the Taita Hills near Mount Kilimanjaro before the Galla; some coastal Bantu tribes were probably assimilated into the Arabic coastal empire. The Bantu tribes in central Kenya did not arrive until much later. The Kikuyu, now Kenya's major tribe, may not have reached its present location until about 1800. The whites and Asians, Kenya's two newest "tribes," began to move to the interior at the end of the nineteenth century.

Remains OPPOSITE of *Homo erectus* are displayed at the archaeological site of Koobi Fora on the shores of Lake Turkana. Nairobi University, with starkly modern architecture and art ABOVE, has students from every corner of Kenya and the world.

THE COAST — A DIFFERENT HISTORY

The Kenyan coast, on the other hand, has been visited throughout history by personages familiar to students of western and eastern civilizations. Alexander the Great certainly sailed the Indian Ocean, but whether he reached Kenya is not known. During the first century, a Greek merchant named Diogenes (not he who went looking for an honest man) undoubtedly spent a portion of his life here: his log, *The Periplus of the Erythraean Sea*, is one of western civilization's earliest documented records of East Africa. It describes Kenya's coastal inhabitants as "men of the greatest stature, who are pirates…and at each place have set up chiefs."

These coastal chiefs were probably Arab traders who had settled and intermarried among the Bantu tribes. Their communities were actively involved in trade with Arab, Indian, and Indonesian merchants. They sold foodstuffs (wheat, rice, sesame oil, and sugar), cloth, hardware, porcelain, and glassware in exchange for ivory, rhinoceros horns, tortoise shell, palm oil, and, in some areas, slaves and gold. Here, native and foreign influences merged into a new culture and a new language, Swahili, today one of Kenya's official languages (English being the other).

A century later, the Greek-Egyptian geographer and mathematician Ptolemy included Kenya, which he called *Parum Litus*, in his *Geography*. Despite its many errors, this work remained the authority on Africa until the sixteenth century. There is no record that Ptolemy ever visited inland Kenya, yet he documented lakes and mountains with relative accuracy.

Trade followed the rhythm of the monsoons. Numerous dhows, pushed by the northeast winds, or *kaskazi*, arrived in Kenya between November and April, departing between May and October when the *kusi*, or southeast winds, began. Coastal communities, each with its own autonomy, developed, but trade remained under Arab control until the fourteenth century.

Local builders make skillful use of natural papyrus to fashion their dwellings.

From the time of Ptolemy (second century) until the eighth century, no major changes took place in the coast except for the advent of religion. Schisms within Islam over the selection of Mohammed's successor drove religious refugees to Kenya in search of a new homeland.

These new Arab immigrants, who were neither merchants nor sailors, helped turn the Kenyan coastal settlements into sophisticated cities built from blocks of coral carved from the barrier reef: crisp, white architecture with narrow streets, ramparts, numer-

ous mosques, sultans' palaces, and urban housing with elaborate courtyards for the well-to-do. Remnants of these cities still exist at Manda, Malindi, Mombasa, Pate, Lamu, and Kilifi, and are most visible today at Gedi, where the extensive ruins of an ancient city still stand.

Kenya's coastal treasures were traded in the richest kingdoms of the ancient world. India, China, Indonesia, Malaysia, Ceylon, Persia, Arabia, and the countries of the eastern Mediterranean were favored destinations for ivory, rhinoceros horns, and palm oil. El Idrissi, a thirteenth-century Andalusian historian of the court of the Norman king of Sicily (a distant cousin of Richard the Lion-Hearted), claimed that iron ore exported from Malindi was the reason for the high quality of Toledo's swords and knives.

Similarities in style, culture, and language among Kenyan coastal peoples gave early voyagers the impression of a unified empire. In fact, except for brief periods, they existed independently and in relative peace, until the arrival of the Portuguese in 1498. This marked the end of the most prosperous period for coastal Kenya.

PORTUGUESE DOMINATION

During the late fifteenth century, under the reign of King John II and his son, Henry the Navigator, Portugal began a period of extensive ocean exploration aimed at breaking the Arab monopoly of the spice trade from India.

After Dias rounded the Cape of Good Hope in 1488, the Portuguese decided they had found the route to India, and began planning an extended expedition up the East African coast. With four vessels under his command, Vasco da Gama left Portugal on July 8, 1487. In November, he passed the Cape and began traveling the East African coast, whose residents soon discovered the Portuguese preached "vulgar" Christianity, and responded with reserve and hostility.

News of the Portuguese predated their ships' arrival in Mombasa on April 7, 1498; they were attacked and quickly retreated to Malindi. Da Gama's log reports that they were warmly received by Malindi's sultan: "For nine days we had fetes, sham fights and musical performances." Having replenished the ships' stores and acquired a navigator, they set sail with a favorable *kusi* and reached Calcutta on May 23. Three months later, da Gama began his return voyage, making another call at Malindi.

On subsequent expeditions, the Portuguese were welcomed at Malindi but met continued open hostility in Mombasa. Cabral, who, on a voyage to Kenya in 1500, accidentally sailed far enough west to claim Brazil for Portugal, sacked Mombasa before returning home.

In 1505, Portugal decided to install itself permanently in its new territory, and sent Francisco d'Almeria as Viceroy of India. For reasons more strategic than commercial, it decided to capture the Arab positions along the East African coast. Mombasa was again sacked during Almeria's four-year struggle for control. Once victorious, the Portuguese imposed strict and often brutal rule, reserving for themselves a better part of the local resources and wealth; only friendly cities, such as Malindi, were spared. The Kenyan coast, for the first time in its history, was unified into a single empire.

It was, however, an empire that no longer enjoyed commercial supremacy, but one that strained from the antipathies between conqueror and conquered. The Portuguese were never able to revive the once prosperous trading cities, perhaps because they failed to provide traditionally traded commodities, or perhaps because the Kenyans ignored their European goods and culture. The result was a shift by the coastal people from a mercantile to an agricultural way of life.

The Portuguese stayed for almost three centuries. At Mombasa, they ultimately felt compelled to build Fort Jesus in 1592 to maintain control, but even this imposing Italian-designed fortress did not put an end to local hostilities.

In 1595 or 1596, the Swahili governor of Pemba was poisoned for becoming a Christian; at the beginning of the 1600s, Sultan Ahmad of Mombasa, generally considered an ally, repeatedly complained of insulting treatment by the Portuguese. His son and successor, Hassan, quarreled openly with Portuguese officials in 1614 and fled inland. His brother was then allowed to rule for four years before the Portuguese replaced him with a young nephew, Yusuf Chinguliya, whom they promptly sent off to an Augustinian priory at Goa, India for 13 years of "education."

Upon his return to Mombasa, Yusuf renounced Christianity for his native Islam, and massacred all the Portuguese at Fort Jesus. After defeating a punitive force of 800 Portuguese sent from Goa in 1632, he demolished the fort and left Kenya for Oman. He continued naval raids on the Kenyan coast, but by 1635, the Portuguese had regained control of Mombasa and rebuilt Fort Jesus.

The Portuguese never recovered from their defeat at Fort Jesus; for the next half-century, they battled raids from Omani merchants exercising Yusuf's claim to sovereignty and anxious to regain control of the East African waters. A three-year siege of Fort Jesus brought an end to the Portuguese presence in Kenya in 1698, except for two years (1728–1730) when they briefly held Mombasa.

> "You have concealed and preserved
> Dreadful secrets
> Unrevealed.
> Nothing remains
> But deathless fascination."
>
> — Amin Kassam, *Fort Jesus*

The Portuguese departure, however, did not bring independence to the Kenyan coastal cities. The Iman of Oman appointed governors who too often quarreled among themselves; commerce continued to wane. In 1741, Mombasa's Mazrui family claimed sovereign control of the island. Opposed to any foreign domination even though it be Muslim, it began the task of unifying the political and economic structures of the coastal cities.

Some coastal cities soon tired of Mazrui domination. In 1817, Pate requested the aid of the Sultan of Oman, one Seyyid Said, a

Johann Rebmann OPPOSITE, one of several proselytizing eighteenth-century missionaries who also explored the hinterland, notably Mount Kilimanjaro. ABOVE: Children at a present-day missionary school.

resolute, aggressive, young ruler who at age 15 had assassinated his regent for supposedly not acting in his best interests. Pate's request opened the way for Said to reestablish the Omani empire in East Africa. He easily gained control of Pate and the northern Kenyan cities, but failed to take Mombasa when the Mazrui allied themselves with English forces in the Indian Ocean that were at the time trying to stop French slave traders.

With the British flag flying over Fort Jesus, Said admitted the futility of attacking, and

began negotiations. In 1822, he signed an anti-slave-trafficking agreement; the English removed their protectorate from Mombasa, giving Said control over the entire Kenyan coast.

Finding East Africa more to his taste than the Omani countryside, Said moved his capital to Zanzibar in 1832, and began an intensive, highly-successful commercial development program. He transformed Zanzibar into a gigantic clove plantation and directed the planting of sesame crops on the mainland. The British remained in East Africa with their headquarters in Zanzibar, ostensibly to enforce and strengthen antislavery agreements, but actually to obtain a foothold in the prosperous new land.

On Said's death in 1856, Zanzibar and East Africa were split from Oman. His successor, Seyyid Majed, with support from the English, maintained control of the African portion of the empire, and continued both Said's policies and his close association with England. His brother, Seyyid Bharghash, took over in 1870. Under severe pressure from the English, Bharghash forbade all slave trading in East Africa, by sea or land, and prohibited the entrance of slave vessels into his territorial waters. His reign saw the beginning of the partition of East Africa and the fusion of the two separate histories of Kenya.

THE INTERIOR EXPLORED

The antislavery movement drew European attention to the great expanse of Kenyan land waiting to be claimed, and the legions of "heathen" that could be converted to Christianity. During the second half of the nineteenth century, a handful of missionaries and explorers were lured to Kenya by these challenges, and provided the first more or less complete geographic picture of the interior. In previous centuries, coastal Arab traders had established trade routes to Lake Victoria; these, however, did not cross Kenya, but went south of Mount Kilimanjaro through Tanzania, then up the western side of the Rift Valley. This was the general route taken by Burton, Speke, Stanley, and Livingstone on various expeditions seeking the source of the Nile.

In 1846, German missionaries representing the English Lutheran Church Missionary Society settled in Rabia, about 20 km (12 miles) northwest of Mombasa. Although not truly the hinterland, Rabia was beyond the coastal belt of Muslim influence. The missionaries, Johann Krapf, Johann Rebmann, and Jakob Erhardt, made several proselytizing expeditions to the interior, but did not find the residents much more interested in Christianity than had the Portuguese. From Krapf came Europe's first geographical information about Mount Kenya; Rebmann provided data on Mount Kilimanjaro. Krapf also transcribed Swahili into Roman letters, and published a Swahili dictionary, grammar, and translation of the New Testament.

In 1872, a well-armed German exploratory expedition led by Dr. Gustav Fischer came to investigate the possibility of colonizing the interior. His forces reached the Lake Naivasha region but were ambushed in Hell's Gate Gorge by *moran*, or Maasai warriors. Defeated, Fischer retreated to the coast; German colonial activities shifted south to Tanzania.

The English Royal Geographical Society funded the next major European expedition. Its president, Lord Aberdare, intrigued by the descriptions of Krapf and Rebmann, sent a young Scot, Joseph Thomson, with a small expeditionary force to find a direct route for European traders from the Kenyan coast to Lake Victoria.

Thomson left Mombasa in March 1883, with 143 men, and was soon met by Maasai warriors who arrived in the guise of a peace party. But "as the day wore on," Thomson later wrote, "matters became ominous. The warriors grew boisterous and rude. One of them tried to stab me because I pushed him away and we had to remain under arms from morn till night. On the morning of the third day, our worst fears were realized. We had been deluded and entrapped and we knew they were about to take their revenge on our small party for their failure to annihilate Fischer."

Thomson retreated hastily to Mombasa, regrouped, and began again. Choosing a more northerly route, he crossed the slopes of Mount Kenya, named the mountains to the west after his patron, Lord Aberdare, located Nyahururu Falls (for many years called Thomson's Falls), and arrived on the shores of Lake Victoria near the present-day Kenya-Uganda border. On his return, he detoured north to map Mount Elgon.

Thomson's adventures were filled with encounters with hostile Maasai, countless animals, sundry illness and injuries, witchcraft, stunning panoramas, and intriguing discoveries, all of which he recorded and published on his return to England. His tales captured the imagination of Europeans looking for adventure. And the safari business was born.

Kenya's most isolated region, the north, was explored by Count Teleki von Szeck in 1887; he named Lake Rudolf in honor of a Hapsburg prince (now Lake Turkana).

COLONIALISM

And so began what historians have termed the colonial period of Africa, when individuals at negotiating tables in Europe decided, with the stroke of a pen, the fate of the African peoples and the boundaries of present-day African countries. In 1879, it was estimated that more than 90% of the African continent were self-governed. By 1900, all but a tiny percentage were governed by European powers.

In 1886, the present-day boundaries of Kenya and Uganda were set by Prime Minister Lord Salisbury and Chancellor Otto von Bismarck; an international commission ruled that Sultan Bharghash's holdings on the coast extended only 16 km (10 miles) inland. England then negotiated a £17,000/year lease of the Kenyan coast that remained in effect until the nation's independence, when the Sultan ceded the territory to the new Kenyan government.

The Imperial British East African Company, chartered in 1888, became the admin-

OPPOSITE: An anchor outside Fort Jesus in Mombasa, one of the few reminders of Portuguese domination of the Kenyan Coast. ABOVE: Some of Kenya's colorfully dressed city dwellers.

istrative and development arm of British colonialism. It purchased valuable goods from Kenya, particularly ivory, in exchange for less-valuable English goods. The enterprise collapsed in July 1895, causing a Victorian financial crash. The British government acquired the floundering company for £200,000, and the territory became officially known as British East Africa. Construction of the Uganda Railway from Mombasa to Lake Victoria began, fulfilling a Kikuyu/Maasai prophecy of an iron snake breathing fire and smoke.

Mombasa retained its position as the major port, with the remaining coastal cities losing all of their previous prosperity. A new nation built around the railroad emerged. As Sir Charles Eliot, Commissioner of British East Africa in 1903, put it, "It is not an uncommon thing for a line to open up a country but this line literally created a country."

The building of the Mombasa-Uganda Railway, so-named because it would connect Uganda with the Indian Ocean, aroused controversy in England, which had made an interest-free loan for its construction. The £5.5 million loan for this "Lunatic Line" was later written off as a gift. The saga of this railroad is well-told in Nairobi's **Railway Museum**, and in Charles Miller's *The Lunatic Express* and P.H. Patterson's *The Man-eaters of Tsavo*. They tell the heroic story of man's defeat of nature, of thousands of imported Indian laborers who came to build the railroad, of those who stayed permanently and of scores killed by man-eating lions.

Nairobi emerged as the administrative and business center of a country thrust into the twentieth century by the influx of Western (primarily British) settlers, entrepreneurs, developers, explorers, and missionaries.

Kenya's colonial history reads very much like that of the Americas, with the appropriation of native lands, smallpox and measles epidemics, mass slaughter of wild animals, clearing of forests for agriculture, subjugation and confinement of indigenous peoples to reserves, and massive campaigns of "depaganization."

The colonial government chose the temperate plateau between Nairobi and the Rift Valley, the best agricultural land in the country, as Crown Land. In these White High-

lands, the government adopted a policy of not selling to Asians, and an unwritten policy of assuming that no land belonged to the Kenyan tribes. Officially, if the government mistakenly sold or leased lands still occupied by an African, the European purchaser was supposed to advise the government and give up title to the land. In practice, this policy was rarely implemented.

With little or no regard for African rights, white settlers cultivated large expanses of land, using virtually free African labor to plant a variety of crops. The most profitable of these was coffee, which Africans were banned from growing. Big-game hunting and safaris came into vogue, especially after visits by Winston Churchill and Theodore Roosevelt. Although Roosevelt sought fame as a hunter, existing accounts portray him as a terrible shot and a very poor sportsman.

The great variety of African animals, principally lions, leopards, elephants, rhinos, buffalo, and antelope, as well as countless species of birds and reptiles, were slaughtered without quarter. A European community, somewhat loosely organized by the eccentric Lord Delamere, developed with all the trappings of genteel colonial life: antique furniture, European-style homes, formal dinners, polo matches, horse races, and clubs.

The easy lifestyle was briefly interrupted by the First World War. Husbands left their wives in charge of plantations, or shipped them home to England, and rode off to fight the Germans in nearby Tanzania. The war in East Africa was not a major British military effort, yet it brought Tanzania under British control via a League of Nations mandate.

In the first years after the war, British veterans were lured to Kenya under the "Soldier Settlement Scheme," whereby land was given away in lotteries and sold on long-term, low-interest credit. The influx of settlers caused a labor crisis; Africans were understandably reluctant to work their own land for someone else at a tiny percentage of the return. The colonial government began to put pressure on the chiefs to direct their subjects into European employment.

Many of the old settlers returned to neglected plantations in need of both labor and money. As Elspeth Huxley describes it in *The Mottled Lizard*:

"So it was a question of starting again, more or less from the beginning, and in the meanwhile everyone had spent his capital. To balance this, the managers of the three main banks in Nairobi were in an expansive, benign and optimistic frame of mind. They conferred large overdrafts upon their customers, rather with the air of monarchs dispensing orders and stars, and details such as rates of interest and terms of repayment were considered by both parties to be almost too insignificant to be brought into the conversation at all. Happily for the banks, who

"Many other farmers were in the same boat. Some went off to hunt elephants, others to work as transport contractors or as road-gang overseers for the Government, one man to collect the skeletons of hippos on the shores of Lake Victoria, pound them up and sell the resultant bonemeal as fertilizer. Another way to turn a modest penny was to recruit labor for the sisal companies, or for some other large employer. One of our neighbors... had taken to this.

"One day he rode over to propose to [Father] that the two of them should go together

in fact charged eight percent, their liberality was rewarded by the stabilization of the rupee, which had been worth 1s. 4d., at the rate of 2s. This meant that one evening [you] went to bed owing £2,000, and woke up next morning owing £3,000; by a stroke of the pen, the banks had gained a bonus of fifty percent at the expense of everyone who had borrowed from them, which meant almost every farmer in the country.

"Because of the state everything had fallen into during the war we could not expect an income from the coffee for three or four years, and... [Father] doubted whether Mr. Playfair and the overdraft would support us, unaided, for as long as that. So he... cast about in all directions for ways of tiding things over...

to a district he knew of, hitherto neglected by other recruiters, in search of stalwart young men willing to put their thumb-marks on a contract binding them to work for six months on some distant plantation... They would get one shilling for each recruit delivered to a prospective employer."

In 1920, there were approximately nine thousand Europeans in British East Africa, most clamoring for London to give them self-rule. London responded by renaming the territory the Kenya Colony and Protectorate, for lofty Mount Kenya, and restating its policy in the Devonshire White Paper of 1923: "Primarily Kenya is an African territory, and

Many photography shops take photos of their customers: selling film is often only a sideline.

His Majesty's Government thinks it necessary definitely to record their considered opinion that the interests of the African natives must be paramount, and that if and when those interests and the interests of the immigrant races should conflict, the former should prevail… In the administration of Kenya His Majesty's Government regard themselves as exercising a trust on behalf of the African population."

Until after the Second World War, to which Kenya sent many native regiments, a succession of colonial governors administered

TOWARD INDEPENDENCE

It was from the educational system, a random assemblage of missionary establishments, that Kenya's national spirit, principally a story of Kikuyu dissatisfaction and resistance, sprang. The Kikuyu population was growing, yet was hemmed in by the White Highlands and the forest around Mount Kenya. Many members of the tribe went to work on European plantations; others left the land for Nairobi.

Kenya with little regard to the Devonshire Paper. Julian Huxley, after a 1929 tour to evaluate education in Kenya, summed up the prevailing situation: "On top of all this variety of nature and man there impinge Western civilization and Western industrialism. Will their impact level down the variety, insisting on large-scale production to suit the needs of Europe and Big Business, reducing the proud diversity of native tribes and races to a muddy mixture, their various cultures to a single inferior copy of our own? Or shall we be able to preserve the savor of difference to fuse our culture and theirs into an autochthonous civilization, to use local differences as the basis for a natural diversity of development?"

Out of the Jade Sea

After the Second World War, Harry Thuku, a Kikuyu government clerk, began organizing Kenya's first nationalist group, the Young Kikuyu Organization, for which he lost his job, was arrested, and eventually banished to Kismaiya, a small town on the northern Kenyan coast. This fractured the movement but only briefly. In 1924, the Kikuyu Central Organization (KCA) was formed, with Jomo Kenyatta as secretary.

The Africans were particularly incensed about colonial interference in tribal customs, such as female circumcision, and the

OPPOSITE: Musicians TOP and a gourd craftsman BOTTOM are part of a more variegated coastal lifestyle. ABOVE: Mzee Jomo Kenyatta, first president of Kenya.

misappropriation of native lands for European settlement. These and other grievances were carried to London in 1929 by Jomo Kenyatta, who remained abroad in London and Moscow for 15 years, organizing the African rights movement, studying anthropology at the London School of Economics, and publishing a study of Kikuyu life and customs, *Looking on Mount Kenya*.

London responded to Kenyatta's pleas with a series of studies and reviews. One conducted by the 1934 Kenya Land Commission found that 47.5% of the 4.4 million hect-

ares (17,000 sq miles) of the Highlands reserved for European settlement were not being cultivated. Twenty-five percent lay fallow and another 20% was occupied by African squatters allowed to reside so long as they worked part-time for the European farmer on his terms. At that time, the coffee ban, in which the government prohibited Africans from planting coffee by requiring a license that was virtually impossible to secure, was also still in effect.

These conditions catalyzed the nationalist movement, primarily under the KCA. In 1940, the leaders of all African organizations were arrested, detained, and their groups banned. The government invoked a "defense regulation," to justify its actions, claiming

that a copy of *Mein Kampf* had been found at KCA headquarters and that its leadership had been suspected of consorting with the Italian Consulate in Nairobi.

The ban did not stop the nationalist movement. It gave rise instead to the Kenyan African Study Union, a multi-tribal organization which became the Kenya Africa Union (KAU) six years later. On Kenyatta's return from England in 1946, he assumed leadership of this party that was to form the government of independent Kenya.

After the Second World War, there were four Kenyan communities — African, European, Asian (primarily Indian), and Arab — all demanding independent and equal representation. Even though the KAU was multi-tribal, it was primarily Kikuyu, and the Africans were divided by tribal affiliations, the Asians by religious beliefs, and the British by the differing attitudes of farmers, businessmen, educators, and missionaries. Only the Arabs had a common front, but they were too few to be a major political force. Everyone, however, found fault with colonial rule; some made their viewpoints known in -unorthodox ways:

"After the Legislative Council passed an ordinance requiring men of all races to carry an identity card with fingerprints, many whites erupted in fury. Until that time, only Africans had been required to carry identity cards, a measure which they intensely resented. Across the White Highlands, angry meetings were held at which the more zealous whites advocated open defiance of the new law... At one stormy meeting in Nakuru, a member of the Legislative Council who supported the ordinance was faced with an opponent who strode up and down the gangway of the hall with two large pistols hanging from his belt, fixing a threatening eye on anyone voting against him. In the end, the administration retreated. A compromise was reached by which those who could complete a form in English and provide two photographs were not required to be fingerprinted." (Martin Meredith, *The First Dance of Freedom*.)

Others used traditional avenues in opposing unfair laws. The Kikuyu chief, Mbiyu Koinage, asked the Land Commission for the return of his lands, which had been appropriated for a European coffee farm.

He was awarded about one-tenth of the acreage he claimed and ordered to comply with the coffee ban by removing the coffee bushes growing there. Koinage took the case to court and lost.

But the KAU grew stronger. Government policies were challenged by strikes which were often ruthlessly suppressed. In his 1948 annual report, the District Commissioner of Nakuru in the Rift Valley noted that there was thought to be a clandestine movement among the Kikuyu called "Mau Mau." What had caught his attention were oath-taking

England proclaimed a state of emergency. Jomo Kenyatta and 82 other nationalists were arrested. Rather than crippling the Mau Mau, this seemed to incite them.

"On March 27, 1953, they pulled the worst of their raids, the Lari Massacre, in the course of which more than 200 Africans of all ages and sexes, living in a compound whose chief was a friend of the British, were murdered and mutilated hideously. And with this horror the Mau Mau war entered a grim phase… And as counterbalance, the whites began to direct their determination and their superior

ceremonies that took place among the inhabitants of the Mau Escarpment. These bound individuals to political objectives such as land reform. Oath-taking ceremonies were outlawed in 1950, during a rash of ritual murders in the Rift Valley, whose victims were primarily Christian Kikuyus who had refused to take the oath.

The killings increased in 1952 and began to include outlying English farmers. Chief Koinage's son organized the Kenya Christian Association advocating peaceful change. The KAU organized a meeting, attended by more than 25,000, where leaders including Jomo Kenyatta denounced the Mau Mau movement. But the Mau Mau now had too much momentum. On October 20, 1952,

weaponry into complementary savagery: torture, subversion, and bribery of captured Kikuyu; morbid floggings at the prison camps, where African soldiers were instructed to use Mau Mau methods on suspected inmates, often supervised in these outrages by English officers; the berserker mania that seized the minds of so many 'civilized' Europeans…" (Peter Ritner, *The Death of Africa*).

Meanwhile, Kenyatta was brought to trial, convicted of organizing the Mau Mau, and sentenced to seven years in jail in Lodwar and Lokichar. The trial was a farce—the chief

OPPOSITE: A Maasai's head is shaved by his mother to prepare him for the *Eunoto* ceremony wherein he becomes a *moran*, senior warrior. ABOVE: The Tana River, red with erosion, seasonally greens the arid eastern plains of Kenya.

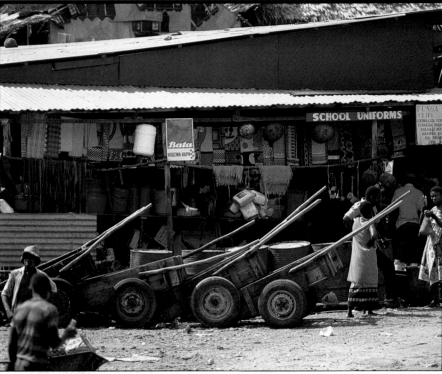

witness was bribed with two years' study in an English university with all expenses paid, and guaranteed government employment on his return. The magistrate received £20,000 to leave Kenya immediately after announcing his verdict.

Even though the KAU leader was no longer Kikuyu, but a Luo, Walter Odede, the government banned the organization and all native groups. It also created fenced "protected villages" where Africans were required to live, and brought in British troops to "enforce" the peace.

During this time, a new constitution, which promoted multiracial participation, was adopted. African politicians complained that democracy was impossible while hundreds of people remained jailed and political organizations banned. In 1955, the colonial government announced that regional political parties could be formed "to encourage a simple and orderly development of African political life."

Under the new constitution, eight communally elected Africans would represent five million constituents, and 14 Europeans would represent 5,000. The Africans refused the Colonial Office's offer of six more seats; in the 1958 elections, all African candidates pledged to refuse office in a move to reject

the constitution. Boycotts and protests followed. These maneuvers finally resulted in the all-party, all-race "Lancaster House Conference" in London in 1960.

From the start, the British Government, which had regained political control of the country during the Mau Mau war, made it clear that Kenya was destined to become an African country. A transitional multiracial government, tipped slightly in favor of the African majority, was endorsed, and national political parties allowed. Two parties emerged: the Kenya African National Union (KANU), which supported a strong central government with its seat in Nairobi, and the Kenya African Democratic Union (KADU), which advocated a federal, decentralized government.

UHURU

When the British released Kenyatta from detention in 1961, he gained the leadership of KANU and a seat on the Legislative Council. Two and a half years of disputes between the two parties resulted in a compromise constitution which provided for considerable regional autonomy and a date for the end of colonial rule:

"Kenya regained her *Uhuru* (Freedom) from the British on December 12, 1963. A minute before midnight, lights were put out at the Nairobi stadium so that people from all over the country and the world who had gathered there for the midnight ceremony were swallowed by the darkness. In the dark, the Union Jack was quickly lowered. When next the lights came on the new Kenya flag was flying and fluttering and waving in the air. The Police band played the new National Anthem and the crowd cheered continuously when they saw the flag was black and red and green. The cheering sounded like one intense cracking of many trees, falling on the thick mud in the stadium." (Ngugi wa Thiong'o, *A Grain of Wheat.*)

Four days later Kenya was admitted to the United Nations. With a Kikuyu, Jomo Kenyatta, as President and a Luo, Oginga

OPPOSITE: Coastal Kenyans TOP have turned their mangrove swamps to a profit — poles for construction. BOTTOM: The narrow, dusty streets of old town Malindi remain the domain of hand-pulled carts and pedestrians. ABOVE: Kenya's jungles are paradises of birds, dense vegetation, and cascading water.

Odinga, as Vice-President, independent Kenya adopted policies to encourage foreign investment and participation in the economy while internally restructuring the government to overcome tribalism.

Since agriculture was the basis of the economy, the new government gave priority to the problems of land distribution and ownership. Within five years of independence, through a land resettlement program, mainly financed by Britain, one-fifth of the Highlands reverted to African hands. During the fifteen years of Kenyatta's rule, Kenya's economy flourished and social services reached a greater number of people. On the political front, the KADU merged with the KANU in 1964, making Kenya a single-party state. The KANU was challenged only briefly, when Vice-President Odinga formed the Kenya People's Union (KPU) in 1966, after he was forced to resign from the government because of his "leftist" views. Three years later, when a Luo, Tom MBoya, then Minister for Economic Affairs, was assassinated by the Kikuyu and violence broke out in Kisumu, the Luo heartland, Odinga and his KPU were blamed. Using tactics learned from the colonial government, Kenyatta detained Odinga and other KPU leaders and banned the KPU.

Kenyatta remained in office until his death on August 22, 1978. He was succeeded by David Arap Moi, a Kalenjin who had become vice-president when Odinga resigned in 1966.

Moi continued the basic policies of Kenyatta and remained in power after elections in 1983 and 1988, but amid growing controversy that included amendments to the constitution from secret ballots to voting by queue, widely and correctly seen as a step backwards for democracy. Councilors from the country's majority Kikuyu tribe were removed from many positions of power and further constitutional changes dissolved the separation between judicial and executive areas of government. Despite this divided opposition, intertribal violence in key areas enabled Moi to win further elections in 1992, held over the Christmas holidays, but many international agencies were dissatisfied with the results: aid programs were suspended and the economy suffered. For the 1997 elections,

Moi changed the constitution to allow himself a further term of office and in an atmosphere of increasing tribal unrest — especially in the Rift Valley and around Mombasa — scraped in for what is widely considered to be his final term of office. Over the last ten years, freedom of speech has increased greatly in Kenya and the voices that are heard are expressing widespread dissatisfaction with a political regime riven with corruption and cronyism. Thirty-five years after independence, Kenya remains the most stable country in East Africa and perhaps in all of Africa. Nonetheless, it faces problems of overpopulation, unemployment, and insufficient foreign exchange to buy needed imports.

To the casual traveler, tribalism is not readily apparent, except perhaps in the obvious difference in dress. But tribal problems exist and can be fanned for political ends: many political analysts feel that therein lies the greatest threat to Kenya's stability. Moi's amendments to the constitution, the basis of Kenya's independence, might also prove to be to be significant threats to Kenya's democratic tradition.

Central to Kenya's economic survival is the creation of jobs and industries to generate foreign exchange. Tea surpassed the traditional "big money" export, coffee, in 1988, while tourism led both in foreign revenues. However tourism is a fragile industry. Kenya's main international draw is its national parks and most visitors come to see the animals. A rash of poaching in late 1988 caused such a dramatic fall in animal numbers and security in the national parks that tourism suffered. Increased pressure on the government by the East African Wildlife Society and tour operators brought about more stringent anti-poaching measures. No sooner were the most pressing environmental problems brought under control than human factors started to threaten. Tribal conflict surrounding the 1997 elections and the occasional, internationally reported, incidents of violent crime brought personal security to the top of the agenda: the tourist industry all but collapsed, bringing the economy grinding to a halt and starving the Kenya Wildlife Service of funds. Tourists can be sure of a warm welcome in Kenya: just as well. Without tourism Kenya's wildlife has little chance of survival.

LAY OF THE LAND

Slightly smaller than the state of Texas, but larger than France, Kenya lies on the equator and is bordered by the Indian Ocean, Somalia, Ethiopia, Sudan, Uganda, and Tanzania. In a stretch of 800 km (500 miles) from east to west, the land rises from the reef-fringed sandy beaches of the Indian Ocean to the mile-high plateau of Nairobi, higher still to the lofty snow-capped summit of Mount Kenya (Africa's second-tallest mountain), then drops across the Great Rift Valley to Lake Victoria at 1,157 m (3,795 ft) above sea level. From south to north along another 800-km (500-mile) axis, the Kenyan countryside contrasts jagged, forested mountains, and lush red-soil agricultural lands with Lake Turkana and the timeless, sandy-colored dusty desert that covers more than one half of the country.

Before the formation of the Rift Valley, Kenya's climate and vegetation were probably uniformly tropical. The gigantic eruption that created the Rift also triggered dramatic climatic changes. After millions of years of evolution, Kenya's climates are now dramatically varied — semiarid, tropical, temperate, alpine, and arctic. Only the visitor who wishes to climb to the peaks of Mount Kenya, Mount Elgon, or Tanzania's Mount Kilimanjaro, however, need prepare for temperatures below freezing. Some day, nowhere in Kenya will warm clothing be necessary, according to United Nations Environment Program (UNEP) scientists in Nairobi. The country's overall climate is warming and its desert growing, due to the greenhouse effect.

Kenya's varied climates and vegetation are home to an endless parade of animals, ranging from miniature antelope only 25 cm

(10 inches) tall to six-ton elephants. To enjoy this animal carnival to the fullest, patience is needed. Kenya has approximately 90 species of ungulates or grazing animals, innumerable predators and scavengers, 1,500 different birds, hundreds of aquatic and reptilian species, and countless types of insects and arachnids. With 10% of Kenya's land and a portion of its coastal waters devoted to the preservation and protection of flora and fauna, you are never more than a few hours from one of 48 national parks and game preserves where animals still reign supreme, and where man is only a spectator.

Cooling themselves lazily in the Mara River, hippopotamuses look more tranquil than they actually are. They kill more people than lions!

Out of the Jade Sea

THE COAST

Kenya's 480 km (300 miles) of coast along the Indian Ocean is world-famous for its sand beaches lined with palm trees, and rocky inlets and mangrove swamps teeming with miniature aquatic life. The beaches are protected from harsh ocean waves by extensive, multicolored coral fringe and barrier reefs. These shelter hundreds of aquatic species, such as the graceful black-and-white striped Moorish idol, electric blue striped blinny, lacy basket starfish, prickly sea urchins, and spongy sea cucumbers, which are protected in the **Kisite**, **Watamu**, and **Malindi Marine National Parks**.

The reefs have for centuries also provided building material for coastal cities, and served as a deterrent to sharks wishing to visit waters near bathing beaches. But there are exceptions! Those who swim or dive on the eastern side of the reef should *always* be alert for sharks.

Inland of the beaches runs a narrow coastal plain of three to twenty kilometers (two to twelve miles) wide in the south and 150 km (90 miles) wide along the Somalia border in the north. The wider northern plain was formed by Kenya's largest river, the **Tana**, which meanders from its source on the slopes of Mount Kenya for 1,120 km (700 miles) to empty into Ungwana (Formosa) Bay between Lamu and Malindi. Some areas of the plain are suitable for agriculture; most are dry scrub; a few stretches of thick coastal forest are protected as natural reserves.

An ever-present wind off the Indian Ocean brings relief from the average daytime temperature of 30°C (87°F). Even in the cooler summer season, night temperatures rarely fall below 20°C (68°F).

Along the coast, rainfall is frequent but of short duration, except during the April to June monsoon season. A tropical cloudburst may slow the unsuspecting visitor, but Kenyans casually proceed along their routes, knowing it will soon be followed by sun and drying wind. Annual rainfall along the coast and coastal plain is 1,000 to 1,250 mm (40 to 50 inches); even in May, the peak of the monsoon season, seven hours of sunshine is normal per day (situated on the equator, Kenya has 12 hours of daylight year-round).

CENTRAL PLATEAU AND HIGHLANDS

The plateau beyond the coastal plain ascends gradually to the central Highlands in the south, and across the Ethiopian border in the north. With only a few low valleys and monotonous but unique vegetation — flaming thorn trees, monstrous upside-down baobabs, and scrub — the plateau conveys a sense of endlessness, a place described by Elspeth Huxley as a horizonless void where "you could walk straight across to the rim of the world." Here in **Tsavo East** and **Tsavo West National Parks** roam elephants, buffalo, Grevy's zebra, giraffes, lions, aardvarks, impalas, and antelope including the miniature five- to six-kilogram (10- to 12-lb) dik dik, and gerenuk which stand on hind legs to feed. Guinea fowl, francolin, black-headed oriole, and red-billed hornbill are only some of the birds you can expect to find.

In the northwest, the Rift Valley and Lake Turkana cross the plateau, changing the landscape. The vegetation is much the same but sparser: Kenya's growing desert. **Sibiloi National Park**, along the shores of Lake Turkana, protects several hundred square kilometers of fossil beds of the Pleistocene era and the "cradle of mankind."

The plateau is dry and hot, with average daytime temperatures of 34°C (93°F). Rainfall is minimal, between 250 to 500 mm (10 to 12.5 inches) per year; the area suffers from periodic drought. Yet the meager vegetation sustains a large variety of wildlife, including elephants, giraffe, zebra, and antelope which have been pushed by human and livestock expansion from the more temperate lands.

South-central Kenya, termed the Highlands during colonial days, is split by the Great Rift Valley. High tablelands with forested volcanic mountains, savannas, and a temperate climate, the Highlands have, in modern times, become a highly populated region.

Here, the savannas are interrupted by deep green valleys, narrow canyons with cascading waterfalls, and steep, rugged mountains, the most arresting being Mount Kenya, 5,199 m (17,085 ft) above sea level. Although lower than Africa's tallest, 5,895-m (19,650-ft) Mount Kilimanjaro in Tanzania, this extinct volcano is taller than Europe's tallest, Mont Blanc. The days are pleasantly warm and the nights cool. In **Mount Kenya** and **Aberdare National Parks** live many of the same animals that inhabit Tsavo, but they are joined by other animals not adapted to the arid plateau.

Mount Kenya on the eastern side of the Rift Valley, and the Aberdare Mountains on the west capture up to 3,000 mm (120 inches) of rain per year, while the lower rich agricultural lands receive between 750 and 1,000 mm (30 to 40 inches) primarily from

TROPICAL JUNGLE

The western slope of the Rift Valley descends to an elevation of 1,157 m (3,795 ft) and the world's second-largest freshwater lake, Victoria, which covers 69,490 sq km (26,830 sq miles). With such a large surface area, Lake Victoria — its islands, papyrus beds, creeks, bays, and beaches—has created a tropical microclimate. Hippos and crocodiles inhabit the shores, as well as Egyptian geese, flamingos, cormorants, blue herons,

March to May, the "Long Rains" and from October to December, the "Short Rains." As on the coast, although a lot of rain can fall it generally does so quickly, and in the worst season, April and May, Nairobi and the Highlands still average five hours of sun per day.

In Nairobi and other low-lying plateau areas, temperatures are comfortable year-round at 10° to 14°C (50° to 58°F) at night and 22° to 26°C (72° to 79°F) during the day. When traveling to high altitudes the visitor will generally experience an average drop of 0.6°C (1°F) per 100 m (328 ft), descending to below freezing on Mount Kenya and the Aberdare Mountains. Evenings in the low mountains are usually brisk, with temperatures around 7°C (45°F) not unusual.

pelicans, Marabou storks, and other flying species. And the entertaining hammerkops and jacan or lily trotters go about transported on the backs of hippos.

Only here, on the surrounding hills and valleys near Kakamega, will one still find in Kenya the tropical forest of African jungle movies, with its monkeys, baboons, bush duikers, forest hogs, buffalo, waterbuck, bongos, and eagle owls. Here rainfall is 1,000 to 1,300 mm (40 to 50 inches) per year; day and night temperatures are more distinct — 14° to 18°C (58° to 64°F) at night and 30° to 34°C (86° to 93°F) during the day.

The hardy acacia tortilis survives in soil scorched by drought.

Nairobi
and
About

KENYA'S WELCOMING CAPITAL

With few exceptions, your trip to Kenya will begin in Nairobi, a bustling city with an ultramodern skyline. As Nairobi is over a mile above sea level, its climate is temperate and not too drastic an adjustment for travelers arriving from colder northern climates. However, culture shock and jet lag are enough to give one a negative first impression. Later on, when you come back from safari, Nairobi will seem more civilized and inviting.

Nairobi is today one of the most important commercial centers in East Africa, and the largest city after Johannesburg and Cairo. Its official population is currently estimated at four and a half million, and growing at eight percent a year. Nairobi, "the place of cold water" in the Maa language spoken by the Maasai, was not inhabited until George Whitehouse, chief engineer for the Mombasa-Uganda Railroad, decided in 1899 to make this papyrus bog his construction headquarters and the railway's principal nerve center. Almost overnight, a boom town sprang up on the "black cotton" soil that expands to a sticky, impassable mud when wet and contracts to a solid crust when dry.

Background

"With its irregular lines of weather-beaten tents and faceless, barrack-like corrugated iron bungalows, Nairobi at the turn of the century bore a not altogether inexact resemblance to a miniature Dachau without walls. There was a main thoroughfare called Victoria Street which became a canal of thigh-deep mud whenever rain fell. A proliferation of the cramped, fetid Indian shops known as *dukas* pockmarked the town, and at the western end of Victoria Street sprawled [an Indian] bazaar… Other points of interest were a post office, a soda water factory and a shaky timber structure known as Wood's Hotel which doubled as a general store and which burned down several times before being abandoned as a poor insurance risk. Social life centered on a singularly uncongenial heap of wood and corrugated iron which railway officials and other British resi-

dents were pleased to call their club." Thus did Charles Miller, author of *The Lunatic Express*, a chronicle of the Mombasa-Uganda railway, describe Kenya's future capital.

The railway was finished on December 19, 1901. The British East African Company soon realized that it could not entice the Kenyans to produce enough export crops to keep the £5 million investment paying for itself. Thus began a publicity campaign to attract European settlers with offers of cheap land in return for crops which would provide freight for the new line.

The scheme was only a minor success. It brought settlers by the thousands, many of whom were more interested in getting rich quickly than working the land. Although the land was fertile, it was difficult to clear and maintain. European crops were often attacked by tropical blights and parasites.

Nonetheless, many European settlers fell in love with Kenya and stayed. Nairobi, not their homesteads, became the center of commerce and society.

In 1906, the colonial offices were moved from Mombasa to this new city that now had the air of a Wild West town. Men carried guns; brawls were not infrequent. Parties were wild and uninhibited, lasting for several days until the participants staggered out of town back to their farms and ranches. Businesses were dominated by Indian merchants, Europeans controlled the banks and administrative services, and Africans were relegated to a subservient role, a formula that has remained

Modern buildings, interspersed with jacaranda, ABOVE, bougainvillea and palm trees, are features of urban Nairobi.

much unchanged to the present day. As the naturalist I.N. Dracopoli described Nairobi in 1914, it was "neither African nor European but seems to combine in one city the discomforts of two civilizations without the advantages of either."

Today, Nairobi has evolved into an international center with a character all its own, having kept a touch of the frontier. The **Norfolk Hotel**, from which Elspeth Huxley began her journey to Thika, has been restored and enlarged, and is now an international class hotel. Another popular European

throughout the city. The dust and mud still exist, and the population is still exploding faster than jobs can be created and houses constructed.

The inhabitants are warm and helpful. The city offers every modern comfort but on Kenyan terms. It is good to remember that Nairobi is Africa and the tropics. Little happens immediately, but it happens. A phone call to Europe or the United States during business hours can go through instantly or take up to an hour. Faxes usually go through instantly, especially outside office

watering hole in the early days, the Stanley Hotel, has been replaced by a modern structure housing the five-star **New Stanley Hotel**. Still in its more or less original condition is the **Green Bar** which claims to have been open 24 hours a day since 1919. Even today, it is raucous and the site of frequent brawls.

The city is cosmopolitan with its mosques, temples, churches, and a synagogue, its international organizations such as the United Nations Environment Program, Food and Agriculture Organization, and World Health Organization, its multinational businesses and foreign embassies. Yet it has retained some of its original flavor. The Indian *dukas* have grown up into a great variety of shops

hours in the United States or Europe, and Internet access is just starting to open up international communications. Meanwhile domestic communications remain in the dark ages. Trying to make internal telephone calls is one of Kenya's great frustrations: lines often drop out of service, ring endlessly or just don't work. Industry and commerce carry on their business in a quiet vacuum untroubled by effective or efficient communication, and to avoid ulcers it is easiest to regard this as a liberating experience. Satellite communications have started to improve the situation in Nairobi and it is hoped that coverage will bring effective and affordable communication to the hinterland over the coming years.

AROUND TOWN

The **city center** lies on both sides of Kenyatta Avenue, bounded by Uhuru Highway to the west, University Way to the north, Moi Avenue to the east, and Haile Selassie Avenue to the south. It is compact and enjoyable to walk in daylight hours. At night and weekends, taxis are recommended.

The boxy skyline is dominated by the distinctive gold-bronze tower of the **Kenyatta Conference Center** in **City Square**, south of

and will bargain whether you are in the mood or not.

Your first day in Nairobi, however, is probably not the best for bargaining: due to your lack of a suntan (if you've arrived from a cooler climate) you will be pegged as a naive newcomer and easy prey for these astute business people. Their aim is to get you to place a value on their offerings: say a price and you're hooked so just stay quiet. After a safari or two, schedule a day in Nairobi for shopping; you'll feel much more in control and be able to enjoy the frantic excitement of

Kenyatta Avenue. Walking tours of the center are provided and a roof walkway (100 KSh) gives a panoramic view of the city. Numerous flowering trees (jacarandas bloom after the short rains and bougainvilleas year-round) line the streets and sidewalks, offering a canopy from sun and rain.

City Market and Jamia Mosque, north of Kenyatta Avenue, are a colorful relief to the otherwise somber concrete structures. **City Market**, once the main food market for Nairobi, still sells some food but the mezzanine level is tightly packed with open stalls selling colorful baskets, graceful wood carvings, native jewelry, batiks, soapstone carvings, paintings, and other crafts and trinkets. Vendors compete avidly

the market. The market is open from 7:30 AM to 6:30 PM, Monday to Friday, 7:30 AM to 6 PM Saturday, 8 AM to 1 PM Sunday.

Jamia Mosque can be enjoyed from the outside by non-Muslim tourists, who are occasionally allowed to enter. The delicacy of its architecture and calm ambiance is unique in Nairobi. As you travel Kenya, other mosques will appear when you least expect them, as on the dirt track to Meru National Park, 20 km (12 miles) from the nearest town.

In the vicinity of the Bus Station (Mfangano and Hakati Roads) is the **open market**.

OPPOSITE: The Parliament Building on City Square is a landmark of Kenya's Uhuru (Independence). ABOVE: Friday prayers outside Jamia Mosque in downtown Nairobi.

Nearly 50% of Nairobi's population inhabit this area bounded by Moi Avenue and the Nairobi River. Here, the market is similar to those of country villages, where a great variety of dried beans, *ugali* (white maize meal), rice, potatoes, cabbages, and the other essentials of everyday Kenyan life are sold.

The **Bus Station** itself is a fascinating hub of human activity at the end of a working day. Drivers stand, bidding for passengers to overfill their already crowded buses. Vendors hawk food, toys, and other items to passengers through the open windows — often having to run alongside to collect money or give change as the bus pulls out. Buses are loaded with every type of cargo imaginable, all strapped helter-skelter atop. A more unusual sight was a gentleman holding his live chicken upside down out the open window: most of the other chickens were safely on passengers' laps.

Nairobi has several parks and green spaces. Although **Uhuru Park** across Uhuru Highway from the city center, is not generally safe even during the day, the **Nairobi Arboretum**, five kilometers (three miles) northwest of the city center on Arboretum Road, has been restored to its former glory and **City Park**, three and a half kilometers (just over two miles) northeast of the city center on City Park Road, is the third largest. Here, you can enjoy the tropical vegetation and bird life while taking a relaxing stroll, but only in daylight. None are safe after 6 PM, but on weekends all are crowded.

To the north of City Park are the rich, formerly all-white suburbs with beautifully-manicured and heavily-guarded grounds. On **Muthaiga Road** are the palatial residences of foreign ambassadors, of which you can only catch a glimpse through rarely opened gates or small cracks in the tall fences and dense shrubbery.

As a newly arrived tourist, don't be surprised if you are approached frequently by young men offering their services as guides to help you find a hotel, safari operator, or car rental. They can be helpful but more often are annoying. Once you get a tan and have found your way around town, you probably won't be bothered as much.

If you do decide to deal with one of these young men, never follow him down alleys or to businesses that do not have offices. Even some of the Nairobi offices are nothing more than a front for services that are not readily available. There is an abundance of legitimate tour operators, car rental businesses, and travel agencies, so don't deal with sharks.

WHAT TO SEE AND DO

First on the list should be the **National Museum**, located just over two kilometers (less than a mile and a half) from the city center on Museum Hill. It provides an informative orientation to Kenya's paleontology, geology, ornithology, ethnology, history, and wildlife. It also has a small gift shop whose prices may be slightly higher than some of the downtown shops, but the proceeds go to the Museum, a worthy cause. Entrance fee is 200 KSh. Adjacent to the museum is the **Snake Farm**, which houses an extensive collection of poisonous and nonpoisonous African snakes, crocodiles, tortoises, and fish. Admission is 200 KSh. It is safer to see these creatures here than in the wild.

Near the railway station, at the end of the potholed Ngairia Avenue south of Haile Selassie Avenue, is the **Railway Museum**. It has an extensive photographic display of the building of the "Lunatic Express," and a collection of memorabilia from the railway and Lake Victoria steamers. Outside are old locomotives on which you can climb. Coach No. 12, from which Superintendent C. H. Ryall was dragged and eaten by one of the man-eaters of Tsavo, is also here: look in the main museum for the picture of the lion dragging the body clear. The locomotive that was used in the filming of *Out of Africa* is also preserved. Open from 8:30 AM to 4:45 PM daily, it charges 200 KSh for entrance.

You can also visit **Parliament** and the **Kenyatta Conference Center**. Both are situated around City Square where you will find the statue of Mzee Jomo Kenyatta and his mausoleum with an eternal flame. When a conference is taking place or there are visiting dignitaries in town, City Square is brightly decorated with flags and drapes. For a fee you'll be taken to the top of the conference center, for a panoramic bird's-eye view

Mosques built by Kenya's Muslim minority are among Nairobi's most graceful buildings.

of the city. Security guards at most of Nairobi's highrise buildings are happy to take you to the roof on this basis and the Kenyatta Conference Center is no longer the highest. Less trodden are the stairs of **View Park Towers** on Loita Lane who will even let you up at night to watch the parade of mismatched headlights thread through the potholes of the city's main roads.

Parliament is open to the public, but during a session you must obtain a permit from the gatehouse on the corner of Parliament Road and Harambee Avenue to visit the

public or speakers' gallery. If Parliament is not in session, the guards can usually arrange a tour of the building.

The children found the National Museum and Snake Park nice but the city a bore. They wanted to see real animals immediately. So, in the late afternoon after our arrival, we made our first safari to **Nairobi National Park** on the outskirts of the city limits. Through the park gate was the vast open land populated by animals the children had only seen in zoos, circuses, and films.

Seconds after paying the entrance fee (steep at US$20 for adults, US$5 for children, 200 KSh for the car, although this is standard for this class of park in Kenya), we encountered a troop of olive baboons who are

residents of the main gate area. Within the next two kilometers (just over one mile) we had seen Maasai ostrich, common zebra, impala, gazelle, jackal, Maasai giraffe, and warthog. It is hard to describe the sudden thrill of being surrounded by such a variety of wildlife with the noise of Nairobi traffic faint in the distance.

For us, the two-hour game drive was a grand success, but our friends thought we were unlucky not to see lions, rhinoceros, cheetahs, hippos, or crocodiles. But if we'd seen then all on the first day, what would there be left to look forward to?

On our second trip to Nairobi National Park, after we had logged 6,000 km (3,720 miles) of safari, it was just as exciting and we finally did see rhinoceros and lions. This time, we spent five hours in the park and now knew to ask the rangers where to find the rhinos. They usually have a good idea where to find these threatened animals. In fact, Nairobi National Park is your best bet for seeing the rhinos in Kenya on your own.

For Isak Dinesen fans, her house in **Karen**, 15 km (nine miles) south of Nairobi, has been restored and turned into a museum featuring a small exhibit of her life and work. The grounds contain early farm machines and are well maintained. Entrance fee is 200 KSh. Many tour operators offer half-day tours that take in the **Karen Blixen Museum** and the nearby **Giraffe Sanctuary**, where each afternoon visitors can feed cattle nuts to endangered Rothschild's giraffe. It's not just their necks that are long: so are their tongues!

Denys Finch-Hatton Memorial in the Ngong Hills used to be one way to recapture the romantic isolation of colonial times: now the private owner charges entrance fees and the atmosphere has gone. Better to stroll off alone, relax under the trees and let Kenya seep into your soul as it did into the young author's.

From the top of the Ngong Hills is a magnificent view, but it is not safe to go alone. In the past few years, there have been several muggings and robberies. In spite of an ever-present security force, the Tourist Information Bureau suggests that you park your car at the police station at the foot of the hills, and that single women, or even two women alone, not make the hike.

A carry-over from colonial times are the races at **Nairobi Racecourse**, 10 km (six miles) northwest of town on Ngong Road that take place one weekend out of two. Check the sports pages of the *Nation* newspaper to see if there's racing scheduled during your visit. They are usually a lively gathering where everyone knows both horses and riders and the even the bookies seem to know the winner in advance. Admission is 200 KSh and the first race at 2 PM. Racecourse Road, outside the grounds, is lined with traders and a good place to hunt for folding chairs, wicker furniture, and large-sized earthenware pots.

WHERE TO STAY

On arrival, if you have not yet reserved a room, the **Kenya Tourist Information Office** ((02) 604245 FAX (02) 501096, on Mama Ngina Street, is unlikely to be much help finding a lodging. Better to walk in to any travel agent or take your pick from the list below.

At the high end of the spectrum are the international-class hotels. Most famous is the **Norfolk Hotel** ((02) 216940 FAX (02) 216769 WEB SITE www.kenyaweb.com/lonrho-hotels/norfolk/norfolk.html, Harry Thuku Road, Box 5851, Nairobi, now rather expensive at US$242 for a double. Traditional landmark and rather more central, the **New Stanley Hotel** ((02) 333233 FAX (02) 229388 E-MAIL reservations@sarova.com, Kenyatta Avenue and Kimathi Street, Box 30680, Nairobi, has double rooms for US$154: even though the famous message-board thorn tree has been cut down it still offers better value. **Hilton International** ((02) 334000 FAX (02) 339462, Watalii Street off Mama Ngina Street, Box 30624, Nairobi, charges US$165 for a double, while **Hotel Inter-Continental** ((02) 335550 FAX (02) 210675, City Hall Way and Uhuru Highway, Box 30353, Nairobi, charges US$180. Set in 26 hectares (64 acres) but far from the action, the **Safari Park Hotel and Country Club** ((02) 802493 FAX (02) 802477, Box 45038, Nairobi, is located 14 km (nine miles) north of the city center and charges US$256 for a double. Best of the luxury range is perhaps the **Serena Hotel** ((02) 725111 FAX (02) 725184, Nyere Road, Box 46302, Nairobi, at US$200 for a double. These prices do not include meals.

There are two good middle-range hotels orientated towards the package market in the up-and-coming suburb of Westlands: the **Landmark** ((02) 540780 FAX (02) 543810, Chiromo Road, Box 40075, Nairobi (US$118 per double) and the **Mayfair Court Hotel** ((02) 740920 FAX (02) 748823, Parklands Road, Box 74957, Nairobi (US$176 per double). For a bit more character head just above the center to Nairobi Hill for the graceful and welcoming **Fairview Hotel** ((02) 723211 FAX (02) 721320, Bishops Road, Box 40842, Nairobi (5,400 KSh per double). Near the National

Museum is the **Hotel Boulevard** ((02) 227567 FAX (02) 334071, Harry Thuku Road near Museum Hill, Box 42831, Nairobi (4,730 KSh per double), whose main advantage is the location; and on the edge of the city center is the **Hotel Ambassadeur** ((02) 336803 FAX 211472, Moi Avenue, Box 30399, Nairobi (US$76 per double). Most hotels in this price range include breakfast.

There are several town center hotels in the 1,000 KSh to 2,000 KSh range, filled mainly — but not exclusively — with a Kenyan clientele: best is perhaps the friendly **Terminal Hotel** ((02) 228817, Moktar Daddah Street, Box 66814, Nairobi, (1,100 KSh per double), or the idiosyncratic **Parkside Hotel** ((02) 333348 FAX 334681, Box 53104, Nairobi (1,500 KSh per double), overlooking the Jeevangee Gardens (not safe at night). The **Iqbal Hotel**, Latema Road, Nairobi, is the most popular of the "cheap"

OPPOSITE: The lights of the Hilton International Hotel sparkle in Nairobi's clear night air. ABOVE: During the day streets are crowded with overloaded *matatus*, or communal taxis, and private vehicles for Nairobi's ever-growing population.

downtown Nairobi hotels in the rather dodgy River Road area (210 KSh for a bed in dormitory, double, or triple rooms). You cannot make reservations and may even have to put your name on a waiting list. It is secure, usually has hot water and is handy for the infamous Green Bar. There are several other dirt-cheap lodgings in the surrounding River Road area, but it's not a good place to-be looking for accommodation after dark.

For the cheapest rooms, with nothing like the Green Bar or its equivalent for your neighbor, try the **Nairobi Youth Hostel (** (02) 721765, Ralph Bunche Road, Box 48661, Nairobi, for 330 KSh per bed. It is an International Youth Hostel Association member.

In the suburb of Parklands, which is reached by the No. 107 bus, is **Mrs. Roche's Guest House**, Parklands Avenue, Nairobi, where you can take a bed in one of her cabins (400 KSh) or camp in the garden (300 KSh per person). Mrs. Roche has been renting beds for more than 25 years and can provide you with interesting and sometimes helpful information. It is popular with overlanders on their way from Cape to Cairo or the Ivory Coast to Kenya.

WHERE TO EAT

Nairobi offers a superb variety of restaurants in every price range. According to the Tourist Information Office, there are over 200 different cafés, restaurants, and snack bars offering a choice of more than 20 different cuisines, but there are probably twice as many as their estimate. Nairobi is one of the few places in Kenya where you'll be able to pick and choose your meals; Mombasa, on the coast, is the other.

In Nairobi, nearly every nationality is well represented, but there are few American fast-food chains. There is, however, Kenyan fast-food — fish and chips (the fish is fresh Nile perch, but the chips usually greasy), curries, sausages, kebabs, and stews. These "stand-up and eat" shops are found everywhere in Nairobi; often the food is good at 50 KSh to 150 KSh per serving. Before selecting an establishment, look discreetly at what others are eating. If it looks appealing and the surroundings relatively clean, try it. Avoid salads and cold meals. Your best bet in a tropi-

cal environment is hot food, because cooking keeps bacteria to a minimum.

Be sure while you're in Nairobi to try some of its internationally renowned restaurants. A gastronomical treat is the **Carnivore (** (02) 501775, Langata Road, Nairobi. The Carnivore serves spit-roasted wild and domestic meats on an "all-you-can-eat" basis, accompanied by homemade soup, salad, relishes, baked potato, dessert and coffee or tea for 1,000 KSh. For meats, there are the standards — spare ribs, lamb, beef, chicken, and pork — and countless varieties of game — eland,

hartebeest, crocodile, zebra, giraffe, Cape buffalo, warthog, ostrich or wildebeest — depending on availability. The wild meat comes from game farms in Kenya. For example, the crocodile comes from a farm at the coast that grows crocodiles for their skins. The skins are exported to Italy and the Carnivore buys the meat. If you have a non-carnivore in your party, there is a good vegetarian menu or fried trout, fresh from the Carnivore's trout farm on the slopes of Mount Kenya. They also serve the best Irish coffee to be found outside San Francisco.

OPPOSITE: At Nairobi's Carnivore restaurant, wild and domestic meats are roasted in the open hearth. ABOVE: For more conventional meals, Nairobi has an abundance of good seafood and European-style restaurants.

The Carnivore is very popular with Kenyans, thus reservations are advisable. Lunch, from noon to 3 PM, and dinner, from 7 PM to 10:30 PM, are served daily except New Year's Day, when they close to recover from a lavish New Year's bash in the adjacent Simba Saloon (see NIGHTLIFE, page 133). If you make reservations early enough, you can request a table inside around the open hearth where the meat is roasted, or outside on the terrace which is airy and cool. It is a good idea to bring a jacket or sweater in case you are seated outside. The Carnivore is a 10-minute drive from the city center. You can take a *matatu* or bus, but there's a kilometer (half-mile) walk: at night a taxi is always recommended, which shouldn't cost more than 600 KSh.

Nairobi has numerous, generally excellent Indian restaurants. Best is currently the **Minar** ((02) 330168, with three outlets but the original at Banda Street, Nairobi; they serve some of the best Indian Mughlai cuisine outside India. Their closest rival is the **Haandi** ((02) 448294, Westlands' Shopping Mall, Nairobi. Prices reflect the quality; you can expect to pay between 600 KSh and 1,000 KSh per person for dinner. The menu is extensive and at Haandi's they are happy to prepare special orders off the menu. If you have difficulty deciding, the waiters can explain what each dish is.

A fine Japanese restaurants is the **Restaurant Akasaka Ltd.** ((02) 220299, 680 Hotel, Kenyatta Avenue, Box 47153, Nairobi, formal and traditional in decor and service, especially in the evenings: their lunch boxes make a perfect meal while shopping downtown. The sashimi (raw fish) is fresh (as is most fish in Kenya).

The **Delamere Coffee Shop** ((02) 216940 in the Norfolk Hotel on Moi Avenue has been and still is a favorite tourist hangout. Its atmosphere is relaxing, a good place to sit and watch the passersby while adjusting to the pace of Africa, but the food is pricey and disappointing.

Another popular tourist stop for coffee, tea, or buffet meal is the **Thorn Tree Café** ((02) 333233 of the New Stanley Hotel. The four-story tall thorn tree, once covered with thumb-tacked messages left by travelers, has been cut down, but the location, in the heart of the city, is some compensation.

There are several good continental restaurants: best for French food is the expensive (by Kenyan standards: 1,000 KSh to 1,500 KSh — US$15 to US$20 — for dinner) **Allan Bobbe's Bistro** ((02) 336952, Cianda House, Koinange Street, where reservations are essential and where the food is either homegrown at their private ranch or flown in fresh from the ocean off Somalia.

Drinkable wine has also started to become available in Kenya, mainly imported from South Africa though some is produced domestically. The local vineyard, Naivasha

Winery, produces an excellent white wine, but the reds and rosés are more variable.

For Kenyan food, just look through any number of steamed-up windows: special offerings include *ugali* (maize meal), roast meats, *mboga* (vegetable stew with some meat), and *pilau* (rice with meat) at very reasonable prices (30 KSh to 60 KSh). The **Chic Joint**, on Uhuru Avenue, is one good place for local food and they often have good live African music at weekends. In the city center, the **Harvest House**, Kenyatta Avenue, Nairobi, half a block from the Kipande House branch of Kenya Commercial Bank, offers an African Platter

OPPOSITE: Kenya boasts several styles of fine Indian cuisine. ABOVE: The Uhuru Monument celebrates Kenya's struggle for independance.

(300 KSh) with a variety of local dishes. In concept, it is like a Mexican combination plate, but not in taste. If you like cornmeal or polenta and baked or refried beans, you'll enjoy Kenyan food. It is subtly spiced and hearty. Perhaps Nairobi's best Kenyan food is served at the **Utalii Hotel**, eight kilometers (five miles) out of the city center on the Thika Road: owned and run as the practical part of the university's tourism department, it is where student chefs and waiters hone their craft with enthusiasm and skill. Tuesday lunchtime is a special Kenyan buffet, but the restaurant

offers great value every day and is a favorite with Nairobi residents.

There are also moderately-priced Chinese, Korean, and Ethiopian restaurants in Nairobi. All are worth a try.

SHOPPING

Curio and craft shops and stores are found everywhere in the city center. You can bargain in most but generally only with cash. Expect to pay near full price if you use a credit card. Before buying, shop around, because prices and quality vary greatly. To get some idea of the best available check out **African Heritage**, a combination café/museum/shop and, on weekends, live music venue on Banda Street. Prices reflect quality. For possibly the worst quality and value head to the **Central Market**, where a central core of vegetables are ringed by balconies of sharp salesmen. Many visitors prefer to head out of town and buy where they know excess profits are going to a good cause: the **Undugu Shop** in Woodvale Grove, Westlands, has a wide

range of handicrafts and Ethiopian antiques sold to benefit a number of charitable projects around Nairobi. An even wider range of products is available at the **Utamaduni Crafts Center** in Langata, where 18 specialist shops trade in a center opened by the Kenyan Wildlife Service. For safari clothes, try **Colpro** in Kimathi Street: it outfitted Michael Palin on the BBC *Pole to Pole* television show. Behind banked and junky tee-shirts they run a specialist outfitting department with a full range that can be tailored to fit.

The **East African Wildlife Society** runs a shop on the mezzanine floor of the Hilton Building, on Mama Mgina Street and City Hall Way, and proceeds help support their wildlife projects. Several artists sell their work only here. Some unusual items are produced with the American or European buyer in mind, such as hand-painted animals on handkerchiefs and scarves. The Society sell its own "impala" tie and a safari board game that makes a great present for children and adults alike. From it you can learn Kenyan geography and the names of animals in Swahili. The Society also has a selection of books on Kenya.

Books in Kenya are not expensive, and the selection is excellent. It is a good idea to bring a book or two on safari because, in the game parks, you will generally have a couple of hours in the mid-afternoon when reading on the verandah of your room or tent or around the swimming pool will be as energetic as you feel. At the end of this book, we have included a list of RECOMMENDED READING, page 306, if you want to select books about Kenya or by Kenyan authors. There is a wealth of good literature available. There are also many coffee table books on Kenya and its animals that you may want to take home. Our eight-year-old fell in love with the pictures of Jonathan Scott after we gave him a copy of *Safari Guide to East Africa's Animals and Birds* (printed in English, French, German, Italian, and Spanish), and he spent his Christmas money on Scott's *The Leopard's Tale* (890 KSh).

For children, the East African Publishing House has two beautifully illustrated legends, *The Hot Hippo* and *The Greedy Zebra* for 230 KSh. They are good for the read-aloud-ages and are written on a third-grade reading level.

The best bookshops in Nairobi are the bookstore in the New Stanley, **Select Bookshop** on Kimathi Street, and the **Text Book Center** in the Sarit Center, Westlands.

If you're having trouble deciding on exactly the right souvenir to take home or to give to family and friends, consider a membership to the **East African Wildlife Society** ((02) 574145 FAX (02) 571335, Box 20110, Nairobi. It costs US$50 a year for overseas membership for Europe, for which you get six issues of the well-produced and fascinating bimonthly color magazine *Swara*—a little bit of Kenya every other month. In addition you are contributing to the survival of Africa's threatened wildlife. The larger the international membership of the Society, the more clout it can wield when confronting government laxness in fighting poaching and protecting the national parks.

NIGHTLIFE

Nairobi does not have a roaring nightlife and, in general, it is best not to walk around at night. Even for short distances it's wise to use one of the many taxis. Their minimum fee is 200 KSh so this can make bar-hopping an expensive business.

Popular bars with expatriate workers in the town center start with the **Delamere Terrace** at the Norfolk Hotel and the bistro at the New Stanley. Most of the hotels have their own bars with their particular characters: in the Hilton, for example, the **Jockey's Bar** gives an evening's free beer to anyone successfully downing a yard of ale. Unless you know the trick of twisting the yard to avoid a sudden flood of beer halfway through don't try this: you'll end up with a soaked shirt, a laughing audience and paying for the yard.

Travelers who don't mind being the only white face in a Kenyan crowd are always surprised by the welcome they receive in local bars, for security reasons often located on the first floors of city center office blocks: try **Tanager Bar** in Rehema House, Kaunda Street, to mix with senior civil servants or **Invitation Bar**, opposite the New Stanley, for a younger crowd of office workers. The infamous **Green Bar** in the River Road area is featured in so many guidebooks it is constantly packed with hustlers and petty criminals geared up to

fleece the tourist market: go prepared if at all. Smarter drinkers head out to the smarter suburbs: Westlands is home to **Gypsies'** and **Papa Loca**, both lively and best found by taxi, always the best way to get about at night and especially to visit discos or night clubs.

The **Simba Grill** at the Carnivore (see WHERE TO EAT, page 129) usually has a disco or live music from Wednesday to Sundays. Wednesday is rock, Thursday jazz, Friday groove, Saturday disco and the only noticeably African night is Sunday. The cover charge (after 9 PM) is 150 KSh. This is a fairly

standard charge for Nairobi discos. As the disco scene changes relatively quickly, it's best to ask at your hotel for other recommendations. Many of the large hotels have their own evening entertainment.

Nairobi's most infamous nightspots are the German-owned **Florida 2000** and sister establishment, the **New Florida**, lively from 11 PM until 6 AM.

In which context, a word of caution about AIDS. Surveys show that more than 80% of the prostitutes in Nairobi—and other Kenyan cities—are AIDS carriers and the figures are almost as high for the single mothers and good-time girls who just fringe over into transactional sex. In Africa the disease is heterosexual, and any sexual contact constitutes a risk. Although some people place their confidence in condoms, perhaps the best advice is to bring your own companionship.

OPPOSITE: Cotton and silk fabrics in Nairobi shops are as colorful as the butterflies and birds of the national parks and reserves. ABOVE: The temperate climate means every sort of fruit and vegetable can be found in Nairobi's markets.

TO THE SOUTH

OLORGASAILIE

A long day excursion or relaxing overnight trip (if you're willing to rough it) from Nairobi is to the prehistoric site of Olorgasailie and the pink-tinged waters of **Lake Magadi** in the Rift Valley: entrance costs 200 KSh which includes a guided tour.

In 1890, geologist John Walter Gregory discovered stone tools and other evidence of prehistoric habitation of this Rift Valley crater that probably contained a lake some 400,000 to 500,000 years ago. It was not until the 1940s, however, that the site was systematically excavated by Louis and Mary Leakey. The Leakeys concluded that the lakeshore had been inhabited by *Homo erectus* of the Acheulian culture, early men who had the same culture as those who had lived in St. Acheul, France. A variety of tools for skinning animals, crushing bones, and hunting, as well as hand axes for which this culture is best known, were unearthed and are displayed *in situ*. Despite the large concentration of tools, no human remains have been discovered. The Leakeys also found a gigantic fossilized leg of an extinct species of elephant. Your entrance fee includes a guided tour by a usually well-informed ranger.

Where to Stay

The only accommodations at Olorgasailie are self-service bandas or bunkhouses (500 KSh per person) and a campsite (100 KSh per person) run by the National Museum ((02) 742131, Box 40658. Olorgasailie, but you'll need bedding and cooking equipment. Without this it's perhaps best treated as a day trip.

How to Get There

Leave Nairobi heading south past Wilson Airport and the national park and turn left onto the C58. After 40 km (25 miles), just after the village of Oltepesi, follow the signpost to Olorgasailie and turn left to drive one and a half kilometers (one mile) to the site. Alternatively buses do occasionally leave from

Technicolor Lake Magadi has the hottest climate in Kenya and an unusual resident population of aquatic birds.

Nairobi bus station, usually early in the morning. It's not a busy route and it is more convenient to rent your own car or reserve a vehicle and driver from an operator such as **Let's Go Travel** ((02) 340331 FAX (02) 336890, Box 60342, Nairobi, or **UTC** ((02) 331960 FAX (02) 331422 WEB SITE www.unitedtour .com, Box 42196, Nairobi.

LAKE MAGADI

At 600 m (2,000 ft) above sea level, **Lake Magadi** is one of the hottest spots in Kenya

and the world's second largest trona deposit (first is California's Salton Sea). This alkaline lake acts as a gigantic evaporating pan in which trona (a solution of sodium salts) deposits are 30 m (100 ft) deep, giving the lake its unlikely pink or green color, depending on the season. The lake is leased by the Magadi Soda Company Limited: signs by the road warn visitors to report their visit to the police station; permission is freely given.

Lake Magadi once received international attention when the flamingos left their normal breeding grounds in Lakes Nakuru and Baringo and laid their eggs here. The hatchlings were unable to free themselves from the sticky sodium deposits. A massive rescue operation ensued that took thousands

of the stranded birds to safety. The bird life at the southern end of the lake and in the small freshwater swamps is varied enough to make the trip worthwhile for the dedicated bird watcher. This is the only place in Kenya where you are likely to see the chestnut-banded sand plover.

Geologically, the site is unique. Each year, Magadi receives less than 500 mm (20 inches) of rainfall and has an average temperature of 20°C (68°F), varying between 15°C and 41°C (59°F and 106°F). Its evaporation rate is 3,500 mm (120 inches) annually. Thus, theoretically, the lake should be dry. But it is not, and the trona deposits are growing more rapidly than they are mined.

Obviously, local rainfall is not keeping the lake alive, but rainfall from the neighboring areas of the Rift Valley drains into the lake underground. In addition, this underground seepage is being geothermally heated, which accelerates the rate at which the water can leach soda salts from the subsurface rocks. Once the hot water, already rich in soda, reaches Lake Magadi, evaporation takes place quickly, leaving solid trona crystals on the surface of the lake. Some deposits are so solid that cars can drive across them; in spite of the heat, it's fascinating to walk over these technicolor fields on the factory causeway. The two factories operated by the Magadi Soda Company produce approximately 166,000 tons of soda ash and 40,000 tons of table salt annually.

Where to Stay
The town has, thanks to the factory, a public pool that is free to all comers. You might want to cool off here before beginning the journey back to Nairobi. Camping is possible here if you ask permission, although you're more likely to be invited to stay by a company employee. Alternatively, check in to the **Lower Guesthouse** ((0303) 33000 or (0303) 33278.

How to Get There
Leave Nairobi heading south past Wilson Airport and the national park and turn left onto the C58. After 83 km (51.5 miles) you will reach the end of the road and Lake

OPPOSITE: Longonot Crater towers over the Rift Valley, and ABOVE an ox-cart safari travels the shores of nearby Lake Naivasha.

Magadi. Alternatively, most days a bus does leave from Nairobi's bus station early in the morning. It is easier to rent your own car or reserve a vehicle and driver from an operator such as **Let's Go Travel** ((02) 340331 FAX (02) 336890, Box 60342, Nairobi, or **UTC** ((02) 331960 FAX (02) 331422 WEB SITE www.unitedtour.com, Box 42196, Nairobi.

TO THE WEST

Because Longonot Crater, Lake Naivasha, and Hell's Gate National Park are so close

here has been a problem in recent years, so don't hike alone. You will be accompanied by a Kenya Wildlife Service ranger in any case. Admission to the park is US$10.

On reaching the rim your response might be similar to that of Major Joseph Thomson, the first European to describe his visit here, in 1884. "The scene was of such an astounding character that I was completely fascinated, and felt under an almost irresistible impulse madly to plunge into the fearful chasm. So overpowering was this feeling that I had to withdraw myself from the side of the pit."

to Nairobi (within a two-hour drive), it is easy to speed by them in haste to get to more distant safari destinations. Each can be a day-long trip from Nairobi, but more enjoyable would be an overnight or a two-day trip around Naivasha before continuing west or returning to Nairobi.

LONGONOT NATIONAL PARK

The attraction of Longonot National Park is hiking and picnicking in the ragged volcanic crater, which takes its name from the Maasai "Oloonong'ot" meaning mountain of many spurs or steep ridges. A trail starting at the Longonot police station takes you to the rim. Like the Ngong Hills, security

You can descend into the crater but the walk around the rim offers better views. It takes over two hours to make the circuit as the path is narrow and often crumbly. You will need a sturdy pair of shoes. If you are not interested in the climb, there are superb views of the crater and nearby **Suswa Crater** from the Nairobi–Naivasha road, where there are scenic overlooks (which unfortunately are lined with souvenir vendors). Don't leave your car unlocked anywhere in Kenya, especially here.

How to Get There

To reach Longonot from Nairobi take the Naivasha Road northwest towards Limuru. After 28 km (17.5 miles) the road splits: the new Uplands Road heads on to Limuru and

Lake Naivasha, while the B3 forks left. After a further 22 km (14 miles) turn right onto the C88 signposted for Longonot. Park at the Police Station after 16 km (10 miles).

LAKE NAIVASHA

Lake Naivasha is one of the most beautiful of Kenya's Rift Valley lakes, surrounded by feathery papyrus, marshy lagoons, and grassy shores. It was the setting for M.M. Kaye's mystery, *Death in Kenya*. The story isn't great, but it describes the Naivasha area accurately.

Over the centuries, the size of the lake has fluctuated greatly. In the 1920s, a Swedish geologist, Eric Nilsson, found a buffalo skeleton in sediments of a former, larger Lake Naivasha. This buffalo had a horn span of over two meters (six feet) and its teeth indicated that it fed on soft juicy foliage rather than the tougher, drier vegetation that the buffalo of today eat. Nilsson suggested that this buffalo lived in an environment more moist than at present prevails in the Naivasha basin. Other research supports Nilsson's hypothesis; it is now generally agreed that the Rift Valley as a whole had a colder, wetter environment 10,000 to 20,000 years ago.

Early explorers such as Thomson and Fischer in the 1880s described it as a smaller

lake: records from the 1890s show that during that decade it rose 15 m (50 ft) and was much larger than it is now.

Today the lake water irrigates the surrounding countryside, where much of the fresh vegetables for Nairobi markets are grown. On the south shore is Kenya's only vineyard, and a plantation that employs approximately 4,000 people to grow flowers that are exported throughout the world. Many of the flowers in the world famous Amsterdam market are flown there daily from Kenya.

From all waterfront hotels you can take a boat to **Crescent Island** (200 KSh to 400 KSh per person), a private game sanctuary, where you can walk around the island and view, at close range, zebra, waterbuck, giraffe, and several species of antelope. Hippos are almost always seen and heard during the boat ride. Bird life around the lake is also abundant.

Where to Stay and Eat

Around the lake are several places to stay. In town is the excellent and fun **La Belle Inn** ((0311) 21007 FAX (0311) 21119, Moi Avenue, Naivasha, one of the oldest hotels in Kenya; the rate is 1,900 KSh for a double, bed and breakfast. On weekends, it's often full; people from Nairobi flock here for lunch and dinner. Sometimes, it is even difficult to find a seat for coffee or tea. The establishment is small, much like its counterparts in the French or New England countryside. White rabbits nibble the courtyard grass and a caged python provides a touch of local color. In addition to the French fare, it offers American-style milkshakes, pizza, and superb Italian sandwiches.

On the lake shore are the **Lake Naivasha Country Club** ((02) 540780 FAX (02) 543810, Block Hotels, Box 40075, Nairobi, (US$162 per double, full board); and **Safariland Club** ((0311) 20241, Box 72, Naivasha (US$138 per double, full board). Both have a golf course and swimming pool. You can also camp at Safariland on a lovely shaded lawn.

As an early refuge for Nairobi's elite, Lake Naivasha is a good place to take a break from hotels with a stay in private ranches or

OPPOSITE: The dramatic landscapes of Hell's Gate National Park. ABOVE: Fischer's Tower is a landmark.

homestays. If interested in conservation, consider a stay at Joy Adamson's famous house, **Elasmere** ((0311) 21055 FAX (0311) 21074, Box 1497, Naivasha (7,000 KSh per double, full board), set on the Lakeshore towards Kongoni Game Valley. This was where her life was spent working with lions immortalized in her writing that put conservation issues onto a world stage. Less a hotel experience and more like staying in a private house, it prefers guests to have an interest, if not in Joy Adamson's life and work, at least in conservation.

volcanic forces millions of years ago. It was here that the German explorer, Dr. Gustav Fischer, was attacked by the Maasai during his 1882 expedition. Fischer's Tower, a volcanic plug near the north entrance, identifies the approximate site of the ambush.

The park has an abundance of herbivores (zebra, impalas, gazelles, klipspringer, and buffalo), an outstanding bird population, a small Maasai population centered in several *manyattas*, and a spectacular red-cliffed gorge with a resident pair of lammergeyers (bearded vultures).

How to Get There

It's a two-hour drive to Naivasha although the frequent buses and *matatus* that leave Nairobi from the lower end of River Road will take rather longer. Drive northwest on Uhuru Highway, which turns into the Chiromo Road, and climb out of Nairobi on one of the country's few stretches of dual lane road — shared, unfortunately, with a lot of heavy traffic, to climb the shoulder of the Rift Valley. It's a spectacular drive.

HELL'S GATE NATIONAL PARK

Nearby is one of Kenya's unsung, but most accessible national parks, Hell's Gate (entry US$15, children US$5), shaped by violent

Because there are few or no predators (although lions may soon be introduced to control the herbivore population), it is possible to hike throughout the park. During and after the rains, the road to the gorge is impassable and you will probably have to walk most of the way from the gate if you wish to see the 180-m (600-ft) cliffs, formed by Lake Naivasha's prehistoric outlet.

It is a full-day's hike, 25 km (16 miles) round trip from the park gate to the south end of **Hell's Gate Gorge**. If you don't want to hike the full distance you can usually drive at least to the head of the gorge six kilometers (four miles) inside the gate. While hiking you will need to carry water and food; a hat and sun screen are highly recommended.

The descent into this miniature Grand Canyon is steep at first, but becomes very pleasant as you reach the bottom of the gorge. At the south end, you will see, but hear first, the steam of the **Olkaria geothermal station** that now produces much of Nairobi's electricity. Here underground water temperatures exceed 304°C (579°F), one of the world's hottest geothermal sites. Olkaria is expected eventually to supply half of Kenya's energy requirements.

Hiking in the park gives one a sense of the freedom, open space, and wildlife that abounded a century ago in Kenya. It is a

How to Get There

Access to Hell's Gate National Park is usually from Naivasha: drive south around the lake on South Lake Road where two left turns lead to Elsa gate and Ol Karia gate respectively. Alternatively, in the dry season, Hells Gate can be reached along a rough track from the B3 Narok-Limuru Road.

LAKE NAKURU

Lake Nakuru, another of the Rift Valley lakes, can be visited in a long day trip from Nairobi

pleasure to travel on foot with wildlife grazing along the route. The terrain is rolling, and you need not make the trek to the gorge. Even a two-hour walk around the plains looking out on **Longonot Crater** is an experience not to be forgotten. During the week, there are few visitors, and one can explore undisturbed. **Fischer's Tower** and **Hell's Gate Gorge** offer every level of rock climbing difficulty. We watched several climbers scaling the east face of Fischer's Tower, while dozens of rock hyraxes sunned themselves unconcernedly below.

There are several primitive campsites in the park (US$2 per person), but you must bring your own water and food. Ask the rangers at the gate for the best locations.

or an overnight stopover on safari going north or west. There is enough to see in the area to merit a two-day or weekend trip if Menengai Crater and Hyrax Hill Archaeological Site are included.

Alkaline Lake Nakuru was first mapped by Major Thomson, as was the nearby, smaller **Lake Elmenteita**, which is privately owned by the descendants of Lord Delamere. During a dry period from 1939 to 1940, Lake Nakuru completely evaporated, but filled up again during the mid-1940s. By the end of the 1950s, it was dry again, and dust devils whipped up and scattered white soda

OPPOSITE: Hiking in Hell's Gate National Park is a highlight of any visit. ABOVE: Flocks of lesser flamingo pink the lakes of the Rift Valley.

sediments over nearby farm fields. The dust often traveled 64 km (40 miles) away, threatening the productivity of the agricultural lands. The lake refilled in the 1960s and has remained wet ever since.

The lake is world-famous as the feeding ground of both lesser and greater flamingos, which can be distinguished by size and color of the bill. The lesser flamingo has a deep carmine-red bill, the greater a pink one with black tip. The lesser also has a deeper pink plumage, but unless both species are present, it is difficult to use this as a basis for identification.

Lake Nakuru and a wide strip of shoreline were made a national park in the 1960s and entry is US$27, US$10 for children. It was estimated then that there were, at times, more than a million flamingos on the lake. Ornithologist Roger Tory Peterson described it as "the most fabulous bird spectacle in the world." The concentration of flamingos fluctuates greatly, depending on which of the soda Rift Valley lakes (Magadi, Elmenteita, Bogoria, Turkana, or Nakuru) has the best food supply, but even when food is more abundant elsewhere, there are sizable flocks of flamingos on Lake Nakuru.

A species of alkaline-tolerant fish, *tilapia*, was introduced into the lake in the 1970s and the number of resident white pelicans has since increased substantially. On the southern and northeastern shores are blinds and viewing platforms, from which you can watch the pelicans and flamingos.

Besides the more then 400 species of birds that can be seen in the park, there are hippos, reedbuck, waterbuck, bushbuck, and the recently introduced Rothschild's giraffe and black rhinoceros, which are now fenced and under tight security since the poaching of the white rhinoceros in Meru National Park in 1988. Between the lake and the cliffs in the west, large pythons inhabit the dense woodland, and can often be seen crossing the roads or dangling from trees.

Where to Stay

Accommodations are available in the park or Nakuru town just north of the main gate. In the park are **Sarova Lion Hill (** (02) 713333 FAX (02) 715566, Box 72493, Nairobi (US$120 to US$180 per double, full board); and **Lake**

Nakuru Lodge ((02) 226778, Box 561, Nairobi (US$100 to US$160 per double, full board). There is camping (US$15 per person) inside the park. Most campsites have running water and some facilities but you are warned not to leave anything valuable at your campsite.

The best of the town lodgings is the **Midlands Hotel (** (037) 212125, Box 908, Nakuru (1,900 KSh per double, bed and breakfast). As Kenya's fourth largest city, Nakuru also has a great variety of *hotelis* — which can mean anything from the most basic foodhut to a modest hotel — and small restaurants, but the town itself has little charm and what character it has is not very prepossessing.

How to Get There

Nakuru is three to four hours drive from Nairobi, an hour and a half beyond Naivasha on the A104 Uplands Road. The lake is 158 km (99 miles) northwest of Nairobi. Motorists should watch out for Nakuru's mechanics: they're famous for staging or faking mechanical breakdowns and then dragging out repairs. A steady stream of buses and *matatus* link Nakuru with Nairobi.

MENENGAI CRATER

The 11-km (seven-mile)-wide Menengai Crater is one of the largest in the world. Although you get the best view of it from the Nyahururu–Nakuru road, the easiest access is from Nakuru. When the first European settlers arrived, they found the crater and the surrounding area surprisingly void of inhabitants. Later archaeological finds, however, indicate that the area had been inhabited since prehistoric times.

Legends about the Menengai volcano, whose name in Maa means "corpse," may account for the lack of nineteenth-century inhabitants. Several tell of scouting and raiding parties who ventured into the crater never to be seen again. One story relates how the now extinct Ilaikipiak tribe celebrated their victory over the neighboring Ilpurko by throwing themselves to death in the Menengai. They supposedly gathered at the edge of the crater, gorged themselves on looted meat, and finally called upon God to witness their mass suicide, as there was nothing left for them to live for since they had defeated everyone worthy of their prowess. Yet another version claims that the Ilpurko pushed hundreds of Ilaikipiak warriors over the crater rim. Today, there is a satellite tracking station on the rim. The bush-covered lava floor 500 m (1,600 ft) below is still relatively uninhabited.

The crest of the crater is about eight kilometers (five and a half miles) from Nakuru; follow Menengai Road to Crater Climb. There is a path from the signed, but now defunct,

burial mound, and a great variety of bones, utensils, obsidian fragments, and pottery remnants.

Most of the site has been dated to the late Kenyan Iron Age (the fifteenth and sixteenth centuries AD), but one burial ground is Neolithic. A large stone slab that once sealed it has been removed to display the bones of Stone Age inhabitants. In another site to the north, 19 more Neolithic graves were discovered in an Iron Age burial site. It is interesting to note that in the Neolithic graves, women were buried with their tools, while

"Campsite and Picnic Area," past the satellite tracking station to a lookout tower. Only on a clear day will you be able to see the opposite wall of the crater.

HYRAX HILL

Six kilometers (four miles) east of Nakuru is Hyrax Hill, one of three archaeological sites managed by the National Museum (Koobi Fora and Olorgasailie are the others). It is open to the public at 50 KSh per person. Here, in 1926, Louis Leakey discovered utensils and bones, some dating from the Neolithic period. Mary Leakey's excavations during 1937 and 1938 uncovered dwellings, a fort, livestock enclosures, a

men were buried alone. This might indicate that even then African women did the bulk of the physical labor: they certainly do today.

There is a small museum housing the finds from the dig and you can walk along the rocks to see the dwellings and burial mounds. An excellent guide, which will help you identify the sites, is on sale in the museum and your entry includes a guided tour by the museum's curator. The site is a bumpy two kilometers (one and a half miles) off the main Nairobi road five kilometers (three miles) southwest of Nakuru town.

Remnants of a prehistoric dwelling on the slopes of Hyrax Hill, one of several archaeological sites open to the public.

North to the Mountains

THIKA

The journey to Thika which took Elspeth Huxley three days to complete in an ox-drawn wagon at the turn of the century now takes less than an hour on a four-lane free-way. The red dust is still there (though you won't be covered with it) but the papyrus and tall grasses have been replaced by government buildings, apartment complexes, a sports stadium, Kenyatta University, cattle ranches, and sisal, pineapple, and coffee plantations.

Thika is now a Nairobi bedroom community and manufacturing center that sprawls haphazardly on both sides of the freeway. The **Blue Posts Inn** ((0151) 22241 Box 43, Thika, the first permanent business site in Thika and a gathering point for the early European settlers, is still in operation. Situated at the junction of the Thika and Chania Rivers, it has attractive gardens that overlook two spectacular waterfalls and is an ideal spot to stop for lunch, coffee or tea. The restaurant is good and reasonably-priced (200 KSh to 300 KSh for a plate), and the rooms have recently been refurbished. The rate are 1,500 KSh for a double, bed and breakfast.

The original structure, built in 1907 by a British captain affectionately nicknamed Major Breeches, got its name from its blue hitching post. Most of today's Blue Posts buildings were added in the 1930s and renovated in 1988.

From Thika or Nairobi, you can make an interesting side trip to **Ol Doinyo Sapuk National Park** and **Fourteen Falls** on the Athi River.

OL DOINYO SAPUK NATIONAL PARK

Ol Doinyo Sapuk (big mountain in Maa) or **Kilima Mbogo** (buffalo mountain in Kikuyu), rises to 2,146 m (7,043 ft) and is the major attraction of this park. It is here that the colonial owners, William Northrup McMillan and his wife Lucie, are buried.

McMillan, a Canadian, and Lucie, an American, came to Kenya in 1905. He apparently won Ol Doinyo Sapuk in a poker game at the Norfolk Hotel. The couple also owned land at Juja, Saba Saba, and Ondiri; their 16,000 hectares (40,000 acres) at Juja was a private game sanctuary as well as a farm. McMillan spent much of his time studying animals as well as hunting them. Lucie was an avid photographer.

After the First World War, McMillan was knighted for his services in the 25th Fusiliers. He and Lucie spent most weekends at their cottage known as "Lucie's Folly" on the slopes of Ol Doinyo Sapuk. McMillan died in 1925 and was buried on the slopes of the mountain. In 1958, a year after her death, Lucie's executors began the long and tortuous proceedings to carry out her last wishes that Ol Doinyo Sapuk be given to the government as a park. There was much interference from relatives. For a long time, nothing appeared to happen though the colonial government gratefully accepted the gift of land and, with it, the stipulation that the area should be known as the McMillan Memorial Park, and that the graves should be cared for.

By 1964, illegal *shambas* or farms dotted the hillsides, and it would have been easy for the new Kenyan government to assert that the squatters needed the land. But it honored the stipulations of the will and today Ol Doinyo Sapuk is a national park.

The view, on a clear day, is superb — Nairobi and the Athi River to the south, and Mount Kenya to the north. The dirt track to the top is rough and steep, thus a four-wheel drive is advisable, particularly after heavy rains. During the period of long rains, from April to June, the road may be closed and it's best to ask in Thika or Nairobi before making the trip.

Even though walking is not permitted during periods of road closures, a climb can sometimes be arranged with rangers at the gate for a nominal fee. Under no circumstances will a single individual be allowed to hike, due to hostile buffalo, the predominant inhabitants of the park. If you are lucky, you can also see Sykes' monkeys or black-faced vervets. Unsubstantiated rumor has it that there are still leopards in the forest. During both the long and short rains, butterflies are abundant as is a multitude of wild

Vervet monkeys look sweet but watch out: they are skilled at stealing your lunch.

flowers. Year-round, the ravines are alive with hundreds of species of forest birds. There is no entrance fee.

FOURTEEN FALLS

It's a short drive from the park to Fourteen Falls on the Athi River. After a heavy rain, the numerous small cascades merge into a spectacular rush of water. Unfortunately, upstream overgrazing and farming have caused erosion that turns the water a murky red. The avid waterfall lover can descend to the base of the falls along a rocky and often slippery trail. The falls are surrounded by dense tropical vegetation and were used years ago as the setting for one of the many Tarzan movies. Just which one, no one seems to know.

KIKUYULAND

The freeway ends abruptly a short distance north of Thika, as you travel toward the dwelling place of the Kikuyu god, Mount Kenya. This is Kikuyuland, home of Kenya's largest tribe and its first president, Mzee Jomo Kenyatta.

The countryside is cloaked with an infinite number of green tones on terraced hillsides where corn, beans, peas, bananas, coffee, and tea are grown. After the short rains (October and November), the flame trees dot the hillsides with orange. A month later, the jacarandas bloom, casting an otherworldly purple glow across the fields.

The land is always a hub of female activity. Brightly-dressed women, with infants and toddlers in tow, fetch water, weed and harvest crops, gather and carry firewood, wash clothes in the rivers and ponds, and do whatever is necessary to manage their households. The more affluent women with babies tied on their backs have the luxury of going about their journeys with an umbrella to shade them and their offspring. Older children tend cattle, goats, and sheep that graze in wooded strips between fields or along the roadside.

Many smile and wave to travelers in passing cars. Once, a young boy who stood against

Fourteen Falls on the Athi River, a short hour's drive from Nairobi.

a rock watching his mother hoe the corn-field inspired us to stop and ask if we could take a photograph. His mother agreed if our two boys were in the picture also. We walked back to the car to call our boys, returning to find our subject had vanished, nerves having got the better of him at the idea of having his image captured by a black box. Many Kenyans do not want to be photographed; it is important to respect their privacy, and occasionally unsafe not to.

What intrigued us about the episode was the mother's attention to detail. We had

driven past and parked our car out of view. Yet, she had obviously seen us pass and remembered that we had children in the vehicle. Throughout Kenya, we found this not uncommon. Waiters will remember what you liked or didn't like at previous meals, and if you preferred coffee or tea. Merchants and street vendors will remember your previous purchases and are quick to offer similarly-priced items.

Of the towns along route A2 — Maragua, Muranga, and Sagana — only **Muranga** has much to see. Formerly Fort Hall, Muranga is still the district headquarters, with modern

Kenyan women do most of the heavy household labor, planting crops, carrying firewood and water, and caring for their large families.

administrative buildings and the **Church of St. James and All Martyrs**. In the church is a mural of the life of Christ as an African, designed by the Tanzanian artist Elimo Njau. It was consecrated in 1955 by the Archbishop of Canterbury as a memorial to the Kikuyu victims of the Mau Mau revolution.

At the turn of the century, Muranga was little more than a military outpost administered by officers of the King's African Rifles. Many of the commanders spent their time shooting animals and leading occasional punitive expeditions to settle intertribal dis-

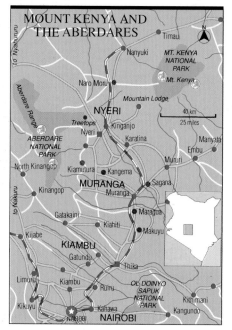

putes or settlers' problems with their Kenyan workers. Justice was frequently expedient rather than fair.

At Muranga, you can find rooms at a number of inexpensive *hotelis* such as **Rwathia Bar** on Market Street. However, an hour north, in the market town of **Karatina**, there are good and inexpensive accommodations in the **Karatina Tourist Lodge** ((0171) 71522 FAX (0171) 72520, at 1,000 KSh for a double, bed and breakfast.

Karatina has one of the best open markets in the area and is a popular stop for tour vans going to Aberdare and Mount Kenya National Parks. There are a few stalls selling tourist items, but inside the concrete-walled open market is all local business —

fresh fruits and vegetables, dried beans of every color and size, rice, *ugali*, houseware, and soap. It is worth stopping just to see the cabbages as large as basketballs. Woman vendors pass the time weaving baskets and the ever-popular Kenyan bags.

In the market's southeast corner, women operating treadle sewing machines repair torn garments or sew new ones to the buyer's specifications. The best market days are Tuesdays, Thursdays, and Saturdays. Usually, no one objects to your taking an overall picture of the market, but be sure to ask if you want to photograph a single individual or a small group.

Twenty kilometers (12 miles) north of Karatina, the road splits. The left branch leads west to **Nyeri** and **Aberdare National Park**, the other north to **Mount Kenya**.

THE ABERDARES

Nyeri, formerly a market center for European Highlands farmers, is a busy commercial and industrial center and the dropping-off point for **Aberdare National Park**. Its cemetery attracts visitors to the graves of the famous author and hunter of man-eaters, Jim Corbett, and of the founder of the Boy Scouts, Lord Baden-Powell, who spent the last years of his life in a cottage on the grounds of the nearby Outspan Hotel, and who once said, "Nearer to Nyeri, nearer to heaven."

Here, you can find a variety of places to spend the night. In town is the inexpensive (500 KSh to 600 KSh) **Bahati Restaurant and Lodging** among others, or the **White Rhino** at 100 KSh. Out of town and more expensive are the **Aberdare Country Club** ((02) 216940 FAX (02) 216796, Box 58581, Nairobi (US$173/double, full board), 10 km (seven miles) north of Nyeri in Mweiga; and the **Outspan Hotel** ((02) 540780 FAX (02) 543810, Box 40075, Nairobi (US$112 for a double with full board), opposite the CalTec Garage on the Nyeri Road, Nyeri. Both operate night game viewing lodges (The Ark and Treetops, respectively) in Aberdare National Park.

At the time of independence, the land around Nyeri still in the hands of European farmers was purchased by the government,

The spectacular Gura Falls in Aberdare National Park.

divided, and distributed by drawing lots among the Kikuyus. These farms are some of the most prosperous in Kenya, harvesting up to four crops of maize per year. However, farming has not always been easy with the park nearby. Elephants frequently devastated the crops until the Park Service dug a boundary ditch, strung an electric fence, and established a migratory right-of-way for these giants. During migration, a herd of elephants will push an unknowing neophyte through the electric fence, and the rangers must then radio farmers along the route to Mount Kenya to have them open their gates so the elephants can pass.

ABERDARE NATIONAL PARK

Established in 1950, the Aberdare National Park (entry US$27, children US$10) covers 590 sq km (230 sq miles), mostly at altitudes greater than 3,000 m (10,000 ft). To Kenyans, these mountains had always been the Nyandaraus, but in 1884, Major Thomson renamed them after Lord Aberdare, president of the Royal Geographical Society that funded his expedition.

Because of its high altitude, the park has chilly weather — high rainfall and almost freezing night temperatures — and some of Kenya's most unusual vegetation, bamboo forest and open moorland with tussock grass and giant heath. Year-round, a four-wheel drive vehicle is recommended; sometimes, even this may not get you through the park's black cotton soil, as the roads wind along the sides of steep, wooded valleys and across the moors and there is little maintenance of any kind.

We last traveled in the Aberdares after the short rains, and sections of the road to Karuru Falls and Gura Falls were closed. Even the open roads were not a treat. After helping a Danish family get their four-wheel drive out of the mud, we managed to get ourselves stuck in a patch of black cotton only a short distance from a pride of feeding lions.

The road to **Chania Falls** is usually passable, even for two-wheel drives, and the walk down to the base of the falls is like a fairy tale with rolling mist, giant lianas, Spanish moss, and innumerable flowering plants and trees. Above the falls, the **Chania River** has superb brown trout fishing. Arrangements for trout fishing in the Gura, Karuru, or Chania Rivers should be made through the park rangers.

From the peaks of **Ol Doinyo Lasatima**, 3,994 m (13,125 ft), and **Mount Kinangop**, 3,903 m (12,810 ft), are beautiful views of the Rift Valley and Mount Kenya, but these may be shrouded with mist after early morning.

Wildlife is abundant but often difficult to see. Along the roadside are many places where elephants have dug into the soil with their tusks in search of salt. Buffalo, baboons, and impalas are the easiest to find. Lion sightings are becoming more frequent and the Aberdare lions, most of whom have been transported in from ranches, are known to be very aggressive and have attacked tourists. Don't hike to the falls alone.

Leopards, including the rare black panther (a melanistic leopard), are found near the Wanderis gate, but it's a good idea to ask the rangers where they were last sighted. A game driver from the Aberdare Country Club tells the story of an American couple whom he was taking on a private game drive en route to their overnight stay at The Ark. The driver came upon the elusive black leopard on the road while the couple were having an argument. Ignoring the leopard, they refused to let the driver stop, insisting that they be taken immediately to their rooms. On arrival at The Ark, the couple were not speaking. The guide, irate that they did not understand the rare opportunity they had missed, was even more upset that he had not been able to watch the leopard himself.

Four species of sunbirds and 200 other bird species inhabit the park. Whether you can identify the birds or not, their songs, color, and activity are a delight. The best time for viewing Aberdare's wildlife is during first light.

The only full-service hotel accommodations in the park are The Ark and Treetops. Because of the difficulty in negotiating the roads, visitors who come to view animals, not the falls and mountains, stay at one of these two forest night-viewing lodges. Being older, **Treetops** is better known to tourists, but is far less frequented by lions and leopards than The Ark since its surrounding forest has disappeared into firewood and *shamba* construction. By all accounts, the Treetops experience is good, but you are paying for the prestige of staying in the place where Queen Elizabeth became Queen (her father died while she was viewing the animals), than for the accommodations (tiny bedrooms with paper-thin walls and a bathroom down the hall).

We spent one night at **The Ark** and it was among the most exciting game watching we've had in Kenya. Although Treetops does not allow children under 12, the cutoff age

You enter along a 100-m (330-ft)-long catwalk and the gate is closed behind you, remaining so until your departure the next morning. (Meanwhile the vehicle drives down a side-road straight to the lodge's service entrance but for guests to do this would rather spoil the entrance.) Quiet voices inside and whispers only on the open balconies and catwalk are the order of the day and night.

A hostess assigns you to your rooms and your baggage is delivered while tea is served. Any variety of animals is likely to be eating

at The Ark is seven, and the management has been known to bend the rules with the understanding that your child must be well-behaved and quiet (this rule applies to all guests regardless of age, rank, or nationality). Another plus for The Ark is a no-smoking viewing lounge, which is very much appreciated when the outside temperatures drop.

As it is impossible to drive to The Ark (or Treetops) to decide if you want to stay, let us give you a scenario of what to expect at The Ark. At 2:30 PM, you are taken from the Aberdare Country Club up to The Ark, elevation 2,293 m (7,525 ft). It has been designed to look like Noah's original, though the animals are not encouraged to come aboard.

at the salt lick, grazing, or drinking at the pool on your arrival, and sightings are recorded in vast ledgers that record the waterhole's status over the years. Buffalo, giant forest hogs, and the resident pair of Egyptian geese greeted us.

A naturalist, called The Hunter, is there to answer questions and to point out the animals and birds. On duty during our visit was Mike Clifton, an entomologist by training, a naturalist by vocation, and a lover "of all things big and small." At 5:30 PM, The Hunter on duty gives a brief description of the park, a history of The Ark, and a sum-

---

ABOVE: The Aberdare Country Club has magnificent facilities and food.

mary of what you are likely to see. During its 25 years of operation, the hotel has maintained a record showing that there is a 50% chance of sighting a lion, 88% for an elephant, 40% for a rhinoceros (probably lower now), 20% for a leopard (baited), and 2% for the rare bongo. Buffalo, baboon, bushbuck, and bush baby are almost guaranteed.

The northern part of the park where The Ark is located is a mist forest. There is little rain and the forest depends on the mist shadow coming from Mount Kenya for its water. In August and September, The Ark is

frequently covered by clouds and there are fewer animals.

About 6:30 PM, the staff feed the birds along the catwalk. It is a colorful sight — yellows, bright greens, red, orange, and iridescent blue. Thanks to Mike Clifton, we learned that there were golden-winged and eastern double-collard sunbirds, African rock martins, the pesky speckled mousebirds, and several varieties of weavers, montane warblers, streaky seedeaters, yellow-vented bulbuls, and olive thrush. He identified many more, far too many to remember them all.

Usually the birds are joined, or rather chased away, by genet cats (both black and spotted) and mongooses which arrive to pick

up the scraps that fall to the ground. Though the genet cats look remarkably like domestic cats, they are not related at all, belonging like the mongoose to the weasel family.

At nightfall, 7 PM, the bush babies are expected. These primates are as cuddly as a teddy and incredibly brazen. They stay at The Ark until the early morning hours, keeping those who remain awake company. They will try to follow you indoors. Don't be surprised if they tug on your clothes or sit beside you on a bench. Though it is tempting to pet them, they are wild and may bite.

After dark, there is usually more activity at the salt lick and floodlights are turned on. During the night we were there, buffalo were constantly present. We were also visited by a bull elephant who demonstrated how to use one's tusks as an earth mover, by forest hogs who were chased away by the buffalo, by a spotted hyena who just waltzed through, by a white-tipped mongoose, and by 50 or so bushbuck who were continually harassed by a lioness.

While the carnival continues outside, at 7:30 PM dinner is served inside "galley style" at communal tables. It is a nice way to meet your shipmates. After dinner, you watch the game or catch some sleep between the arrival of new "big game." When elephants, lions, or leopards make their appearance, the ship's bell rings in the rooms to alert everyone of a new act. (Anyone who wishes to get a full night's sleep can turn off his bell.) At 7 AM, everyone is awakened, breakfast served, baggage loaded, and all are transported back to Aberdare Country Club.

One of the most exciting hunts we've ever seen occurred at The Ark. About midnight, as a herd of bushbuck were grazing, a shape moved slowly in from the forest beyond the lights. At first, it seemed a shadow, but it moved with the authority of the great cats, lethal but extraordinarily beautiful, tan-golden and huge.

It was a young lioness, her body glimmering in the lights as she lithely picked her way through grass and brush upwind toward the unsuspecting bushbuck. She reached the last clump of brush that could shield her, the bushbuck only 20 m (60 ft) away, and crouched to wait, only her pointed ears visible above the bush.

The bushbuck grazed closer. Buffalo approached from the other side, driving the bushbuck nearer the lioness. One, a young female, was now less than 10 m (30 ft) from the lioness. Still, she waited patiently, knowing the bushbuck's leaping agility and speed. The wind changed, bringing the lion's scent; several bushbuck barked an alarm call, and the herd nervously sidled away, peering toward the darkness.

For the next two hours, the lioness lay motionless as the bushbuck edged nearer, and scampered away, hungry for the grass

Before going to The Ark, we stayed the night at the unparalleled Aberdare Country Club. We would however recommend you to do this in reverse, because there were so many animals at The Ark that we got little sleep and could have used the following day to rest in the comfort and beauty of the club, which is as elegant as any hotel in the world. The rooms, many of them brand new, are large and beautifully furnished. The architecture is reminiscent of an Italian estate and the grounds, looking out on Mount Kenya, are alive with

but suspicious. Finally, she made a dash at one and missed, and they all bounded into the forest. Untill nearly 4 AM, we could hear their sharp barks as she stalked them down the mountainside.

By 5 AM, the bushbuck were grazing peacefully and again the lioness made her move. Again she almost got one and this time padded after them down the other side of the hill.

Many tourists feel they have to see a "kill" before they leave Kenya. But it's as valuable to watch the hunt itself, and to learn what it's like to be a hunted animal, never to be able to relax one's guard, knowing always that eventually, as soon as you're old, sick, unwise, or just unlucky, a predator will get you.

colorful flowers and shrubs, and flocks of peacocks. There is an aviary, a nine-hole golf course, tennis courts, and a swimming pool; the trout fishing is reputed excellent in the section of the river on the grounds. For an overnight stay in the Aberdares, you'll want to bring film of 1,000-ISO or higher. Warm clothes can be useful too: year-round night temperatures are near 3°C (40°F). Long pants, wool sweater, and windproof jacket are a must, and even then you'll probably feel cold if you stay outside during the night.

OPPOSITE: Lionesses can be tender with their cubs but be prepared to be shocked when they get hungry ABOVE.

Where to Stay

The only full-service accommodation in the national park is at the famous **Ark** ℂ (02) 216940 FAX (02) 216796, Box 58581, Nairobi, (US$352 for a double with full board), or at **Treetops** ℂ (02) 540780 FAX (02) 543810, Box 40075, Nairobi (US$218 for a double). The Ark has a higher concentration of predators and is more comfortable than Treetops, which is no longer surrounded by trees. Reservations are a must for The Ark and Treetops; both can provide transportation to and from Nairobi if you don't have your own

(at US$75 round trip) and in any case insist on providing transport from the Aberdare Country Club or the Outspan Hotel respectively. You may also camp or rent the self-service bandas or bunkhouses at the **Aberdare Fishing Lodge** ℂ (0171) 55024 ᶜ/o Warden, Aberdare National Park, Mweiga, near the Kiandongoro gate. The rate is US$15 per person for bunkhouse accommodations, US$10 per person for camping. Bring your own bedding, food, and cooking utensils. Perhaps the best option, if driving yourself or in a party, is to stay at **Tusk Camp**: for 5,000 KSh, up to eight people can camp in the wilds of the park. Reserve through Let's Go Travel ℂ (02) 340331 FAX 214713, Box 60342, Nairobi.

MOUNT KENYA

No trip to Kenya is complete without a view, or even better, an ascent of Africa's second-tallest peak, Mount Kenya. Named by the various tribes as Ol Doinyo Ebor, Ndur Kegnia, or Kima ja Kegina, it is at 5,199 m (17,057 ft), taller than Mont Blanc, the Matterhorn, the Rockies, the Sierras, and most of the peaks of the Himalayas and Caucasus.

Composed of a huge volcanic base and plug whose outer mantle and crater have eroded away, Mount Kenya has three main peaks and a series of subsidiary cones scattered about its crest. The first European, and perhaps the first person, to reach the mountain's top was the British geographer H. H. Mackinder, on September 13, 1899. He named the taller two peaks **Batian**, 5,199 m (17,052 ft), and **Nelion**, 5,188 m (17,017 ft), in honor of two famed Maasai medicine men. The third and lower peak, **Lenana**, is 4,985 m (16,361 ft).

During the early era of human history, six to three million years ago, when our ancestors were wandering the shores of Lake Turkana and probably the foothills of Mount Kenya, the mountain was even taller, estimated by geologists at over 7,000 m (23,000 ft). Since then, the mountain's mass has caused it to sink into the earth's crust, and the combined effects of glaciation, wind, and weather erosion have further lowered its peaks.

Both Batian and Nelion are glaciated spires set in a gleaming array of snow-clad cirques and arêtes, like the Matterhorn and many of the Himalayan peaks. They are the province of skilled mountaineers only, with a variety of routes from Grade IV and above, depending on the time of year, and should *never* be attempted without the requisite experience, equipment, and guides. Lenana, however, is far more rounded, slightly lower, and beloved by Kenyans because it is accessible to hikers who are fit and reasonably conditioned to altitude.

OPPOSITE: Marabou storks confer in the branches of a thorntree. ABOVE: Mount Kenya, considered the home of God by many Kenyan tribes, is Africa's second-tallest mountain.

CLIMBING LENANA

Climbing Lenana is one of the peak experiences of the Grand Safari; a view of all Kenya awaits you on the top, and if you're lucky enough to reach Lenana at dawn, after a short climb from a hut below, the sunrise across the vast plains and hills of Africa will stay with you all your life.

Mount Kenya is visible from afar, its peaks usually covered with clouds by noon, but often glitteringly free in early morning or just

welcoming, and a variety of options are available for those who wish to hike or drive to Mount Kenya's lovely lower slopes or ascend Lenana Peak.

There are four main routes up Lenana. The most direct and popular, though perhaps less scenic, is the **Naro Moru Route**. Its advantage is that you can stay a night at the marvelous **Naro Moru River Lodge** ((0176) 62212, Box 18, Naro Moru (reservations also available through Alliance ((02) 337501 FAX (02) 219212, Box 49839, Nairobi), its lovely cedar cabins spaced among giant podocarpus

before sunset. On his epochal safari from Mombasa to Lake Victoria in 1883, the explorer, Joseph Thomson, was one of the first Europeans to see the mountain:

"Suddenly there was a break in the clouds far up in the sky, and the next moment a dazzling white pinnacle caught the last rays of the sun, and shone with a beauty, marvelous, spirit-like, and divine, cut off, as it apparently was, by immeasurable distance from all connection with the gross earth."

Thomson did not reach the mountain itself, having been threatened with extermination by Maasai while encamped on the Ewaso Ngiro River 24 km (15 miles) away, and forced to flee westward toward Lake Victoria. Today, the locals are more

trees, green lawns, and gardens along the south bank of the **Naro Moru River**. The lodge charges US$110 for a double, full board, and US$55 for self-service cabins. It also offers a bunkhouse and an exposed campsite. It has excellent cuisine, a very friendly staff, more birds on the grounds than you can count, and great fishing for rainbow trout literally at your doorstep.

First stocked with trout in 1910, the **Naro Moru River** stays clear most of the year, except during and just after the rains. Good fishing for browns and rainbows is also available in the nearby **Burguret** and **Nanyuki Rivers**, although overgrazing, logging, and intensive farming have led to increased turbidity and sedimentation of spawning

160

beds, diminished minimum flows, and reduced fish habitat.

You can rent fly tackle at the Naro Moru River Lodge, as well as all the gear you'll need for a hike around the mountain and up to Lenana Peak. The lodge has everything from boots (it's better, of course, to bring your own) to backpacks and even climbing hardware. It will arrange porters if you wish, and organize your stays in upper mountain huts depending on your pace and aspirations. Steven Wahome, a member of Kenya's 1989 Mount Everest team, is the manager of the

lava flows, then into towering conifer forest with vast clearcuts where potatoes have been planted between the new seedlings. During the rainy seasons, this section of the road may be totally impassable due to the huge ruts gouged into it by trucks bringing down harvested potatoes. Usually, you cannot drive beyond the park gate at 2,400 m (7,874 ft); however, if the road's good, you can take your vehicle all the way to the **Meteorological Station** at 3,050 m (10,000 ft).

In any case, it's a beautiful walk from the park gate up to the Meteorological Station,

lodge's climbing office, so, needless to say, you're in very good hands.

To reach Naro Moru, follow the road north through Thika, Muranga, Karatina, and Nyeri. If you've come from Aberdare National Park, you can return to Nyeri or take the back road shown on the map to the town of Naro Moru. An intersection just north of the town of Naro Moru leads either two kilometers (one and a quarter miles) west to the Naro Moru River Lodge or 17 km (11 miles) east to the **Mount Kenya National Park** gate (US$10 per day adults, US$5 children) and the start of the Naro Moru route to Lenana Peak. This first 17 km (11 miles) takes you through gradually ascending farmlands and scattered forest over ancient

as the conifers give way to hardwoods, then thick bamboo forest with magnificent vistas over thickly vegetated, mist-shrouded valleys. Once common throughout much of Kenya, the hardwood forests diminished as tectonic movement raised the earth's crust and split the Rift Valley, decreasing rainfall in much of East Africa. They are now found in isolated areas such as lower **Mounts Kenya** and **Elgon**, in the **Aberdares** and the **Mau Escarpment**. This mixture of hardwoods begins at about 1,800 m (5,600 ft) on Mount Kenya, shifts to bamboo and then moorland and heath at about 3,200 m

OPPOSITE: Mount Kenya's Nelion Peak rewards fit climbers. Much of the route up the mountain passes through montane forest ABOVE.

(10,500 ft), with the hardwoods more dominant on the south and east slopes due to the prevalence of rain-bearing winds.

Buffalo are common on the road all the way from the park gate to well beyond the Meteorological Station, and may be dangerous, particularly if they are solitary. If you're hiking, don't get too close: they are very bad-tempered, likely to charge, and much faster than they look. If you encounter them on the trail, try throwing rocks to chase them into the bush; if that doesn't work or if they move toward you, try climbing a tree or

become a problem if you're not acclimated; it's usually better to spend an afternoon hiking up to treeline (3,200 m or 10,500 ft) and enjoying the view. In the afternoons, the weather frequently turns rainy and visibility drops; the trail to Mackinder's Camp has a section known as the "Vertical Bog" which is best left alone in the rain.

From the station, you break out above treeline in less than an hour, slog up through the bog past the rain gauge and Picnic Rocks in another hour, and soon cross the Northern Naro Moru River, coming upon a

retreating *posthaste* until they lose interest and go elsewhere. Similarly, avoid hiking off the main road unless you have a local guide and he's willing to go first; buffalo have a habit of exploding out of the bamboo thickets and trampling the unwary wanderer.

The Meteorological Station has a campsite and self-help bandas with cooking facilities and mattresses but no food. Bushbuck, Sykes' and colobus monkeys, giant forest hogs, eagles, and, of course, buffalo are common near the station, and leopards not infrequent in the boggy meadow below the bandas. If you arrive before noon, it's possible to ascend further to **Mackinder's Camp** the same day. But the altitude can suddenly

marvelous view up and down narrow **Teleki Valley**, the imposing snow-covered peaks glittering above you. Since the station, the vegetation has changed from bamboo and hardwood forest, to stunted trees, to heather and tussock-grass moorlands, with giant yellow-flowered groundsel (*Senecio*) and giant lobelia standing up to 10 m (33 ft) tall.

While not luxurious, the concrete and rock bunkhouse of Mackinder's Camp will seem more than welcoming. If the clouds have not descended, there is a fine view of the peaks; from the ridge above camp it's possible to climb northward to **Two Hut Tarn** and other small lakes. Sunset on the peaks is beautiful beyond description, but Elspeth Huxley, in 1919, comes closest:

"The land stretched it seemed forever into a setting sun that had inflamed the whole sky with purple, crimson, and gold. And then the peak emerged from its sheath of cloud, incredibly sharp and delicate, its snow-covered glaciers a deep pink and little whips of violet hovering above its icy pinnacles. The black rock-faces, tooth-edged crags, all the weight and massive solidity of those twin towering peaks, Batian and Nelion… was transmuted into something as light, as airy and ethereal as a phantom ship riding upon a fleecy ocean…

"The night was cold, our single fly-sheets scarcely broke a chilly wind, damp rose from the ground to penetrate our blankets. So clear was the sky that the Milky Way looked like a plume of spray thrown across it by the bursting of some colossal breaker and held there in myriad frozen droplets. Above us, the peak loomed silently in darkness. Rocks were black as tarn water, grass a misty gray, mysterious shapes waited on the fringe of our vision, and we seemed to be afloat on some motionless vessel high above all the oceans of the world."

Three other routes up the mountain deserve special mention. The **Chogoria Route** from the eastern side is the most scenic and strenuous of all the ascents, more popular now, the road on the east side of the mountain has been paved to the roadhead at 3,200 m (10,500 ft). Above this point, there are spectacular views of the incised **Gorges Valley** and **Lake Michaelson**, a "trough lake" dug by glaciation. To reach this route, turn off the Embu-Meru highway north of Chuka at the sign for **Meru Mount Kenya Lodge**. The lodge is 30 km (19 miles) from the highway and offers self-service bandas at 2,100 KSh per person, no food or beverages, and a good campsite; reserve through Let's Go Travel ((02) 340331 FAX (02) 336890 E-MAIL info@letsgosafari.com, Box 60342, Nairobi. If you wish you can hike an hour further up to **Urumandi Hut** at 3,060 m (10,050 ft), and pay 300 KSh per bunk bed.

There are magnificent rain forests and bamboo jungle on the way up to Urumandi, and from there, it's an exhilarating four- to six-hour hike to **Minto's Hut**, spectacularly set into a bowl of three small tarns. You can stay in the hut or camp, again leaving early

(3 AM) if possible. It's a two-and-a-half- to four-hour hike from Minto's to Lenana Peak, with a long scramble over slippery scree, which at this altitude can be more than exhausting.

Alternatively, the **Sirimon Track** is the longest and driest route, much of it through thick rain forest and fabulous moorlands with long views of the peaks. Noted for its wildlife, Sirimon begins 13 km (eight miles) east of **Nanyuki** before the bridge crossing the **Sirimon River** and Timau. Leaving the highway, drive 10 km (six miles) through open farmland to the national park gate at 2,440 m (8,000 ft), then another nine kilometers (over five and a half miles) to the roadhead at 3,200 m (10,500 ft), where you'll find a campsite.

From the roadhead, it can take a day to climb the Barrow to **Liki North Hut** at 4,000 m (13,123 ft). If you're in very good condition, you might like to continue round the wall above Mackinder Valley past **Shipton's Caves** at 4,150 m (13,615 ft) — an emergency shelter — and thence straight up to **Kami Hut** at 4,425 m (14,518 ft). After Kami, it's possible to circle eastward below Batian across **Simba Col** and pick up the Chogoria route up Lenana. It's also possible, but inadvisable, to climb Lenana from this side, as the scree makes for significant danger, particularly in the dark if you're trying to reach the peak by sunrise.

A fourth approach is via the **Burguret Trail**, from the **Mountain Rock Hotel** ((0176) 62625 FAX (0176) 62051, Box 333, Nanyuki, eight kilometers (five miles) north of Naro Moru on the Nanyuki road, where there is a campground (US$5 per person), bandas (US$60 per person) and a restaurant. As at Naro Moru, you can get guides and can drive to 3,000 m (9,840 ft), thence following the **Burguret River** to the Highland Castle Camp at 4,000 m (13,120 ft), and ending at **Two Tarn Hut**, whence a three-hour scramble will take you to the top of Lenana.

The scree, or talus, at the top of Lenana, particularly when wet or icy, is difficult for the average hiker. Originally formed by the freeze-thaw weathering of the mountain's

OPPOSITE: Large farms on the plains surrounding Mount Kenya produce much of the country's wheat.

glaciated upper slopes, it is loose enough in some areas to take a great deal of high-altitude energy just to get through. Thus if you're not experienced in mountain trekking and scree climbing, consider hiring a guide, who will make your trip a lot more relaxed and see that you don't miss things that are easy to pass by. At 500 KSh to 1,000 KSh per day, it's an inexpensive way to double your pleasure and minimize potential danger.

Another option, if you're not pressed for time and love the mountains, is to ascend

huts on the mountain, and has extensive information and guidebooks. Call or find out more at its clubhouse at Wilson Airport, Nairobi where it holds public meetings every Tuesday at 8 PM.

Guided hikes can be arranged through the following contacts. For the Naro Moru Route, contact **Naro Moru River Lodge** ((0176) 62212, Box 18, Naro Moru. To head up the Sirimon and Burguret Routes get in touch with **Tropical Ice Ltd.** ((02) 740811, Box 57341, Nairobi, who operate from Mountain Rock Hotel. The operators who spe-

Mount Kenya by one route and descend by another, such as Burguret and Sirimon, which makes an easy circle. If you can, try to spend a day or two on the high peaks, as the huts are inexpensive and the views majestically different from each side. Remember that no food or beverages are available, so bring plenty.

If you're thinking of climbing Lenana Peak or just want to hike some of the lower trails of Mount Kenya, it's best to pick up a copy of the excellent *Mount Kenya Map and Guide* by Andrew Wielochowski and Mark Savage. It is available at most lodges round the mountain and sometimes in Nairobi. The **Mountain Club of Kenya** ((02) 501747, Box 45741, Nairobi, has built and manages many of the

cialize in the Chogoria Route are **Savage Wilderness Safaris** incorporating **East African Mountain Guides** (/FAX (02) 521590 WEB SITE www.kilimanjaro.com, Thigiri Road, Box 44827, Nairobi. If you want to try technical climbing on the peaks (ice and rock to Grade VI), you have a choice of operators. Call Steven Wahome at **Naro Moru River Lodge**, **Tropical Ice Ltd.**, or **Savage Wilderness Safaris** incorporating **East African Mountain Guides**. For hiking and climbing all routes, try **Joseph Muthui** ((02) 242627 FAX (02) 250734, Box, Naro Moro., a previous member of the mountain rescue team, who is famously patient and good-humored, as well as being very reasonably priced.

WHERE TO STAY

Where you decide to stay will partly depend on which route you choose. For the Naro Moru route the **Naro Moru River Lodge** ((0176) 62212, Box 18, Naro Moru (reservations also available through Alliance ((02) 337501 FAX 219212, Box 49839, Nairobi), is a logical choice. It charges US$110 for a double, full board, and US$55 for self-service cabins. Alternatively there are cheap *hotelis* in Naro Moru village, including a **Youth Hostel** ((0176) 62412 FAX (0176) 62211, Box 27, Nyeri, at 400 KSh per night, which is a good place to meet up with other climbers if you want to team up. For the Chogoria Route head to **Meru Mount Kenya Lodge**, 30 km (19 miles) from the rough road that runs from Embu to Meru. Don't let the word "Lodge" deceive you. Huts are more like it: for 2,100 KSh per person, there is no food or beverages, but a good campsite; reserve through Let's Go Travel ((02) 340331 FAX (02) 336890 E-MAIL info@letsgosafari.com, Box 60342, Nairobi. On a budget — or just to get ahead — hike an hour further up to **Urumandi Hut** at 3,060 m (10,050 ft), and pay 300 KSh per bunk bed. For the Burgeret Trail carry on through the village of Naro Moru for eight kilometers (five miles) to **Mountain Rock Hotel** ((0176) 62625 FAX (0176) 62051, Box 333, Nanyuki, where there is a campground (US$5 per person), bandas (US$60 per person) and a restaurant, and full equipment/guide rental facilities.

If, on the other hand, you want to just have a gentle stroll around the area but haven't the slightest intention of climbing any mountains whatsoever, a good place to stay is the very smart **Mount Kenya Safari Club**, operated by Lonhro ((02) 216940 FAX (02) 216796, Box 58581, Nairobi (US$341/double per night); just before Nanyuki turn right and thread up the mountain for six kilometers (four miles). And 40 km (25 miles) from Nanyuki along the C76 towards Nyahururu, one of the worst main roads in the country, is **Sweetwaters Game Reserve** with Sweetwaters Tented Camp, also operated by Lonhro, a center for rhino research (Ahmed, their tame rhino, follows you around like a dog) and a chimp sanctuary.

HOW TO GET THERE

Most of the routes up Mount Kenya approach it from the western flanks. Leave Nairobi on the Thika road heading north and continue to Karatina, turning right just before Nyeri (signposted Naro Moru River Lodge and Samburu Lodge), and continue on towards Nanyuki. The drive will take about four hours but it can take longer: the road surface is bad, especially in the latter stages. Public transportation will take longer and unless you start very early (leaving by five or six in the morning) will probably involve a change of *matatu* at Karatina and Nyeri. Alternatively, perhaps because it is Kenya's air force center, Nanyuki is well served by air. **AirKenya** ((02) 501421/3 FAX (02) 500845, Box 30357, Nairobi, flies every day between Nairobi and Nanyuki, with round-trip tickets costing US$120, and even have a daily service between Nanyuki and the Maasai Mara costing US$142 one-way.

For the Chogoria Route, on the mountain's eastern flank, turn right at Sagana or Muranga for Embu and continue towards Meru. At the village of Chogoria turn left for the 16 km (10 miles) of rough track to the self-service Meru Mount Kenya Lodge. Take your own food and bedding. On the eastern slopes of Mount Kenya check locally about the current security situation as this area is at the heart of Kenya's production of *miraa*, the fairly intoxicating drug made of the leaves and stems of a bushy plant common to the Meru area; and drugs and safety rarely go together.

A Driving Story

Last time we drove back down the mountain after climbing the Naro Moru route, it had been raining heavily, and the potato trucks had left their crater-sized ruts in the dirt road below the conifer forest. In places, the road was a lake, with four-wheel drives, five-ton potato trucks, and lesser vehicles marooned here and there like remnants of the Spanish Armada. At one huge pool, we backed up and roared through, casting great sheets of brown water like outriggers on each

Young leopards are among the most appealing of Kenya's cats.

side. Midway through, there was a loud thump; thinking we'd bottomed out, we kept going, arriving drenched but still running on the far side.

The road ahead looked like it had been carpeted by thousand-pound bombs, with stuck vehicles on either side, but the Isuzu never stalled, never slowed. Its windows coated with mud, it wrenched and roared round and over two-foot ruts, and when the road was totally impassable, took to the steep shoulders like a goat. Suddenly our middle son, Luke, called out, "The oil gauge! There's no oil pressure!" Our hearts sank as we pulled to a stop — the oil pressure gauge read zero. So busy we'd been fighting our way through the ruts we hadn't noticed.

Thinking we'd broken off the oil pan plug when we bottomed out, we got out to inspect. An enormous bough had driven like a lance right through the radiator. Opening the hood, we saw it had taken clean away a quarter of the radiator, split the air cleaner in half, and lodged against the steel firewall.

We concluded that someone had dropped a tree into the huge pool we had crossed, hoping to thereby drive across it. We had plowed unsuspectingly into its submerged bough. At some point thereafter, another shock had pulled loose the sensor cable to the oil pump — despite running for over six kilometers (nearly four miles) with no water in the radiator, the Isuzu still had not overheated!

It took 10 minutes of hauling and prying to pull the bough free; disconsolately, we surveyed the wreckage of our radiator and surmised that we had a long rainy hike down the mountain in the gathering night. Not to worry, in Kenya, there's always a friendly person willing to take pity on a poor tourist. The first vehicle that passed, a spattered, battered blue pickup truck of indeterminate genealogy, immediately halted, and a small man in a tattered hat asked why we had stopped out here in the middle of nowhere.

He whistled when he saw the hole in the radiator, and shook his head thinking of how far we'd driven with no water in it. "I'm a mechanic, and can tow you down to Naro Moru," he said, "There, I can find you someone who'll solder the radiator so the rest of the cores will be good and you can drive the car. But," he added apologetically, "I'll have to charge you three hundred shillings."

For the next two hours, in rain and darkness, around marooned potato trucks and through puddles that hippos could hide in, Joseph towed us toward Naro Moru. The chain was old and kept breaking; finally, we patched it with bits of parachute cord and wire. Every time Joseph's truck got stuck, people materialized out of the darkness to help push, skinny boys and barefoot men, till finally as the rain cleared he pulled us into Naro Moru, where we left the Isuzu for the night. He drove us back to the Naro Moru River Lodge.

Riding with Joseph, we had a chance to notice that his own truck did not seem to be any particular brand. Its doors were made of sheet metal with slide bolts for locks; the dashboard gauges were of several makes: everything seemed put together out of leftovers, as in fact it was. "I made it myself," he told us, opening the hood to show a small Isuzu engine bolted into a homemade frame, with Datsun electronics, no air cleaner, and a transmission of generic origin. And yet this man was of the first generation of his tribe to own a vehicle; not long ago, mechanics was a foreign skill to the Kikuyus. We wondered how many of our own countrymen, despite a much longer immersion in mechanical and technical things, could build their own truck, one capable of towing another through one of the worst roads in either hemisphere?

Early the next day, Joseph returned to drive us back to Naro Moru, where in two hours he had found a man to solder our radiator. The Isuzu, muddy but hardly worse for wear, was ready to continue the Grand Safari. Ahead lay the Ndare Forest and Nyambeni Hills, and beyond them, the magnificent savannas and rocky outcrops of Meru National Park.

MERU, ELSA'S COUNTRY

On the northeastern slopes of Mount Kenya is the town of **Meru**, the administrative and commercial center of the district of the same name. The Bantu-speaking Meru tribe, related to both the Kikuyu and the Embu people to the south, are thriving and populous; the town itself is overcrowded and the new modern "sculpture" erected in the heart of its nondescript business center is reason enough to bypass the town. However, if you're in need of a meal or a place to stay — and you might well be, since access roads are poor and there's nowhere to stay in the national park — the **Pig 'n' Whistle** ((0164) 20433, Box 1809, Meru, has been in operation since the First World War, with various renovations. Meal prices are reasonable (100 KSh to 250 KSh) and the food is delicious and ample. Well-maintained cabins are

This dirt road, which can be difficult during the rainy season, descends 55 km (34 miles) through former forest now jammed with small farms (*shambas*), and lined from time to time with tiny shops (*dukas*).

The parade of women heavily laden with firewood and water containers, of children herding livestock, and of men promenading while chewing *miraa*, the local drug, is endless. As recently as 1970, this entire region between Meru National Park and the highway was solid forest, wild and filled with animals. Now, every inch is under cultiva-

1,000 KSh for a double, bed and breakfast. The town sees few Western visitors.

Meru National Park

Meru National Park, 85 km (53 miles) beyond Meru town is on few itineraries: recent poor security and the closure of all park accommodation seems to have sealed the park's fate. To reach the park, follow the signs in the center of town, taking the macadam highway 30 km (19 miles) northeast (it has marvelous views opening northward on the Nyambeni Hills). Turn left on a dirt road just before the town of Maua (the highway soon turns to dirt also); there is usually no sign to indicate the turn and you may have to ask.

tion, eroding, or being overgrazed: a lesson in the earth's crying need for population control.

At the national park boundary, the human throng ends abruptly; stretching out before you are the golden, rolling plains where Joy Adamson released the lioness Elsa, the locale of the book and later the movie, *Born Free*. The park, 1,812 sq km (700 sq miles), descends in a series of plateaus from the 1,000-m (3,000-ft) Nyambeni foothills southeast across savanna and open woodland to less than 300 m (1,000 ft) on the banks of the Tana and Rojewero Rivers.

The common zebra, with stripes across its underbelly, populates the open plains of central and southern Kenya.

One of Africa's most beautiful national parks, Meru contains a variety of ecosystems, from near-desert savanna to tropical marshes and riparian zones, even rain forest (the **Ngaia Forest**). Occasional rugged, reddish-yellow rocky outcrops thrust up from the plateau amid combretum and commiphora scrub, grassland, and acacia trees. A series of sizable waterways, including the **Murera**, **Rojewero**, **Tana**, **Kiolu**, and **Ura Rivers**, flow southeast across the plateau, providing water for wildlife and riparian forest zones of towering fig and tamarind trees, and raphia and doum palms. The northwest section of the park has numerous large marshes packed with wildlife such as **Bwatherongi**, **Mughwango**, and **Mururi Swamps**, all accessible by the park's excellent road system.

Sizable animal populations inhabit the park—lion, elephant, buffalo, both common and Grevy's zebra (although you'll probably see only the common), reticulated giraffe, Somali ostrich, waterbuck, impala, Grant's gazelle, beisa oryx, olive baboon, Sykes' and patas monkey, aardwolf, leopard, cheetah, caracal, wildcat, serval-cat, hippopotamus, and crocodile, as well as countless birds. Until November 1988, its major attraction was five very tame white rhinos. They were slaughtered by Somali poachers with automatic weapons who opened fire on the rhinos and nearby rangers, who immediately took cover.

The incident created an international outcry; security at the park tightened, but the poachers, of course, were never found. A major result of the ensuing security crackdown was the closure of several remote campsites. This incident has tainted the park's fame, but rhinos or no rhinos, Meru remains one of Kenya's, and the world's, best parks.

Meru offers superb views of Mount Kenya in the early morning and late afternoon, when the clouds usually clear. It has a well-designed road network and the intersections of the park roads are numbered—note them in your head as you pass and it's less likely you'll get turned around. Also, in the rare event that you can procure a map of Meru, these markers are shown.

During and after the rains, when forage and water are easily available, Meru's wildlife is generally more dispersed, but in the dry seasons, it tends to congregate near the rivers, swamps, and ponds, when the marsh in front of the Meru Mulika Lodge is visited regularly by elephants, buffalo, impalas, baboons, ostrich, and waterbuck.

The northeastern section of the park has the most varied vegetation — magnificent stands of doum palms and whistling thorn. You may not see a lot of game here, but you will often find monkeys and baboons shaking the fruits from the palms. Germination of the doum palm is facilitated by passage through the bowels of an elephant, thus, where you see these palms, it's likely there once were (and may still be) elephants.

There is a nearly endless series of short and long game drives you can take in Meru, alternating riverine roads with open savanna ones. **Elsa's Camp** on the Ura River is near its junction with the Tana, in the southeast corner of the park. From here, it's less than an hour's drive along the north bank of the Tana to dazzling **Adamson's Falls**, where you will often find hippos and a profusion of birds including the loud Pel's fishing owl. Be sure to check with park rangers as to the status of the road before departing on these itineraries; take a guide if they so advise.

Accessible from Meru are the **Bisanadi**, **North Kitui**, **Rahole**, and **Kora National Reserves**, all semidesert except along the banks of the Tana, which they adjoin. The barren, sweeping landscapes and the birds in these areas make the long excursions memorable, but you are also rewarded with excellent undisturbed game viewing.

Before you attempt trips into any of these reserves, however, be *sure* to check with the park rangers on dangers and restrictions. Immediately after the rhinos were poached, it was impossible to make the trip without a ranger/guide. Don't let it disturb you when he climbs into your vehicle armed with an Enfield .303 or a German G-3 automatic rifle. Traveling with tourists offers the rangers a chance to patrol. He's also there for your security; there are few maps and numerous chances to get lost, and the 6:30 PM curfew is strictly enforced in Meru. Chances are he can point out scores of animals you'd miss alone. The times we've taken a guide with us, we found him to be useful, but the experience was not as relaxing as driving on our own.

Meru boasts over 300 species of birds. They are everywhere and of all colors of the rainbow. Meter (three-foot)-tall kori bustards often patrol the entrance to the lodge, iridescent Superb and Hildebrant's starlings flash about everywhere, and there are four species of honeyguides in residence. Guinea fowl and francolin are abundant enough to be annoying as they scurry ahead of your vehicle, refusing to give way. They do give way, but not until the very last millisecond, quite unlike the large land tortoise who simply pulled in his head and legs as we approached.

Where to Stay

Since the Meru Mulika Lodge closed, the only accommodation is at designated primitive campsites for US$2 per person, and that *must* be arranged first at the gate or the park headquarters. In consolation, Meru offers some of the best game viewing for travelers allergic to the sight of other vehicles. The good news is that upmarket operator **Cheli & Peacock Ltd.** ((02) 748307/27 FAX (0154) 22553 or (02) 740721 E-MAIL chelipeacock @attmail.com WEB SITE www.chelipeacock .com, Box 39806, Nairobi, are opening a lodge in Meru. Called Elsa's Kopje, it will offer game packages of day and night game-drives and guided walks for US$280 per person per day.

Lions often rest during the day on outcrops and termite mounds on the savannah.

How to Get There

From Nairobi there are main two routes to Meru: both circle Mount Kenya, to the east or the west. Take the road north to Thika and then the decision whether to turn right for Embu or to continue straight ahead to Karatina and Nanyuki depends partly on the security situation. The western route is perhaps more scenic, while the eastern is dotted with small villages, is more active agriculturally, and less visited. Allow plenty of time — six hours or so — as the tarmac is deteriorating: it can be a grueling drive especially in the wet season. All this will make the journey irresistibly tempting to the adventurous! Thanks partly to it's importance as a hub for *miraa* trading, public transportation is well-developed: early-morning buses link the town with towns as far away as Malindi on the coast and *matatus* regularly leave for Nairobi. Be warned though: if there are traders selling *miraa* from the back windows of your *matatu* you'll find the trip slowed — often by several hours — by endless trading stops.

ONWARDS

From Meru, you have the option of driving north through the Bisanadi gate to the settlement of **Garba Tula**, and from there northeast toward **Wajir** and the Somalia border. In the rainy season, this can be a fiendish road; in the dry season it can be blistering hot. But it's strange country, and if you're a nut about deserts, perhaps worth the trip (for details, see ISIOLO, PEARL OF THE NORTH, page 173).

The Desert: Southeast of the Jade Sea

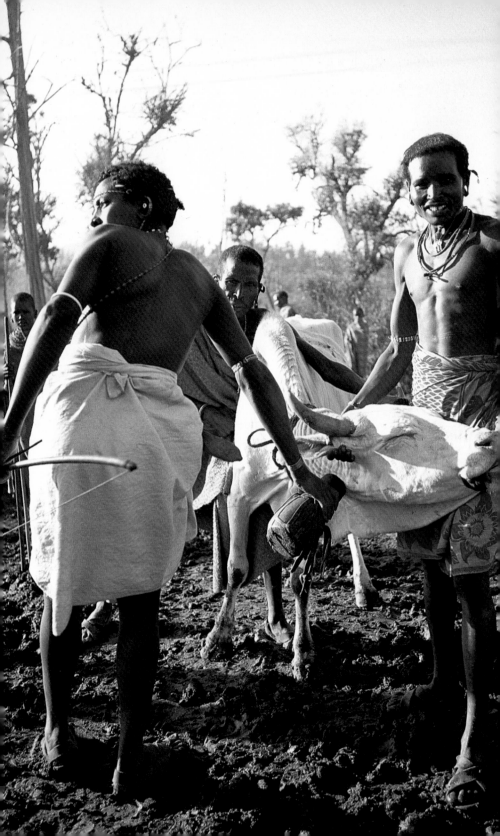

ISIOLO, PEARL OF THE NORTH

It's not necessary to return to the town of Meru to go to Isiolo, as a dirt road branches off at Muthara. This road, however, is often impassable during the rains, and has been the site of several tourist holdups, including one murder, by *shiftas* or Somali bandits. It is wiser to return to Meru and pavement.

From the junction of the Nanyuki-Meru road, it's 30 km (19 miles) of one of Kenya's isolated and often inexplicable stretches of excellent pavement north to the bustling town of Isiolo. On either side are magnificent views: the purple slopes and peaks of the **Loldaika Mountains** to the west, and the soaring **Nyambeni Hills**, where most of the country's *miraa* is grown, to the east.

It's worth spending a little time in **Isiolo**, for the town is a striking clash of southern and northern desert cultures, with an overflow of the more sultry Meru temperament and a strong Somali influence.

Bear in mind that Isiolo is the last sure place to buy gasoline until **Moyale**, some 525 km (325 miles) to the north, at the Ethiopian border; even on the Grand Safari, you may not be traveling that far. **Marsabit**, a mere 275 km (170 miles) north from Isiolo, may have gasoline at the rundown **Marsabit Lodge** ((02) 229751 or (02) 330820, but don't depend on it unless you've called one of these Nairobi numbers to reserve some.

Isiolo's most famous blacksmith, one Mumin Hassan, age 65, known locally as "Ayatollah Khomeini," has almost singlehandedly created a thriving industry in daggers, Somali swords, *kols* or curved knives, and other such instruments of mayhem, which he and his flock of sons cheerfully sell to tourists, Samburu warriors, and *shiftas* alike. Usually, he can be found sitting beneath a spreading euphorbia tree, unfinished dagger in hand.

Isiolo is also a regional center for packing and trading *miraa*, a fairly intoxicating drug. The *miraa* arrives by truckloads early each morning, to be sorted and bound by Isiolo women into bundles of a kilo each (called *kilos*) for resale. Chewed by many northern Kenyans and Somalis, *miraa* is reputed to have a slow, amphetamine-like

effect. Although not illegal, it appears to lead to outrageous fantasies and occasionally, when combined with alcohol, to violence, particularly when imbibers have their swords in their belts. Like "uppers" in the United States, it is a favorite of long-distance truckers, another reason why the tourist is best advised not to drive in Kenya at night.

WHERE TO STAY

There are several cheap inns for the intrepid traveler. The **Bomen Tourist Class Hotel**

((0165) 2225, Box 67, Isiolo, at the end of the alley opposite the new white Barclay's Bank, is the most palatable at 1,200 KSh. However the **Mocharo Lodge** ((0165) 2385, Box 106 Isiolo, is much better value at 400 KSh and has safe parking. A luxury alternative 20 km (12.5 miles) south of Isiolo on the Nanyuki Road is **Lewa Downs** ((02) 571661, FAX (02) 571665 E-MAIL Bushhome @africaonline.co.ke, Box 56923, Nairobi. This wildlife conservancy was established by Anna Merz, famous for her involvement with rhino conservation, and accommodation is either in luxury at Lerai Tented Camp

Once a single tribe, the Samburu and Maasai (FOLLOWING PAGES) maintain many OPPOSITE AND ABOVE original dances and traditions.

($320 for a double with full board) or — with riding — at Lewa Wildlife Conservancy ($530).

HOW TO GET THERE

For Isiolo, head north from Nairobi taking the A2 through Thika and on to Karatina and skirt Mount Kenya's eastern flanks via Nyeri and Nanyuki. Drive on towards Meru and turn left for Isiolo, 30 km (19 miles) towards the Samburu National Park, still along the A2. Early-morning buses and *matatus* link Isiolo with Nairobi, although if you miss the last one (sometimes possible even at 6 AM!) you might face a long hopping journey. Frequent *matatus* link Isiolo with Nanyuki, a center for air travel and with occasional *matatu* links west to Nyahururu.

EAST FROM ISIOLO

The fascinating, if barren, itinerary from Isiolo through **Wajir** to the Somali border is an off-shoot of the Grand Safari, not recommended unless you have time on your hands and can stand incinerating desert temperatures and abysmal roads. But it *is* off the beaten track and, surely, the stuff of adventure.

If this is the adventure for you, take the **Garba Tula-Mado Gashi** road east from Isiolo, being as usual sure that you have sufficient

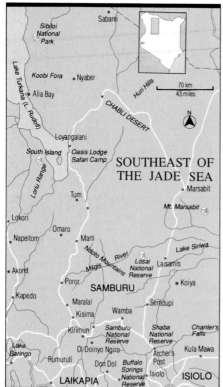

SOUTHEAST OF
THE JADE SEA

70 km
43 miles

(140 miles) across the **Sardindida Plain** to **Mandera** on the Somalian border. You can also take a shortcut, as we did, on the sandy, flat road from Meru National Park up to Wajir through Garba Tula, via the park's gate beyond Leopard Rock.

The Isiolo region and areas north have long been considered the "lawless frontier" of Kenya, a contested area between expanding Somali tribesmen and the older settlers of Boran and Samburus. Cattle thieving is common, with occasional bloody shoot-outs between AK47-toting Somalis and local police and home guards equipped with .303s and other more exotic firearms. Check locally on the security situation before traveling in this region and try to travel in convoy.

SAMBURU COUNTRY

Isiolo is the gateway to Samburu country. These slender, handsome people became our favorites of all the Kenyan tribes, with their inherent grace and friendliness, and their simple, grave demeanor. They are closely related to the Maasai, from whom they separated in tribal disputes some centuries ago during the migration southward from Sudan and Ethiopia. In the Maa language, which both tribes share, "samburu" means butterfly — the Maasai say because the Samburu fled the tribe, the Samburu say because they flutter around and don't stay put.

Like the Maasai, the Samburu are principally nomadic, wandering their vast, often arid territory in search of grazing for their herds of cattle, sheep, and goats. They live on the meat of their sheep and goats, on berries, tubers, and wild fruits, and on cow and goat milk, often mixed with blood taken from a vein in the necks of their cattle.

Young Samburu men and women are permitted to have relations, the man providing his lover with necklaces as proof of his affection. The young women are then betrothed to older men, circumcised on the day of their marriage, and, thereafter, not supposed to continue relations with the younger men. The young men are circumcised at roughly the same age, but cannot marry until much older, long after they become warriors (*morans*), according to an intricate age-set system which provides multiple brides for

gas and water reserves, plenty of spare tires and tubes, and food. The countryside is flat, blistering hot, and sandy all the way to **Habaswein** at the headwaters of the **Lorian Swamp**, with occasional mirages or the lone figures of Somali and Boran nomads breaking the isolation of the desert. From Habaswein east, you're in the **North Eastern Province**, Kenya's least populated, and the most remote from central rule in Nairobi.

Again, don't believe any map that shows gasoline at Habaswein (it can be found, occasionally, at Wajir — call ahead to the Wajir Administrative Center offices ☎ (0136) 21112, though they may say there is some when there isn't). It's an impossibly long 260 km (160 miles) from Isiolo to Habaswein, another 70 km (44 miles) to Wajir, with its single-story white houses, mosque, Foreign Legion-type fortress, cheap hotels (none particularly recommended) and places to eat, and all the camels you can count.

From Wajir, it's another searing 190 km (120 miles) to **El Wak**, with its own fort, camels, and *miraa* traders. Beyond it, the road is potholed but paved the remaining 225 km older, prosperous men who are or will become the elders (*mzee*) of the tribe.

The Samburu family settlement, or *man-yatta*, is most often a kraal of several mud, wattle, and thatch huts, surrounded by a thorn enclosure in which the herds are kept at night for protection from four- and two-legged predators. Family ties are strong, as are the oral traditions of legends and laws which enliven the fireside. Like most women in Kenya, the Samburu wives and daughters do the majority of the physical work around the *manyatta*, but their word is respected and often outweighs their husbands'.

From the *manyatta*, young Samburu *morans* wander with their herds for days, often months, in search of grazing. They are colorfully dressed in blazing red cloaks, their faces and chests dyed ocher, their *simis* — short, lethal swords made of cut-down machetes — at their waists, their razor-sharp spears always in their grasp. The weapons are not for show. Not infrequently, *morans* find themselves attacked by *shiftas*, better-armed and ruthless. No Samburu who sets out to wander the Northern Frontier District with his herds can be assured of returning. When forage in one area is spent, the *manyatta* may be moved also, depending on the season.

Samburu country contains some of Kenya's finest game parks and most beautiful scenery. Less than 30 km (19 miles) north of Isiolo are the linked areas of **Buffalo Springs**, **Samburu**, and **Shaba National Reserves**. They cover a total area of some 430 sq km (170 sq miles). Samburu is the most famous, an expanse of semiarid, often volcanic prairies and hills, divided from Buffalo Hills to the south by the serpentine, crocodile-infested **Ewaso Ngiro River**. Note, however, that the three reserves impose their own daily fees even if you are just passing from one to another or even in transit. At US$15 per adult and with students and children at US$5 this can add up.

Buffalo Springs National Reserve

In many ways, we feel Buffalo Springs is the most beautiful of the three reserves. Its springs and stream of the same name, with

Meal time for a gerenuk who knows the freshest nibbles are higher up.

their volcanic pools and black-rock water chutes flanked with tall grass and doum palms, should not be missed. The graceful doum palm often reaches 20 m (66 ft) in height, towering over other riverine trees. It is the only palm species whose trunk and boughs divide into branches, making it instantly recognizable. Its orange-brown fruit is eaten by baboons and elephants, and its leaves are used by people for weaving baskets and mats, so extensively that in many areas the tree no longer exists. Its widespread, V-branched canopies are good places to look for black-faced vervet and Sykes' monkeys.

Both Buffalo Springs and Samburu are excellent areas for reticulated giraffe, the unusual beisa oryx with its lovely straight, long horns and gleaming black-and-white coat, impala, blue-legged Somali ostrich, waterbuck, Grant's gazelle, dik dik, duiker, warthog, olive baboon, spotted and striped hyena, and lion. Grevy's zebra, the desert race with large, rounded and fringed ears, and narrow stripes that don't meet under the belly, are common in all three reserves. Also frequently seen are gerenuk, the long-necked antelope which graze like giraffe on the upper branches of thorn trees, and are fittingly named *swara twiga* (antelope giraffe) in Swahili.

Elephants are rare, having been poached by Somalis and, occasionally, Samburus during their annual migrations from the reserves towards **Marsabit** and the northern plains. But if you're lucky, you can see hunting dogs, occasionally cheetahs, and leopards along the waterways or in the rocky, inaccessible hills. The cone-like hanging nests of weavers are visible everywhere in the acacias, their gregarious chatter a constant background sound, especially in the mornings.

Where to Stay

Buffalo Springs Lodge ((02) 336858, Box 30471, Nairobi, at US$172 for a double with full board, has both tents and cottages. It is set in a lovely curve of the stream, and in dry season, is a good locale for game drives due to the presence of water. Although campsites exist in Buffalo Springs Reserve, their use is not recommended due to a spate of recent robberies. Champagne Hills Campground is explicitly to be avoided. The lodge

is less than two hours' drive north of Nanyuki, and less than one north of Isiolo along the A2.

SAMBURU NATIONAL RESERVE

From Buffalo Springs into Samburu, you cross Ewaso Ngiro River on a good bridge, often crowded with baboons. You pay another entrance fee. The higher hills at the south end of Samburu Reserve offer lovely views of the Ewaso Ngiro, and the hills and plains of Buffalo Reserve beyond. On the nearer side of the river, the land is dry and thornbush becomes the common vegetation in the barren, sandy soil. The Ewaso Ngiro begins some 300 km (186 miles) to the southwest, on the 4,000-meter (13,000-ft) slopes of Ol Doinyo Lasatima in the Aberdares. It has no outlet, disappearing another 300 km (186 miles) downstream of Samburu in the vast Lorian Swamp.

One evening, we ate dinner at **Samburu Game Lodge**, former campsite of one of the most notorious elephant hunters, Arthur Newman. Set in a bend of the Ewaso Ngiro, its famous Crocodile Bar offers one the chance to get within kissing distance of these man-eaters, with only a foot-tall fence keeping them from nibbling on one's toes (or worse). They often exceeded six meters (20 ft) from snout to tail, and although they seemed harmless in their basking somnolence, we were assured that they were deadly.

The crocodile kills its prey by drowning, gripping it in powerful jaws, and twirling it round and round beneath the water. Often, it stores its meal for weeks in a hole in the mud until it reaches that stage of decomposition that is truly delectable to the crocodile palate, and stories abound of people being taken by crocs and later escaping. River crocs are said to be more dangerous than the lake ones, perhaps due to the latter's more constant supply of fish.

Crocodiles on the Ewaso Ngiro semi-hibernate during the dry season, when the river dries up. They dig deep holes in the river bed, raiding occasionally the larders they have built up during the wetter seasons. Although they don't often carry off humans, they have been known to catch antelope, baboons, and even zebra, and should be treated with the greatest respect. We personally know of two Americans killed by crocodiles in East Africa. Innocent promenades along the river's banks are definitely discouraged.

After an excellent dinner at the Samburu Lodge we returned, our minds on the crocodiles, to our tent near the river's bank. Two trucks of Gametrackers people were camped even closer to the water, which slightly reassured us that hungry crocodiles would probably choose them before us. On the same principle, we mused, zebra often travel with wildebeest, knowing they can outrun the

In the morning, there were leopard pug marks in the sand behind our grove of trees; while we were packing, a baboon snuck up to the car, snatched a box of cookies and loaf of bread from a backpack, and climbed a tree to enjoy them, refusing absolutely to share with his mates.

From Samburu, you can rejoin the Isiolo-Marsabit road by driving east across the barren uplands to the former British military encampment of **Archer's Post**. Here, the red blaze of desert roses contrasts sharply with the tawny landscape. This stocky, thick-

latter when lions arrive. (We were later to notice that lions nonetheless eat more zebra than wildebeest.)

In pitching our tent, we also ensured that it was not astride a trail used by elephants to reach the water. Forgetting this rule can lead to all kinds of dissension in the middle of the night as to who has the right-of-way, with the elephants liable to enforce their point of view by simply walking across one's tent, and anyone within it. We found a lovely spot beneath a huge umbrella tree. With logs crossed on the fire to keep a light going all night and perhaps dissuade at least the more cowardly of lion from visiting, we lay back to watch Africa's countless glittering stars.

stemmed shrub secretes a milky sap which is used as an arrow poison.

Once beyond the arid reserve, the land, now browsed by goats, becomes even more barren. Although most guides and maps indicate gasoline at Archer's Post, this too is a mirage, as it has almost never been available. Archer's Post is a ragtag, sun-blistered, dust-choked assemblage of tin, plank, and thatch huts. It's possible to buy a few rudimentary foods, however, and there is a lovely **Catholic church**, clinic, and school run by an Italian priest (who is reputed to have diesel fuel

Back-country tented lodges, such as Larson's in Samburu National Reserve, offer the ultimate in luxury.

The Desert: Southeast of the Jade Sea

but denies it). The church seems a replica from a late medieval Tuscan village, and is well worth a quick look.

Where to Stay

Accommodations in Samburu Reserve include a campsite at US$2 per person, just downriver from the bridge and the park entrance; the nearby **Samburu Game Lodge** ((02) 540780 FAX (02) 543810, Box 40075, Nairobi, where gasoline is available (US$152 per double, full board); and the even more expensive **Larsen's Tented Camp** ((02) 540780 FAX (02) 543810, Box 40075, Nairobi (US$216 for a double with full board).

We stayed one night at Larsen's, in a spacious tent erected on a wooden platform amid palms on the banks of the Ewaso Ngiro. The tent's polished hardwood furniture looked as if it had been intended for a swank London hotel, the beds were more than comfortable, and the food worthy of a *Michelin Guide*.

SHABA NATIONAL RESERVE

To reach unvisited and fabulous Shaba National Reserve, you must drive three kilometers (two miles) south from Archer's Post and turn east at the sign for the new **Sarova Shaba Lodge** ((02) 713333 FAX (02) 718700 E-MAIL reservations@sarova.com, Box 72493, Nairobi (US$210 per double, full board). From this turnoff, it's about six kilometers (four miles) of rough road to **Natorbe gate**, entrance to the reserve. From the gate, a series of roads branches east and south through an arid, volcanic expanse of rugged hills and sharp valleys. The reserve extends for nearly 30 km (19 miles) along the south bank of the Ewaso Ngiro, with vulture nesting areas visible across the river on the **Bodich Cliffs**, and monkeys frolicking in doum palms along the water.

In central Shaba, a marsh feeds a seasonal tributary of the Ewaso Ngiro. This is a favorite locale for foraging antelope and their predators, including leopards, cheetahs, and lions. It was at Shaba that Joy Adamson was murdered by a deranged member of her staff as she was completing a study of leopards and cheetahs.

Shaba takes its name from a 1,620-m (5,318-ft)-tall volcanic cone just to the south, which has overflowed areas of the reserve with yet-unvegetated black lava. If you feel unusually adventurous, and your four-wheel drive's in good condition, ask the rangers at Natorbe gate for a guide to accompany you on the track descending 30 km (19 miles) along the Ewaso Ngiro beyond the reserve, eastward to beautiful **Chandler Falls**.

Along the river east of the reserve, we saw a number of hornbills. The female, our guide said, encloses herself in a hole in a tree to sit on her eggs, not breaking open the hole until the young are born, at which time, the male returns to feed both her and the nestlings. Excellent camping used to be available at Shaba, but the *shiftas* have destroyed that, along with the elephants and many other attractions of the Northern Frontier District. To be safe, check with the rangers first at Natorbe gate. In fact, *no camping* should be done in any national park or reserve without first checking with the nearest rangers.

NORTHERN FRONTIER DISTRICT

Driving north from Archer's Post you truly enter the Northern Frontier District, lawless, vast, sun-parched, and visionary. Before you, dominating the endless stony steppe, is sheer, towering **Ol Doinyo Sabachi**, a huge table mountain (inselberg) which many of the Samburu people consider the home of *Ngai*, God.

No doubt long before Buffalo Springs you have seen Sabachi looming above the cragged landscape, and now, with the dirt road seeming to rise across the desert to meet it, the mountain gleams like red gold in the sun.

Inselbergs (from the German for 'island mountain') are not uncommon in the plains country of Kenya. Like mesas in the American southwest, they are formed of harder or less-jointed rock which withstands erosion better than the surrounding peneplain. Sabachi is certainly one of Africa's most imposing, often cloud-covered, thickly wooded on its lower slopes and atop its broad plateau, whose springs, marshes, and grassy

Salt deposits among volcanic rock in Shaba are harvested by desert tribes.

The Desert: Southeast of the Jade Sea

meadows are used by the Samburu for grazing in the dry seasons.

We had ample time to enjoy the vista of Sabachi, for the sharp stones of the road sliced through a front tire and we halted to mount a spare, the silent plains extending like the sea around us. It seemed pure, unadulterated isolation, like the American southwest only more so — nothing but the wind, soil, rock, and sky, the muted colors of the desert. For many kilometers you could see the dust trail of an approaching vehicle—a truck that stopped to offer help, as nearly all vehicles do in the Northern Frontier District. By then we'd changed tires, checked the radiator, which despite the heat and despite missing almost a quarter of its elements, refused to overheat.

Once also the home many elephants, Sabachi is a lovely day's hike, with reasonable grazing trails leading you to the top, where the plains appear to extend eastward beyond the horizon, and to the west the beautiful, forested Matthews Range seems like waves of the sea. Do *not*, nevertheless, attempt the hike alone—a guide can easily be found in the *manyattas* at the base of the mountain, or take the left fork of the road toward Wamba and ask at the first mission settlement.

At this fork in the road a great choice awaits you. Following the Grand Safari, you can turn west toward Wamba. If you wish, you can continue past **Wamba** to **Maralal**, and quit both the Grand Safari and the northern frontier at their most civilized edge. However, if you're well-stocked with gasoline, water, and food, have a four-wheel drive in reasonably good condition, with at least two spare tires and extra tubes, why not, after checking the security situation with local officials, continue into the inimitable **Matthews Range**, then north into the badlands, to **Marsabit**, the great **Chalbi Desert**, and **East Turkana**?

WAMBA

The first stop on this magical tour is the mountain town of Wamba, with one of the Northern Frontier District's best hospitals, whether for snakebite or bullet wound. Turning left at the fork below Sabachi, we stopped

to pick up a Samburu hitchhiker and drove the 40 km (25 miles) of reasonably rutted road to Wamba in about an hour. Our passenger, Iban, who spoke excellent English, having been educated at the Catholic mission school in Wamba, wore a San Francisco 49ers T-shirt, and seemed to know more United States and European geography than most American students his age.

Slowly the desert with its camels, huddled *manyattas,* and parched scrub gave way to hills then lushly forested peaks. The tallest mountain, Iban said, is **Mount Wamba**, indicated on most maps as Warges or Ouarges. The name, Wamba, he added, means "where the people gather to go raiding."

"Whom do they raid?"

"The *shiftas*. When they attack us we join together here and then go after them. The mountain protects us."

"How?"

"In the mountain, the people can hide. Now we have home guards — they carry rifles to shoot the *shiftas*."

"And to kill elephants?"

"Not very often. Most of the poachers are Somalis."

The lovely town of Wamba stretched out along the foot of the mountain, cool, windswept, with a broad dirt avenue fringed by the standard tin-roofed, open-faced huts, kiosks, and *dukas*. "You can stay with my family," Iban offered.

"We're trying to get to Kitich," we said, referring to the legendary tented camp in the Matthews Range to which friends had given us directions involving a series of yellow rocks somewhere in the desert.

"It's far." He checked the setting sun, cocked his head dubiously. "I better find you someone quick to fix your spare tire." He returned a few minutes later with Kijo, a friendly teenager in a blue T-shirt, patched trousers and bare feet. "You're in luck," Iban said, "there's some people here from Kitich. They can show you the way."

The people from Kitich were two Samburu warriors in full regalia, faces coated in ocher paint, *simi* swords at their belts and spears in their hands. They agreed to wait while we

The Ewaso Ngiro flows from the slopes of the Aberdare Mountains through arid Samburu country and dries up in the vast Lorian Swamp.

had our spare tire patched, so with Kijo giving directions we drove across the red, sandy scrub to a *manyatta* of forty or so cheerful children and a tall, slender woman who seemed to be the mother of most of them. In the shade of a thorn tree stood a diesel compressor and a clamp for dismounting tires from the rim. The woman, a child in her arms and another five or ten about her skirts, gave rapid instructions to Kijo and his brothers, and in a few minutes our spare tire was patched.

More children arrived with two donkeys pulling a cart laden with water jugs; they

haired and even more slender than the first, both with ivory plugs in their ears. They dismounted their spears and climbed into the back beside the boys, rearranging their swords and pointing the spear points to the rear.

KITICH

The sun was sinking, orange and huge, beyond the desert's distant crags as we drove west out of Wamba through the Matthews Range. The road changed from sandy to

showed us to the vegetable gardens behind the *manyatta*, where they carefully ladled out a tin can of water to each plant. "It feeds us all!" Kijo's older brother said, with the astonishment of a herdsman new to the miracle of agriculture, "and what's left over we sell in town."

The two warriors from Kitich were still waiting when we returned to Wamba. "How far is it?" we asked.

"Oh, about forty kilometers," the younger answered. He had a friendly face; his lower front teeth had been extracted in the Samburu and Maasai fashion, making the upper ones buck outwards—supposedly to make themselves look more like their beloved cows, someone had told us. The other was gray-

rough; darkness fell with the quick curtain of African night, our headlights scampering before us across the dust. The road worsened then worsened still, a savage track cut into the raveling slopes, dry streambeds, bony forest, and sandy luggas, the Samburus' spears and anklebells jangling on each bump, rut, and pothole. "How far?" we asked, after an hour.

"Far. Very far," the younger warrior answered.

Assuming we'd misunderstood, we kept going. With the constant low gear and frequent four-wheel driving, the gas needle began to sink: if we ran too low we'd have to return to Isiolo. The road got rougher, narrower, steeper; the Samburus obligingly got

The Desert: Southeast of the Jade Sea

out and walked on sharpest inclines. After a seemingly endless time the track broke out on a long clear ridge bathed in stars. We approached an unlit *manyatta*. "He will get out now," the younger Samburu said, referring to the other.

When the old man had nodded thanks, and for the first time loosened his iron grip on the backs of our seats, and departed, the younger one directed us back along the ridge and down a wide, dark, jungle valley, where the road had also obviously served duty as a stream bed. "He is a *mzee* [elder]," he said, referring to the other warrior. "This is the first time he has ever traveled in a car."

With thornbrush scraping the car on both sides, and elephant dung like boulders on the track ahead, we crossed this valley, and deposited the young Samburu at the mouth of a side canyon. "My home is up here," he said. "Kitich is just there," he pointed ahead.

Five minutes later we could see lights between the trees — never had a few lanterns seemed so much like civilization! The manager of **Kitich Camp** came out to welcome us, showed us where to pitch our tent and got his cooks, despite the late hour, to fix us fried egg sandwiches and tea. Before returning to his bed he placed kerosene lanterns on both sides of our tent. "There's often leopards in camp but they won't bother you. And the lights will keep the elephants from stepping on your tent."

Camp consisted of luxurious en-suite walk-in tents, each for two people, with individual bathrooms and copious bucket showers filled each morning with hot water from the large wood-fed boiler near the kitchen tent.

The spacious dining tent and the guest tents each look out from groves of shady fig trees onto a magnificent small valley with the shimmering Ngeng River in its center and the rugged ridges of the Matthews Range rising abruptly on the far side. In a tree beyond the river a young female leopard sat guarding a goat hung there for her delectation; birds skimmed the sparkling water and monkeys called from the trees.

Although we've spent years wandering the far corners of the world, and have known many wild places in many countries and several continents, this green valley at Kitich

was certainly one of the most beautiful we had ever seen. On the opposite slopes grew 800-year-old cycads, a prehistoric species of palm which is the most primitive extant seed-bearing plant, and now found few places on earth, as well as some of the largest podocarpus and cedar in Kenya. Other plants include six species of hibiscus, crotons, whose bright flowers produce a very sweet honey, and combretum. The valley boasts a population of butterflies unique in the world, with new species still being found, and is a major stopover for European migratory birds.

From Kitich, accompanied hikes through the Matthews Range can last for periods from one to eight days with food, tents, and baggage transported by horses. Day hikes are also a breeze — from the ridge above camp you can see all the way to the Somalia border.

Where to Stay

Staying in **Kitich Camp** is rather more expensive (doubles cost US$360 with full board; for information, contact **Bush Homes of East Africa** ((02) 571661 FAX (02) 571665 E-MAIL Bushhome@africaonline.co.ke, Box 56923, Nairobi) than most Kenyan tented camps, but the treatment and location are certainly unique, and the difficulty in transporting supplies goes some way to explain the difference. It is also possible and much cheaper to camp by the river but watch out for crocs.

How to Get There

Kitich is an eight-hour drive from Nairobi, traveling north on the A2 to Isiolo, through the Buffalo Springs (paying an entry fee) and forking left for Wamba. Alternatively, travel north to Naivasha, bear left to Nyahuru and complete the second half of the drive on *murram* roads, turning left before Maralal for Wamba. The fact there are two routes raises the interesting possibility of a short circuit lasting anything from four days to a week. If you don't relish the eight-hour drive from Nairobi, it's possible to fly directly to Wamba and have someone from Kitich pick you up there. At the other end of the scale the C78 that links Isiolo with Maralal does not see a

---

Once common nearly everywhere in Kenya, elephants have been reduced by ivory poaching to remnant, threatened populations in a few national parks.

lot of traffic and the trip could take many days if hitching. Wamba itself is five kilometers (three miles) off the main road and Kitich 40 km (25 miles) further still. This doesn't mean it's impossible but you should be prepared to do some fairly serious walking and on the road, to travel very slowly; some days, not at all.

ONWARDS

Before leaving we took a swim in a crystalline pool of the stream, cool, drinkable, and free of crocs and hippos. The road seemed not nearly so bad in daytime; returning to Wamba and Sabachi we made the difficult decision to retreat to Isiolo to top up our gasoline supplies, and by noon teamed up

with a truck convoy headed north back past Sabachi toward the arid frontier. Depending on the *shifta* situation, it may be essential for any traveler in the Northern Frontier District to join a convoy; the place to ask is at the police post on the road just north of Isiolo, where in any case you must register and indicate your destination.

LOSAI NATIONAL RESERVE AND MARSABIT NATIONAL PARK

Swinging east of Sabachi's ramparts we jiggled, bounced, and banged across the potholed scrub, keeping as much distance as possible from the trucks' trail of dust ahead. After a 100 km (60 miles) of flat, inselberg country was the seedy outpost of **Laisamis**,

at the northern edge of **Losai National Reserve**. From time to time gerenuk, suni, or Grevy's zebra were hazily visible in the sunbaked distance, or more frequently bony cattle and Boran or Samburu herdsmen, or the goats responsible, in part, for this denuded landscape.

In the dry seasons it's possible to go by four-wheel drive across the **Kaisut Desert** along the north edge of Losai to **Ilaut** and the **Arsim Valley**, the border between the Samburu and Rendille tribes, and from there it's a short cut to East Turkana. But that way you miss magnificent Marsabit, and so, after a halt for warm sodas in Laisamis we bustled northward, occasional anthills like miniature skyscrapers above the stony, brown **Sagererua Plateau** that extended into infinity

under a burning blue sky with a row of distant puffball cumulus nose to tail like a herd of migrating elephants.

It's a 100 km (60 miles) of bone-crushing corrugations from Laisamis to **Marsabit**, but worth the torture: Marsabit's volcanic mass rising into the fleecy clouds like Shangri-La amid the desert, its coolness paradise after the molten desert. In fact, one of the mountain's crater lakes ("gofs") is **Paradise Lake**, or Gof Sokorte Guda, and no misnomer, for the whole, craggy, cratered, forested wonderland, with its enchanting views across the outspanned desert, has no real comparison in Kenya or the world.

Watered by the mist and clouds of air blown east from Lake Turkana, the volcanic cones of Marsabit contain important remnants of Kenya's upland forest, its often-immense trees cloaked in *usnea* lichens and gray-bearded mosses, its flora and fauna of exceptional beauty and diversity. The country's longest-tusked elephants have traditionally come from Marsabit Mountain, the most famous being Ahmed, who died in 1974, and is now on display, life-sized in fiberglass, at the National Museum in Nairobi (a humorous account of Ahmed's demise and subsequent enthronement is contained in Patrick Marnham's *Fantastic Invasion*).

Although Ahmed enjoyed the protection of President Kenyatta, the President's last wife, Mama Ngina, was more mercenary in her concern for elephants, having by most accounts directed Kenya's largest poaching ring, with the result that nearly all of Ahmed's peers have vanished from Marsabit, their tusks sold via South Africa to the ivory merchants of Japan, China and Taiwan, and the park is seriously encroached. Curiously enough, Mama Ngina's brother followed as Kenya's Minister of Tourism and Wildlife, thus becoming responsible for the safety and well-being of those few pachyderms which escaped his sister's ministrations.

Many other superb animals remain, however, in the 2,100-sq-km (811-sq-miles) **Marsabit National Park**, including greater and lesser kudu, reticulated giraffe, spotted and striped hyena, caracal, serval, leopard, lion, beisa oryx, and the unusual *petersi*

Vervet monkeys await nightfall in the forked branches of a doum palm.

The Desert: Southeast of the Jade Sea

Grant's gazelle, with its near-parallel horns. What's more, the place is an ornithologist's fantasy, its microclimates shifting from cloud forest to blasting desert, the home of 52 different birds of prey. Grebes, herons, spurwing geese, ducks, teal, and pintail can be found around Lake Paradise itself, with the rare lammergeyers (bearded vultures) nesting on the precipitous cliffs of **Gof Bongole**, and many more rare species found in the black lava desert surrounding the park.

Six kilometers (three and three quarter miles) from the town of Marsabit, off the main road from Isiolo, are the **Ulanula** or **Singing Wells**, more looked for than found: ask a local to show you where they are. In the dry season the local Boran herdsmen form human chains to hand up buckets of water from the well's muddy depths, singing when the mood strikes (or for benefit of tourists, when recompense is offered).

Marsabit Lodge ((02) 229751 or (02) 330820 FAX (02) 227815, Msafari Inns, Box 42013, Nairobi (double for US$120 with full board), is a bit run down but beautifully situated on the edge of a tree-lined lake, **Gof Sokorte Dika**. Most importantly, if you've called ahead, you may be able to get gasoline at the Lodge. Cheaper, highly rated and often full is the **Kenya Lodge and Hotel** ((0183) 2221, in Marsabit town; and there's a campground near the Park's main gate; we were told it's also possible to camp at Paradise Lake, but there was no one there at the time and the rangers were less than enthusiastic, due, they said, to "too many lions."

Marsabit's not the kind of place you want to leave, but it *is* the gateway to the wild north, and sooner or later adventure beckons. When it does, you can head north across the stunning, barren, blackened **Dida Galgalu Desert** toward **Moyale**, a simple 250 km (155 miles) from Marsabit, only five to seven hours when the going's good. As usual, be sure to convoy up or check with the police in Marsabit on the *shiftas*.

In his fine novel, *The Hills Are Falling*, Marsabit native Mude Dae Mude, later a Foreign Affairs minister and Nairobi journalist, describes the trip well:

Everything that he saw, from the acacia and *jirme* plains sprawling for miles to the foot of the mountain, to the vast craters

haphazardly scattered about the plain, the stately giraffe, the Grevy's zebra and greater kudu, touched his fancy.

"Presently the plains of Dida Galgalu, an expanse of endless black, mingled in the distance with the bluish gray of the sky to give an impression of total endlessness. The air was calm and translucent. The sun hurried to its night's repose and a solitary bird fluttered over a far-off tree. The horizon was brushed with rays of copper and gold and a few spare clouds stood still against the sky."

Moyale, tacky and barren, is a growing town of nongovernmental organization aid workers with nights periodically broken by the sounds of gunfire. It feels a bit like the end of the earth, with little in the way of comfortable lodging — if you can get permission or a visa, it's better to cross into Ethiopia and stay at the more elegant state-run hotel, two and a half kilometers (one and a half miles) from the border on the Addis Ababa road.

Ten years ago, before Kenya's roads had declined to their present often miserable condition (the money to maintain them, so popular opinion goes, embellishing instead the foreign bank accounts of wealthy politicians), it was adventurous but possible to four-wheel drive from Moyale back down through **Buna** and across the brown, desiccated **Bokhol** and **Gora Dudi Plains** to the oasis of **Wajir**, and thence either up to the Somalia border or back to Meru. Now Wajir is better approached directly from Isiolo, if at all (see ISIOLO, PEARL OF THE NORTH, page 173), and the Buna road is but a memory, marked on obsolete maps.

If you've decided to leave Moyale to the Ethiopians, or have seen it and returned, you strike out from Marsabit for the equally magical, vast desert shores of Lake Turkana, home of the oldest known traces of humankind, the great Jade Sea which has fired the imaginations of explorers from Ptolemy's time. But getting there, as is usual in Kenya, is more than half the fun.

From Marsabit there's a bone-jarring four-hour drive across the **Chalbi Desert** to **North Horr**, past the well of Mayidahad, up the impossibly bleak lower slopes of the Huri Hills and down to scrubby Kalacha Dida spring, mirages hovering over the desert, the track sometimes nothing but the trace of a previous vehicle's tires (if they're not covered with blown sand), sometimes cut across jagged lava and often obscured by seismic highways left by oil prospecting surveys. The scenery is emptily awesome, the heat unconscionable, the dangers of getting stuck, broken down, or lost considerable. It's not intelligent to travel this track alone or without a guide; people have died doing so, and you'll find that no matter how much water and gasoline you have you'll worry that it's not enough.

When it comes, you'll be more than delighted to glimpse, finally, the hill known as Dabandabli, near the police post of North Horr. Here you can turn southwest through the basaltic wastes of the **Chalbi**, being careful to stay on the track, past the Rendille water hole known as **Gusi**, and in two to three hours (85 km or 53 miles) will reach the glimmering shores of **Lake Turkana**, and haven in the form of palm-shaded campsites and lodges with refrigerators.

EAST OF THE JADE SEA

If you wish to visit the blazing moonscape of **Sibiloi National Park** and its fascinating archaeological and paleontological sites, it's best to postpone the drive south to Loyangalani and turn instead northwest from North Horr, driving 130 km or 81 miles (three to four hours) to **Allia Bay** on **Lake Turkana**, south of Richard Leakey's digs at **Koobi Fora**. On a slope overlooking the lake a weird assortment of ochre, brown, and yellow pillars lie like a broken temple among the gray commiphora brush and tawny grass — petrified vestiges of a once-great tropical forest.

At Allia Bay there is a small campground, bandas, and occasionally something to eat. At Allia Bay you can hire a guide (essential if you wish to explore Sibiloi National Park), and drive past the Park offices then two hours north to the peninsula of Koobi Fora, where there's a small museum containing some recent finds. Although it's best to have asked permission in Nairobi (at the National Museum) before visiting Koobi Fora, the resident archaeologists are friendly and if you manifest a reasonable knowledge of and interest in their excavations may offer a quick

tour. As well, there are *in situ* fossil elephant, tortoise, and crocodile exhibits in the nearby uplands at **Bura Hasuma Hill**.

KOOBI FORA

Here near Koobi Fora (the name derives from the local Gabbra tribe's word for the commiphora bush common to the area) have been found many of the fossils that have pushed back millions of years the dawn of human history. Building on many discoveries made by his parents, Louis and Mary

Leakey, at Olduvai Gorge and other locations in Tanzania, Richard Leakey came to the east shore of Lake Turkana because its wind- and water-eroded barrens seemed to offer unusually clear incisions into the sedimentary rocks which bear, like the piled pages of a manuscript, the decodable history of our human past.

Since 1968 Leakey, his wife Meave, and other scientists have made a series of breathtaking finds at over 200 East Turkana sites including, in 1972, the skull of a *Homo habilis* over two million years old, and now considered to be our direct ancestor. Enough information has been gleaned from the over 6,000

Most Kenyan tourist hotel rooms are spacious and comfortable, here in Samburu.

fossil specimens in Sibiloi to form a coherent picture of the development of a gatherer-hunter society as it evolved in language and toolmaking, as its brains enlarged, and, stressed by changing climates and competition, it expanded and diversified until it came to consider itself apart from other animals and favored with dominion over the earth.

In all, the sedimentary deposits of East Turkana have yielded nearly 200 different hominid specimens, including several skulls and other major skeletal sections. Earliest discoveries (three and a half to four million

years old) appear to be of *Australopithecus afarensis*, the earliest recognized hominid. More recent specimens comprise three major hominid groups (*Australopithecus robustus, Australopithecus africanus,* and the *Homo* lineage which led to today's humans); all appear to have lived during the same one-million year period, with *Homo erectus* evolving from the earlier *Homo habilis* about one and a half million years ago.

SIBILOI NATIONAL PARK

Sibiloi National Park is both fascinating and different from any other site in Kenya; considering the terrain and climate, a quite diverse wildlife community exists. It was origi-

nally a haven for elephants (the Koobi Fora museum displays a one-and-a-half-million-year-old example), but these were shot out by white hunters before the Second World War. The park's relatively common large animals include the tiang race of topi, common and Grevy's zebra, reticulated giraffe, Grant's gazelle, gerenuk, dik dik, golden jackal, lion, hyena, a few leopards, a surprising number of cheetahs, with many crocodiles and some hippos near the lake.

LAKE TURKANA

The lake has a majestic splendor all its own. Like its name it seems jade, then turquoise gray as clouds mask the sun, silver at dawn and red at dusk, placid as a pond or wild and wind-tossed as the sea, so elementally vast that its far shore seems to fall beyond the horizon, and the curvature of the earth is visible in its limitless north-south expanse.

The **East African Rift Valley**, in which Lake Turkana sits, supposedly large enough to be seen from the moon with a naked eye, runs over 8,000 km (4,960 miles) from Ethiopia on the Red Sea to Mozambique on the southern Indian Ocean. Initiated some 20 to 40 million years ago by faulting and warping, and continuing still as the tectonic plates floating on the earth's crust pull apart, the Great Rift contains seven lakes in Kenya (**Magadi**, **Naivasha**, **Elmenteita**, **Nakuru**, **Bogoria**, **Baringo**, and **Turkana**), and is liberally punctured with both recent and ancient volcanic craters, of which Turkana's **Central** and **South Islands** (both national parks) are fairly recent examples.

Four million years ago it appears Turkana was a huge freshwater lake four times its present size of 7,200 sq km (2,800 sq miles). By two million years ago, sediments deposited from the Omo River and tectonic shifts had diminished the lake to a wide-based system of rivers, channels, and marshes which may have drained eastward into the Indian Ocean. Since then it has expanded and contracted in the wide low bed of the Rift, has become increasingly saline (average pH is now 9.2), and no longer has an outlet other than evaporation.

The water lost by Turkana to evaporation now generally exceeds inflow from the Omo

River and from the meager seasonal rainfall carried by the Turkwell and Kerio Rivers. Today about 435 km (270 miles) long by an average of 30 km (19 miles) wide, the lake is shrinking again, due perhaps to climatic fluctuation but more so to man-made changes. Foreign-aid irrigation projects in southern Ethiopia have decreased the Omo's flow. Similar French and Italian dam building on the Turkwell and Kerio Rivers will undoubtedly lessen their peak flows and thus their contribution to the lake.

At the same time, explosive population growth among pastoral tribes due to improved health care without the requisite increase in family planning services has vastly increased livestock herds and led to catastrophic overgrazing of the parched uplands surrounding the Rift. The consequent denuding of vegetation and soil erosion has altered the climate, reducing or changing rainfall, and further diminished the lake. All of this strikes home as you look out over Turkana's beaches to its present shores, particularly at **Loyangalani**, next stop on the Grand Safari.

To get there, alas, you first have a four-wheel drive *crawl* back southward to Allia Bay and inland toward North Horr, swinging south at an unmarked track that leads directly to Loyangalani. If you get lost, and have no guide (and haven't expired by this time), then continue to North Horr and take the slightly more visible track through Gusi to Loyangalani.

Bathed by onshore breezes in the palm trees, Loyangalani is a nice place to recover from the rigors of East Turkana. To the east, the imposing ridges of **Mount Kulal**, 2,295 m (7,530 ft), are climbable for those not tired of adventure, and are reputed to offer an inspiring panorama of the lake, the Ethiopian escarpment, and out into the **Chalbi Desert**. It's possible to swim in the lake here with only minimal fear of hippos and crocodiles (however, one local told us an English crocodile researcher was recently devoured).

As always around Lake Turkana, flocks of children will follow you wherever you go, speaking good English, asking to be photographed for a fee or to sell some trinket. The local population is diverse, comprising remnants of the El Molos, considered the most ancient of Turkana's inhabitants, who live

principally on fish, hippo steaks when they can get them, and occasionally crocodile meat. They have largely merged into the overpowering Turkana and Samburu peoples, and their language is now considered lost. The remaining 400 or so of the tribe live on **El Molo Bay**, fifteen minutes' drive north of Loyangalani; for a fee you can visit the village: most visitors find the experience depressingly commercial.

The Turkana and Samburu are more evident, having learned how to fish from the El Molo, and whose herds can be seen watering at the lake edge. If the weather is calm, from Loyangalani you can rent a boat for an hour's ride to fascinating **South Island National Park**, a withered volcanic core surprisingly rich with crocodiles and bird life. Birds are not lacking along the entire east shore of Turkana, with flamingos, pelicans, ibis, cormorants, and avocets being common.

The waters of Turkana have long been famous for their fish, including a world record Nile perch (the largest are supposed to exceed 150 kg or 330 lb), tilapia, golden perch, and the fierce tiger fish, which can weigh up to eight kilograms (18 lb) and which when hooked fights like a trout.

Where to Stay

Lodging is Loyangalani's only disappointment: options are limited to the ex-Sunset Strip fenced-in campsite (200 KSh per person) through the **El Molo Lodge** ((02) 723177, Box 34710, Nairobi, (doubles for US$180 with full board; gasoline available if you've called ahead to reserve it), to the once luxurious **Oasis Lodge**, which you can reserve through Bunson Travel ((02) 221992 FAX (02) 214120, Box 45456, Nairobi (doubles for US$200 with full board). The budget option, at around 500 KSh, is cheap but not luxurious: **Mama Shanga's** consists of a few concrete sheds with a padlocked outside toilet as the only sanitary facilities.

How to Get There

There is no public transportation to Loyangalani: even *matatus* stop at Maralal. With your own transportation, it's a relatively easy three-hour drive to Nyahururu but soon after

One of nature's stranger creations, giraffes can make loving parents.

this the pavement ends, and a rather slower three hours on dirt road to Maralal. From there the road deteriorates markedly and if you complete the last 220 km (137 miles) in less than a further six hours you'll be doing well. Bear in mind that there's no gasoline further north than Maralal unless you call ahead to make sure that there is some waiting for you at Loyangalani. This might not be possible so make sure you have some jerry cans. The only people who do run safaris to Loyangalani are **Safari Camp Services** ((02) 228936 FAX (02) 212160, Box 44801, Nairobi,

Ahead lies the return journey south through Baragoi (gasoline very occasionally, on the black market) and Maralal (gasoline usually at least one of two stations). The nearest sure supply will be at Nyahururu, 360 km (223 miles) to the south — too far to go on fumes. So you might be more worried about how to bet back. This is where it's essential to have planned ahead before you headed north, by calling first the Marsabit Lodge ((02) 229751 or (02) 330820, to check on gasoline supplies there, then El Molo Lodge ((02) 723177, requesting them to set aside or fly

operators of the famed Turkana Bus, which lumbers along the rough road every week or two. There is an airstrip at Loyangalani if you have the budget for it, and some of the Oasis Lodge's rental vehicles might be operational.

BARAGOI BOUND

Getting about in this part of Kenya presents plenty of challenges. If you have cut across from the relatively "civilized" Isiolo, with its gasoline station and fancy Barclay's Bank, through the northland from Marsabit to North Horr, Allia Bay and down to Loyangalani, it is likely your extra jerry cans of gasoline have run dry, as well as your tank.

up several jerry cans' worth for your return trip. True, Loyangalani's fun, but if you haven't planned ahead on fuel (and much of the journey south is in low gears and devours the stuff), you may be there far longer than you wish. And a long stay at El Molo Lodge is not to be courted.

Once gasoline is obtained, your water stocks are full, and your spare tires, tubes, and overall vehicular condition checked, you're ready to continue the Grand Safari through some of the most breathtakingly beautiful landscape on earth. The 210-km (130-mile) trip from Loyangalani to Maralal can take up to 12 hours in the ferocious heat, so it's best to start early or, better yet, stop half way at South Horr and Kurungu.

Driving south along the lake, with sunrise striking the golden battlements of South Island, you ascend the jagged, tire-shredding lava fields of **Horr Valley**, the lower slopes of 2,752-m (9,030-ft) **Mowongo Sowan** to the west, verdant with trees amid the desert, and reach the incised gorge of South Horr, an outpost of jungle with a mission and police post. Here you can hire a guide to explore the **Nyiru Mountains** and forest all the way to the **Tum Valley**, which offers superb views on Lake Turkana and the desolate expanse of **Suguta Valley**. This area is into the El Barta Plains. Baragoi (where gasoline may be available on the black market, with a surcharge) is a mission post and clinic where the black Ndoto Mountains meet the plains, and from where in the 1920s the British led their military campaigns to subjugate the Turkanas. Local children tend to run away from foreigners: any white person, in their experience, is likely to produce a syringe and give them an injection.

South of Baragoi it's slow, arduous driving 80 km (50 miles) south across the plains and up the Lopet Plateau, to **Poror**, where one of

home to **Desert Rose Camel Safaris** ((02) 228936 FAX (02) 212160, Box 44801, Nairobi, perhaps the best-informed and equipped camel safari operators who have a new lodge built overlooking the river (see TAKE A CAMEL SAFARI, page 16, in TOP SPOTS). Just beyond South Horr is **Kurungu**, a shaded streamside clearing where there was formerly a well-run campground with bandas, but now just a simple campsite (ask permission first in South Horr), and from where, with a guide, you can explore the Nyiru forest or even ascend the peak of Mowongo Sowan.

From South Horr to **Baragoi** it's only 41 km (25 miles) on the map but this can take hours on the ground, particularly after the rains, as the road twists and grinds down

Kenya's magic panoramas awaits you. Turning west, take the dirt track (may be impassable during or just after the rains) from Poror six kilometers (three and three quarter miles) through the wheat fields which ten years ago were among the best Samburu grazing lands, to the **Lesiolo Escarpment**, where the **Rift Valley** spreads out 2,000 m (6,562 ft) below in all its grandeur and myriad colors. In clear weather, with binoculars, you can see all the way from the Jade Sea in the north to **Lake Baringo** in the south, a span of over 220 km (140 miles)!

Crocodiles are found at Turkana and many of Kenya's other lakes and rivers. They are both dangerous and swift.

The Desert: Southeast of the Jade Sea

Western
Wonderland

HILLS AND LAKES

MARALAL

Having experienced one of the world's great panoramas, you return to Poror and in an hour reach the mountain town of Maralal in its windswept cleft of hills, cedar forest on both slopes imparting a perfumed, resiny flavor to the cool, thin air. In Maralal you feel on the edge of civilization again: there's electricity, shops, an excellent hotel, a thriving market, usually gasoline, and a throng of souvenir sellers guaranteed to make you wish you were back in the desert.

Two-thousand-meter (6,600-ft)-high Maralal is a microcosm of all the pretensions of modern Kenya: a fancy police post with a spanking new flag, new government buildings overlooking an imposing traffic roundabout from which sign-less, potholed dirt roads unravel in all directions, one leading by chance to the town itself. The main street, with clapboard verandahs and trees not so much lining the streets as growing in it, has a wild-west feel. Cattle and at least one ostrich wander from shop to shop, Samburu tribesmen driven in from the bush by tribal conflict and barefooted gangs of children run around cheerfully. Three bars offer warm beer while there are a number of surprisingly good restaurants.

If you've missed purchasing Samburu trinkets so far, Maralal's a good place to catch up: trouble in the Rift Valley has brought scores of refugees in from the country and they're having to sell their heirlooms. There are two-piece wooden-handled, steel-shafted spears made by local blacksmiths for the tourist trade, and the wicked foot-long double-bladed knives known as *simis* or *lalem*, central to every Samburu warrior's health and longevity.

The true *simis*, those the *morans* carry, are cut down from large machetes made in England — look for the brand name of the machete, such as "Giraffe," or "Birmingham," and the words, "Made in England" which are stamped into the steel just above the haft, and which are carefully conserved when the machete is ground down into a *simi*. The tourist-grade *simis* are made of brighter, lighter Kenyan steel, and will not keep an edge; in either case make sure the goatskin sheath of your *simi* is not split along the edge, or it can give you a nasty cut. The going rate for *simis* is 450 KSh to 600 KSh depending on size and condition; a good spear can cost 1,000 KSh.

Where to Stay

The **Maralal Safari Lodge** ((02) 211124 FAX (02) 211125, Box 15020, Nairobi, about four kilometers (two and a half miles) south of town, is the best place to stay, as it should be with doubles going for US$175 with full board. Their 24 comfortable cedar cabins with fireplaces, a cozy bar, fireplace lounge, and large dining room, all overlook a salt lick and water hole of the **Maralal Game Sanctuary**, with grazing zebra, buffalo, impalas, gazelles, and elands. Guides from the Lodge will take you on a game walk through the surrounding refuge; early in the mornings both birds and beasts are generally abundant.

If the Maralal Safari Lodge doesn't fit your budget or lifestyle, **Yare Safaris Ltd.** (/FAX (02) 214099 E-MAIL travelkenya@ iconnect.co.ke, Box 63006, Nairobi, is a clean and quite classy campground with bandas and bunkhouses just to the east of the main road south of town, with prices from 400 KSh for a banda. There's a well-stocked bar, a restaurant, a fake Samburu *manyatta*, and extensive campsites with a beautiful panorama of the surrounding cedar-clad hills. Yare also organizes camel safaris, accompanied by Samburu *morans*, at unbeatable prices starting at US$500 for a week all-inclusive. Alternatively in town small *hotelis* have basic accommodation at very inexpensive prices starting at US$1 for the **Midpoint Hotel**.

ACROSS THE LEROGI PLATEAU

In case you missed **Wamba**, the **Matthews Range**, and **Kitich Camp** on the way north from Isiolo to Marsabit (see NORTHERN FRONTIER DISTRICT, page 183), you can still catch them by driving south from Maralal 20 km (12 miles) to **Kisima** and turning east across the flat **Lerogi Plateau**, where zebra, gazelles, giraffe, and impalas munch complacently

OPPOSITE: Early settlers brought nineteenth-century technology to Kenya.

among livestock herds under the watchful eyes of red-cloaked Samburu *morans*. The road climbs into the russet mountains, with beautiful views of the **Ewaso Ngiro River** upstream of Samburu National Reserve, and out into the flats of **Lodungokwe**. On the hillsides you can see the line of vegetation commence where the overgrazing stops; on the denuded plain, fenced plots of German anti-erosion projects gleam green against the red, goat-ravaged earth.

If you're anxious to avoid the beaten track, and enjoy torturing your vehicle, there's also the dirt track northeast of Maralal to **Barsaloi** and thence another 60 km (37 miles) to **Wamba**; a cutoff to Kitich is supposed to exist but we couldn't find it. As usual, the countryside's spectacular and the road grievous to all concerned. In addition, there's the threat of *shiftas*, so check the current situation with the local authorities: if you survive you'll have tales for the grandchildren, but if you don't you might not have any.

South from Kisima, you travel the wide open **Lerogi Plateau**, the road rutted and holed but offering stretches for the higher gears. After **Suguta Marmar** the land levels, the grass is greener, taller, and fenced; from here to **Rumuruti** are the remnants of the large cattle ranches which once dominated the plateau all the way to the **Loldaika Mountains**. Many of these vast ranches, cut originally out of Samburu grazing land and some of Kenya's best wildlife habitat, have been bought in the years since independence by Nairobi politicians, who sold the cattle and split the ranches into small parcels which they then sold at great profit to people hoping to farm them. But the plateau is not suited to subsistence farming, and in many cases the new owners could not make a living and overgrazed then deserted the land.

EWASO RIVER VALLEY

Thirty-two kilometers (20 miles) south of Kisima a turnoff to **Lake Baringo** will take you 104 km (65 miles) on a rough road westward through magnificent scenery past Karimadu Mountain and down into the Rift. It's easier, however, to stay on the Maralal-Nyahururu road past the Naibor Springs, where Samburus water their stock, and in

another 37 km (23 miles) take the turnoff east 32 km (20 miles) to **Colcheccio**, named by Italians who once farmed here. At Colcheccio is another highlight of the Grand Safari: the **Ewaso River Camel Hike**.

Run by Simon Evans, member of a local ranching family, the camel hike allows you to travel on foot through the lovely ranchlands and semiarid brush of the upper Ewaso Ngiro, all the way, if you wish, to Samburu National Reserve. All the baggage is carried by the camels, surprisingly gentle and accommodating creatures, which leaves you free to enjoy the ever-changing landscape and marvelous views of the Ewaso Ngiro canyon.

Generally the expedition leaves early each morning, before the heat of the day, and stops around noon to set up camp, usually on the banks of the Ewaso Ngiro, with game hikes in the afternoon and early evening, dinner by campfire, and sleeping out on camp beds under the stars. The safari can vary in length, itinerary, and daily distance depending on the preferences and abilities of the walkers.

One of the virtues of a camel hike, the Matthews Range treks organized by Kitich Camp, or your own itineraries up Mounts Kenya or Elgon or through Hell's Gate, is that they bring you a very valuable side of Kenya that is not available to the average tourist. The normal Kenya trip involves little time on your own two feet, and most travel, unfortunately, is by automobile, little different from the overdeveloped societies most tourists come from. To walk in Kenya at the land's pace, with time to enjoy the slow unraveling of the country's marvels, and to perceive the animals in their environment rather than from the window of an automobile, is an enchanting and timeless alternative to the standard packaged tour.

Costs for a camel safari are a little higher than a standard full board park lodge, it includes food, camels, mattresses, mosquito nets, laundry, and all the bush lore you can ingest. You need to bring your sleeping bag, a good pair of boots, and standard safari hiking gear. For more information, see TAKE A CAMEL SAFARI, page 16 in TOP SPOTS; write to Simon Evans, Box 243, Gilgil, Kenya; or

make reservations with **Let's Go Travel**
((02) 340331 FAX (02) 336890 E-MAIL info
@letsgosafari .com, Box 60342, Nairobi. No
matter your age, if you're "young at heart,"
as Simon puts it, you can leave your vehicle
behind (by now it *needs* the rest) and see
Samburu country the way the Samburus do.

South of Colcheccio the road nears the
Ewaso Ngiro swamp and its outflow into the
Ewaso Narok. On the map, the town of
Rumuruti is shown to have gasoline, but once
again you've been led astray, and tacky
Rumuruti (Maa for "mosquito"), once a

fari of them all, the first to cross Maasailand
and reach the shores of the fabled lake which
would be called Victoria, passing by the cascades now called Nyahururu, which in honor
of himself he named Thomson's Falls.

Already a famed naturalist and explorer
at the age of 24, Thomson was engaged by
the Royal Geographical Society to discover
if a practicable route existed across Maasailand to Lake Victoria and Uganda. He was
soon intercepted by Maasai north of Kilimanjaro, an advance guard of the same
morans who had ambushed Gustav Fischer's

prosperous ranching community before the
European settlers left, now offers little to slow
you down.

The best thing about Rumuruti is that it's
the start of macadam road, with only 35 km
(22 miles) to the larger town of **Nyahururu**,
formerly known as Thomson's Falls, where
for the first time in many hundred kilometers
on the Grand Safari is a guaranteed supply
of gasoline!

NYAHURURU

Leaving Mombasa March 15, 1883, Joseph
Thomson led a ragtag group of some 113
"vagabond" porters and other African coastal
sailors on what was to be the grandest sa-

party at Hell's Gate the year before. Thomson
was forced to retreat to Taveta and then to
make a 323-km (200-mile) dash all the way
back to Mombasa in just six days.

Rather than give up, he recruited more
men and joined an Arab ivory and slave trading caravan as far as Kilimanjaro. From there
the Maasai harassed him all the way through
the Satima mountains, which he renamed the
Aberdares after the president of the Royal
Geographical Society. He finally convinced
the Maasai he was a wizard by removing,
then replacing, a false front tooth, and offering to do the same to a warrior's nose, by use
of a battery to shock them, and by making a
magical potion of fizzy Eno fruit salts. After
an abortive attempt to reach the top of Mount

Kenya, he was forced once more to retreat from the banks of the Ewaso Ngiro by threats of a Maasai attack.

With great relief he passed out of Maasai country, reaching the shores of Lake Victoria on Christmas day, from there traveling north to Mount Elgon, where he visited the Elephant Caves. On the last day of 1883, while hunting for his New Year's dinner, he shot a buffalo which vengefully gored him and tossed him over its shoulder, and which then was killed by one of his men as it prepared to give him the coup de grace.

Badly injured, Thomson was carried on a litter back to Naivasha, where he contracted dysentery and lingered for two months on the edge of death as the Maasai continued to threaten on a daily basis. He finally regained sufficient health to return to Mombasa on May 24, 1884, having traveled 4,839 km (3,000 miles) in 14 months, opened a direct route for the first time to Lake Victoria, and completed one of the most difficult and courageous feats of African exploration.

Thomson's Falls, named after this adventurer, are where the Ewaso Narok River pours roiling and brown over a stony ledge into its narrow, forested chasm, perpetual mist rising from the clash of water and rock, rain-

bows cloaking the green, chilled slopes. An array of souvenir kiosks mars the view of the falls, however, and a quartet of painted "native dancers" may waylay you in an attempt to sell a photo opportunity.

More interestingly, there is a path along the edge of the falls, and a trail you can take to the bottom. However, it is slippery and quite dangerous in places, and easily lost; tourists have also been robbed here, thus it's best to check at the hotel desk on trail condition and safety, and to engage a guide if necessary. At the desk they'll also tell you where to pick up a trail that crosses the river on the bridge above the falls and descends the other side, crossing again lower down and returning to Nyahururu—it's a beautiful walk that takes you into the wall of rainbow and cloud amid the canyon.

Where to Stay

A few minutes walk from the falls is the **Thomson's Falls Lodge** ((0365) 22006 FAX (0365) 32170, Box 38, Nyahururu, which offers double cottages for 2,800 KSh bed and breakfast, which extends comfortably overlooking the Thomson's Falls, with grassy campground behind. Built in the 1930s, the hotel is a relic of colonial times, but has borne the change with considerable grace. The rooms are spacious and very clean, with carefully-laid fireplaces, the food ample and good, and the staff friendly. At 2,375 m (7,800 ft) above sea level, Nyahururu can be cold at night, but the hotel bar usually has a roaring fire, and is a cheerful place to strike up a conversation, far more lively than the average sedate game lodge.

The town of Nyahururu itself has a number of small *hotelis*, including the **Baron Hotel** ((0365) 32056, Box 423, Nyahuru, but nowhere especially recommended.

How to Get There

Nyahururu is easily reached in two hours by *matatu* from Nairobi, but Thomson's Falls and the Thomson's Falls Lodge are four kilometers (three miles) from the town, a steady walk or take a taxi.

OPPOSITE Tranquil Lake Elementeita, another lake where flamingos breed remains the private domain of the Delamere family. ABOVE: Thomson's Falls.

LAKE BARINGO

Lake Baringo is a good stopover site to break the long drive across the Rift Valley, or for a two-day trip from Nairobi. Because it is now accessible by paved road from Nairobi, it has become a popular Kenyan weekend destination. This brown saline lake is the most northern of Kenya's six small Rift Valley lakes and is home for hippos, crocodiles, and over 400 species of birds. It has an average depth of only eight meters (25 ft)

and its three islands (Gibraltar, Teddy Bear, and Ol Kokwa) are breeding grounds for the statuesque one-and-a-half-meter (five-foot) Goliath heron, the largest of the heron species.

The area is home to many communities of Njemps, one of three Maa-speaking tribes in Kenya. The others are the Maasai in the south and Samburu in the north. They are unusual in that they have broken the pastoralist's traditional taboo of not eating fish, and live on a mixed diet of fish and goat meat. Their one-man boats are made from ambach trees which grow around the lake. Like those used by the Turkana, these raft-like craft float semi-submerged, giving the occupant the appearance of sitting atop the water. The predominate inhabitants of

the Lake Baringo area are two Kalenjin tribes, the Pokot and Tugen. President Moi is a Tugen, which may explain the high quality of the roads in this area. They are primarily pastoralists and the land around the lake is severely overgrazed and eroded as a result. If you visit the lake after a rain, the water will have a distinct red tone, while during the dry season it appears more brown.

The surrounding countryside is arid, red-soiled, and sparsely vegetated with several types of the omnipresent thorn trees and candelabra euphorbias. Termite castles of every size and shape abound. After the rainy seasons, the hillsides are dotted with bright-pink but poisonous desert roses.

The shores are a mixture of sand and marsh which provides some cover and shade for the resident hippos. Many visitors swim and water ski in the lake, which is supposed to be free of bilharzia.

We have seen no crocodiles in Baringo, and a few swimmers round the dock at Ol Kokwa Island. By all local accounts there have been more problems with hippos than crocs. Only the month before we arrived, one boat was attacked and another smashed by angry hippopotamuses. Because the lake is shallow, these aquatic giants can be found anywhere, not just along the shores. Apparently the sound of boat motors particularly annoys them; they are also known to kill people for getting between them and the water. If you want to swim, the less accessible **Lake Bogoria** or the swimming pools at Lake Baringo's two lodges might be safer and more relaxing.

Where to Stay

Accommodations at the lake are varied. In the town of **Kampi Ya Samaki** the only town on the lake, are a couple of *hotelis*, but, **Betty Robert's Campsite** on the waterfront, with bandas for 500 KSh per person or campsites for 400 KSh is one of the nicest campgrounds in Kenya with running water and showers, and no extra charge for grazing hippos at night.

Next to Betty Roberts' is the luxurious **Lake Baringo Lodge** ((02) 540780 FAX (02) 543810, Box 40075, Nairobi, which has very comfortable doubles for US$126 KSh with

full board. This is also a good place to eat while staying at Betty's. Because of the influx of weekend travelers, the Lodge has a 100 KSh entrance fee for visitors to their bar, gardens, swimming pool, and hippo-viewing pier but this is often waived. As an added attraction, they offer guided birdwatching walks with 400 species to spot.

Just north of town is the dock for making the journey to **Ol Kokwa Island** where **Island Camp** (make reservations with Let's Go Travel ((02) 340331 FAX (02) 336890 E-MAIL info @letsgosafari.com, Box 60342, Nairobi) provides the luxury tented camp in peace with double tents for US$200 full board. The boat ride costs 600 KSh round trip, and if you have a day to spend at the lake the island is probably the most interesting way to spend it. You can walk on the island, which is inhabited by thousands of birds, a few waterbuck, and several hundred Njemps and their livestock.

How to Get There

The instructions I was given to get to Lake Baringo on my first visit were "Leave Nairobi on the Naivasha Road and at the second roundabout go right" and the directions were spot on. It was more than two hours before I hit the first roundabout at Naivasha and another hour and a half to the second at Nakuru. Overall the drive takes about five hours, with the road starting off laden with

OPPOSITE: Leafy Lake Baringo Lodge is popular with weekend visitors to the lake. ABOVE: The hot springs and geysers of Lake Bogoria.

trucks and buses but improving steadily all the way. By public transportation, frequent buses and *matatus* service Nakuru from Nairobi and other towns, and it is reasonably easy to get to Marigat. From there transportation is likely to become infrequent: carry plenty of water.

LAKE BOGORIA NATIONAL RESERVE

Some 30 km (20 miles) south of Lake Baringo, as the ruddy duck flies, is **Lake Bogoria**, a national reserve. This small equatorial lake has geysers and hot springs. There are relatively few vantage points from which you can see it, but its topaz and green water is strikingly beautiful.

The Maasai know Lake Bogoria as Mbatibat, the Tugen as Makwaria, and before independence the maps called it Lake Hannington, named for the Bishop of Uganda, who was supposed to be the first European to see it. Though history is somewhat vague on the subject, it has been accepted that in 1885 James Hannington, en route to his missionary post in Uganda, sighted the Lake from a point, now called **Hannington's Lookout**, northwest of Nyahururu near Chepkererat, and not easily accessible. Hot and thirsty, Hannington's party climbed down the steep wall of the Rift only to discover the water was saline. His luck did not improve: upon arrival in Uganda he was murdered by the Bagandas as he tried to cross the White Nile.

In 1902, the English adventurer/chronicler, Sir Harry Johnston, wrote that there was a forest of large trees in the center which was slowly dying, and speculated that there must have been recent geological activity or an overflow from Lake Baringo. However, nothing supports these theories, and local traditions claim that the lake had always been here, with or without the dying forest.

Sir Harry also noted a large population of flamingos and photographed their nests. Today you can occasionally see some of these giant, pink birds, but they no longer nest in Bogoria's mud.

Along Lake Bogoria's western shore is a bed of hot springs and blow holes which infrequently erupt two and a half to three meters (eight to ten feet) into the air and constantly emit a pungent sulfur smell. These geothermal phenomena are intriguing, but also dangerously hot. Often the surrounding crust cannot support much weight and recently a visitor fell through the crust and was boiled to death.

Where to Stay

Access to this little-visited reserve leaves much to be desired. No public transportation reaches it, and you need a four-wheel drive, unless the weather has been particularly dry. At present there are no accommodations on the lake, however there are several campsites. The best, and well worth the trip for a relaxing day in the water, is **Fig Tree Campground** (US$2 KSh per person, paid at the Reserve gate). The campground is on the banks of a crystal clear, drinkable spring which flows into several natural whirlpools. Several people told us that plans are underway for a tourist lodge near the hot springs, but there is no evidence of construction now. Undoubtedly someone will capitalize on this unique spot.

WEST OF THE JADE SEA

Going north from Lake Baringo is not currently recommended. Although there are two alternative routes that take you through equally beautiful though different terrain, the area is at the heart of some of Kenya's worst tribal conflict. Take advice locally and see if the situation has calmed. Look forward to some difficult driving conditions in any case: the situation does not encourage road maintenance.

The more difficult route heads north from Baringo through **Loruk** and **Nginyang**, then crosses the **Kerio Valley** and **River** to **Tot** at the foot of the **Elgeyo Escarpment** and swings north to **Sigor**, where it picks up the new section of A1 that goes north to **Lake Turkana** and **Sudan**. North of Tot a second dirt track can be taken roughly following the Kerio River through the **South Turkana National Reserve** and meeting another dirt track from Baringo and Kapedo, then meeting the A1 finally in **Lokichar**. The latter is a four-wheel drive adventure through barren hill and desert scrub, crossing the northern end of the magnificent, desolate **Suguta Valley**, one of the hottest places on earth. During the rains and for several weeks after (or possibly months depending on the scheduling of road crews) these roads are impassible. Even during the dry seasons this route can be dangerous and should only be attempted if you are fully contained (food, water, camping gear, etc.) and have a full tank of gas and at least two full jerry cans.

Timewise it is just as quick to take the longer paved route, a 20-minute drive south from Lake Baringo to Marigat and then heading west. This is itself a beautiful drive and along some of the best roads in the country,

Perched atop the Tugen Hills, **Kabarnet** overlooks the lush Kerio Valley. As the administrative center for the Baringo District, the town has complete shopping facilities, a multitude of government buildings and the recently constructed **Kabarnet Hotel** ((02) 336858, Box 109 Kabarnet, with doubles for US$48, bed and breakfast.

The **Kerio Valley**, with some of Kenya's richest agricultural land, is a welcome relief after the browns and reds of the lakes. (If you are traveling this section in reverse — Eldoret to Marigat — you probably won't be so

a butter-smooth ribbon of little-used pavement, formerly the route of the East African Rally through President Moi's hometown of **Kabarnet** to Eldoret. The route begins at **Marigat**, 19 km (12 miles) south of Lake Baringo.

From Marigat, the road climbs steeply into the **Tugen** or **Ilkamasya Hills**, offering magnificent vistas of Lake Baringo and, from one upper point, Lake Bogoria, as well as numerous volcanic craters, reminders of the turbulent eruptions that have pockmarked the land over millions of years. The high country, only a little less arid than the lake valley floor, is predictably covered with thorn scrub, but where possible the Tugen have terraced the slopes to grow maize.

impressed with the lush greens or the variety of crops.)

Approaching the western slope of the Kerio Valley, the Tambach or Elgeyo Escarpment, you can't help but wonder how the road will ever get to the top of these sheer, wooded cliffs. But it does in 15 km (nine miles) of twisting, hairpin turns that are a challenge to negotiate in any vehicle. Imagine what these must have been like before they were paved!

About halfway up the escarpment just past the village of Tambach you get a full view of **Torok Falls**. If you want to walk to them you will have to do it from Tambach, where

As the sun sets on Lake Turkana the sound of drums come alive in the local settlements.

Western Wonderland

you can usually find a guide who will gladly show you the way or accompany you for 30 KSh and provide some local history as well.

ELDORET

After climbing the western edge of the Rift Valley, the countryside levels out on the 2,100-m (7,000-ft) elevation **Uasin Gishu Plateau**. Here are large wheat and cattle spreads intermingled with cedar, fir, and pine plantations, reminding one of the American Midwest.

It's hard to imagine this area as the early colonists described it — a veritable paradise filled with animals that had never been hunted. None are to be seen today.

During the Boer War, the area was settled by Afrikaners and in 1912 Eldoret became a town when J.C. Shaw opened a branch of the Standard Bank of South Africa. In *The Mottled Lizard*, Elspeth Huxley describes the event. "[He] had arrived in an oxcart with a too heavy safe which he had pushed out at the back onto a wagon track that traversed the bare, brown plateau. As it was heavy to move, a mud hut had been build round it with two rooms, one for the safe and one for Mr. Shaw. The town then consisted of a few little stores and was called Sixty-four, after the survey number on which it stood. Sixty-four served a sparse community of Afrikaners who had arrived together — men, women, children, babies, predikants and household goods — from Bethel in the Transvaal, and trekked in their semi-covered wagons up roadless, forested escarpment to a promised land."

Today Eldoret is very much an ideal village. Very much a Moi area, it has had a great deal of investment, and rather to its bemused surprise, has an international airport. So far, however, the only international flights persuaded to land are those on the so-called "slave run" taking workers to Saudi Arabia. It is a center of industry (fabric and leather) and commerce. On the west edge of the shopping district is a small city park, one of the few found outside Nairobi. Vote KANU!

Whether because it is a commercial center for a large agricultural community, or full of businessmen trying to find some subject to interest Moi over cocktails, Eldoret has an abundance of hotels, and the best is the **Sirikwa Hotel (** (02) 336858, Box 30741, Nairobi, with doubles for 5,000 KSh including bed and breakfast, and a restaurant, bar, and swimming pool. The best of the budget accommodations are the **Kabathaya Hotel and Lodging (** (0321) 22160, Box 832, Eldoret (500 KSh) and while the **New Wagon Wheel (** (0321) 32271 is more expensive at 1,500 KSh, it does allows camping in the garden.

At Eldoret you join the main highway, with heavy truck traffic and as a result a

disintegrating road surface. The 70 km (43 miles) between Eldoret and **Kitale** were so bad when we were last there we almost gave up hope of reaching Lake Turkana that day. However, after Kitale the road improves substantially and much of the truck traffic turns off to Uganda.

KITALE

Kitale is a pleasant town with a wide tree-lined main street, large produce market, and the **National Museum of Western Kenya**. This small museum has a limited wildlife and ethnology section featuring the Maasai, Turkana, Pokot, and Luo tribes. On the grounds are a Turkana village and an agricultural demonstration of "terraced" land to supplement the interior displays on soil conservation; a nature trail leads through a miniature rain forest, a remnant of pre-colonial days. There is also a reasonably priced and usually well-stocked craft shop featuring local wares. Although there's not enough of interest here to plan a lengthy stay, a night here might be inevitable if heading up to Mount Elgon or to break the drive to Lodwar and the western shores of Lake Turkana. In that case the best place to stay is the **Alakara Hotel** ((0325) 20395, Box 1984, Kitale, next

3,068-m (10,066-ft) Mount Kadam, beyond the Uganda border.

Across the Marich Pass we once encountered four boys in circumcision dress. They wore knee-length skin shirts with a rattle attached to the hem to warn passersby of their presence. Their faces and legs were whitened, giving them a ghostlike appearance as they waved their feather-tufted sticks. Only the fact that the rattles were made of soda bottle caps and their feet were clad in plastic sandals indicated that the twentieth century had altered their traditional way of life.

to the Post Office, at 1,200 KSh for a double. *Matatus* go every morning to Nairobi (seven hours), Lodwar near Lake Turkana (five hours) and Kisumu via Kakamega (two hours).

GOING NORTH

The well-paved A1 takes you through the savannas of Trans-Nzoia and along the western and northern slopes of the Cherangani Hills. After Kapenguria, the last gas before Lodwar, the scenery changes from open rolling hills to steep, forested mountains as you climb Marich Pass. On a clear day to the northwest, you can see jagged, unusually shaped mountains, the tallest of which is

Descending the pass, the road follows the Moran River, clear and fast-running over large granitic boulders. Once here we stopped to photograph a steep rocky gorge, not realizing there were two young fishermen below. A passerby came waving a steel bar in his hand to chase us off. We never decided why he was so hostile — perhaps an aversion to having any of his tribe photographed, or the boys may have been fishing illegally. It was another reminder that you should never photograph anyone without asking permission, especially where tourists are not common.

OPPOSITE AND ABOVE: Turkana's El Molo tribe, which subsists principally on fish, is not averse to eating crocodile.

Near the pass you'll see young people selling decorated gourds along the roadside for 10 KSh to 40 KSh a piece. We've seen none of the same style elsewhere in Kenya.

Emerging from the Cherangani Hills, you again look down into the Rift Valley with its extinct volcanoes of varying sizes. To the northwest is 3,325-m (10,910-ft) **Sigogowa** or **Mtelo Mountain**, the Pokot sacred mountain and one of the sources of the Turkwell River. The Pokot bury their dead on the mountain with their heads facing the summit. It's possible to hike to the top of

in the wild. Nonetheless there are plenty of snakes in Kenya and many are deadly poisonous. Generally they are extremely shy and would prefer not to be seen. A heavy footstep will usually send them to cover. Always carry drinking water, matches and some emergency rations. And don't forget a hat!

As you continue north toward the Jade Sea, the scenery becomes less and less varied, more alien. Familiar vegetation begins to disappear as the land becomes more and more arid.

Sigogowa, but you need a full day for the trek and a local guide. The easiest climb is from the village of **Sigor**, the major Pokot market center, on the north side of Marich Pass.

When hiking in Kenya remember that there are always dangers. The more remote the area the more likely you are to encounter wild animals and particularly predators. Never hike alone. Wear sturdy shoes, or preferably hiking boots, and make plenty of noise to alert the wildlife and particularly snakes of your presence. During our most recent trip to Kenya, only our 10 year-old son saw a snake, and a friend who has lived in Kenya for 18 years and run her own safari company has only seen three

It is a long 250 km (155 miles) from Sigor to the west shore of **Lake Turkana**, but the road is excellent and you'll be slowed only by the 47 fords along the way. During rains you must allow extra time because at any moment flood waters can make these fords impassable. You are likely to find yourself waiting for a couple of hours until the water subsides.

In any case, you will be able to watch the subtle changes in the area as you go from tall thorn trees to sparser, squatter thornscrub to golden grasses and doum palms. And the soils change as well. From the traditional African red, it fades to coral, then pastel pink, and finally to sandy white. The few clouds are like puffballs; dust devils swirl about the barren volcanic hills and across dry river beds where women and children dig for water. The hunt for water is endless and if you pass anyone waving a plastic bottle or gourd, he is asking for water. If you have enough, stop and offer some. Water is the most precious gift you can give. Any empty container that can hold water is almost as valuable.

There are the familiar livestock — goats, sheep, and cows — but now there are also camels, blending into the sandy scenery. Hares, squirrels, gazelles, sunis, and jackals are the major, though scarce, wildlife.

LOKICHAR

The only settlement of any size along the route is Lokichar, where a local mission has organized an excellent Turkana crafts co-operative (which is closed on Sundays). The shop is well stocked with baskets and mats, Turkana bead necklaces and bracelets, wrist and finger knives, carvings, bowls, and beaded goat skin aprons. The variety is great, the quality good, the prices fair. Like the Cottage Shop in Nairobi, there is no middleman taking a cut, so we recommend that you not bargain here. The proprietor told us that it took a week to make a basket that we purchased for 40 KSh. It is hard to offer less.

Lokichar and Lodwar have the unfortunate history of being sites of Kenyatta's detention by the English during the Mau Mau rebellion. Even today with a paved road they seem remote and it is easy to imagine how alien they must have seemed to Kenyatta, with no electricity or guaranteed source of water after the lushness of Kikuyuland. Certainly the lack of green was a great deprivation to one so unjustly detained.

LODWAR

Lodwar's inauspicious history began in 1933 when a Pakistani trader, Shah Mohammed, arrived with his donkey on the banks of the seasonal Turkwell River. He eventually built a permanent trading center which today is the last stop on the road to Sudan. It now has a 24-hour gas station, and is a veritable boom town since the road has been paved and Norwegian and Italian fish-canning projects arrived, neither of which have been successful.

The town is an interesting mix of old and new. On its outskirts are traditional Turkana straw domed-huts. In town, radios blare from concrete buildings. There are a few hotelis and restaurants, and large missionary complexes competing for members, one offering "Salvation Music." Best place to stay is the **Turkwel Lodge (** (0393) 21201, Box 14, Lodwar, at 700 KSh for a double including breakfast. This is one town where having a fan is essential!

THE LAKE SHORE

To reach the western shore of **Lake Turkana**, you continue 24 km (15 miles) north of Lodwar before choosing a lakeside destination — turn right on a dirt road for the 48 km (30 mile) trip to **Eliye Springs** or stick to the murram for the 42 km (26 mile) journey to **Ferguson's Gulf**. Only Ferguson's Gulf is regularly served by matatu: there's one most days, and the trip takes about an hour. Get off at the village of Kalokol and walk to the

OPPOSITE: Twenth-seven tons of ivory, confiscated from poachers, go up in smoke. ABOVE: A member of Kenya's northern desert anti-poaching unit. The government has adopted a shoot-to-kill policy in a last-ditch attempt to save its remaining elephants.

lakeshore: this can take an hour and a half and the sun is hot so carry plenty of water.

Eliye Springs had bandas and a lodge, but this is now only a primitive campsite. Water is usually available, but before making the rough 42-km (26-mile) drive, check in Lodwar if anyone knows the latest status of the place. In any event make sure you have enough water for at least one day. The site is usually deserted and tranquil. You will, however, probably be visited by local children once the nearby village becomes aware of your presence. Very few visitors make it here: it is the more attractive of the two settlements on the lake's western shore and worth the drive if you have the vehicle and camping equipment.

In any case you'll be camping at Ferguson's Gulf: the luxury lodge six kilometers (four miles) north is closed and seems likely to stay that way.

Whichever you choose, be ready for an experience of unreality and strangeness. The air is dry, the sun so intense that all color fades. But then there are minute variations in the landscape—bleached sand, golden grasses, and sapphire sky and jade lake. Occasionally there is a dash of green, but only in the first week following the rains in October and November or April and May. They dry all too quickly.

The sun rises red to announce each new day as hippopotamuses return to the coolness of the lake. Young Turkana begin their march to the sea to fill sundry containers with the brackish water. Some pause for a quick, playful swim, always aware they share the water with crocodiles. Sacred ibis patrol the shore, cormorants bob for fish and Egyptian geese float silently.

Later the young men arrive with nets which they lay from their raft-like boats to trap Nile perch. Mothers bring their infants to bathe. Children chase and scream along the shore. Some make a game out of washing clothes, stamping on them in their wash buckets as if they were mashing grapes.

The shore is a hub of measured activity: graceful human figures gliding on shimmering sand, a herd of sheep and goats browsing the tan, gilded grass, a white, glinting scatter

The barren shorelines of Lake Turkana, the Jade Sea.

of shorebirds. Northward, the land leaves a blank horizon, where the Jade Sea extends forever carrying your eye off the edge of the globe straight into space in which this earth floats like a tiny speck in a more infinite sea.

As sunset approaches, a glow creeps across the sky like a giant jacaranda dropping its purple snow, and people glide gracefully, loads atop their heads, back to their dune dwellings. All is silent except for the snorts of hippos as they leave the water to graze along the shore until the sun rises red again.

For the young, school has been added to this rhythm. Most learn the standard Kenyan curriculum in a thatch hut among the dunes; those whose parents can afford it go to the boarding school in Lokwa Kangoli. What changes education will make in their age-old lifestyle in this dry, fragile environment cannot be foretold.

Their survival is constantly threatened. Over the past years Lake Turkana had receded 150 m (500 ft) from Lake Turkana Lodge (now closed). One theory for this recession is the major irrigation projects in Ethiopia on the Omo River that feeds Lake Turkana. The 1998 El Niño rains went some way to bring the levels back up, but growing African desertification and global climate change are certainly contributing to a long-term change.

Regardless of the reason, the "drying" of Lake Turkana has left facilities constructed for fishing projects high and dry. The Norwegians and Italians are still in the area, but their projects have not had expected returns. Fish populations have been substantially reduced. Fishermen frequently have to go now to Central Island in search of a catch, which they dry on the island before returning to sell it to the Norwegian packing plant in Kalokol.

Unlike most national parks and reserves, Turkana's shores can be explored on foot. Crocodiles don't appear to be a problem, but there are many in the area. Early morning and late afternoon are still the best times because the midday sun is unmercifully hot. Along the shore you can find giant Nile perch skeletons, which we first took to be crocodile bones; and some of the many children who will try to accompany you on your expeditions will offer to sell you croc teeth —

the Crocodile Dundees of Africa. They will also pose for a photographic fee, request T-shirts, and give you their addresses if you wish to strike up a friendship. If you want to see crocodile bones ask one of the children to show you the way.

Admittedly there is not a great variety of destinations or sights to see, but the ephemeral quality of the environment weaves its spell.

CENTRAL ISLAND NATIONAL PARK

Another option is a half-day trip to Central Island National Park which costs 2,500 KSh per boat for a maximum of eight passengers, although the park fee will add US$15 per adult and US$5 per child. Approximately 20 km (12 miles) southeast of Ferguson's Gulf, this island sanctuary is the most concentrated breeding ground for crocodiles in Africa. The five-square-kilometer (two-square-mile) island is three connected Park volcanic cones, two of which contain fresh water lakes. The island shores are black lava sand and rock, and the vegetation thorny, bleached scrub.

The southern and smallest cone, a five- to ten-minute hike from the shore, is the domain of the crocodiles, a turquoise rimmed lake with an iridescent, almost algal verdancy of brilliant scrub. From the rim above you can see crocodiles cruising like immense sunken logs, only the knobs of their eyes showing. If you are in Kenya during April and May, this crater can be "the" place to be, and not just to get away from the rain. It's hatching season and the crater is alive with squeaks and yelps of the young, who will spend their first year here before heading out to the Jade Sea. Some, however, spend their entire lives in the crater.

A morning trip is usually the best for viewing the reptiles, while the afternoon excursions frequently include a trip to the northern cauldron and its pink flamingos standing one-legged along the shore. As there are supposedly no crocs here, we once climbed down the steep dusty trail to the water's edge. Scorpions leapt from a trailside boulder as we descended. The flamingos rose and

An El Molo, fishing from his *ambach* raft, pulls in a crocodile.

circled to the far side of the lake, which is larger than it appears from above. Butterflies rode the updrafts. We walked across the hard, cracked mud where scorpions nest. Further on, flat pinnacles of calcified mud rose above the water, where you can walk as if they were stepping stones. The water's edge is thick with algae and almost too hot to touch. Across the lake the flamingos can appear like a pink ribbon edging the brown pleated crater wall.

Central Island has more than its share of shorebirds, a few hippos, and a resident lizard population. We saw several lava-colored reptiles over a meter (a yard) long. As we left, four hippos decided they'd had enough of the tourists for the day and blocked the route of the boat. Making light of what could have been a nasty situation, one of our French companions for the trip joked that the hippos only wanted to have their photos taken and to give us their address. And what's more they didn't ask for 20 KSh!

If you are on a tight budget, you can sometimes find a local fisherman who'll take you to Central Island for about 500 KSh per boat and hope the park ranger isn't around. If you go this route make sure the boat is seaworthy and has plenty of fuel, and that the crew is experienced. Turkana's weather can change suddenly and winds can quickly whip up meter (yard)-tall waves.

For a trip to the island, wear sturdy shoes: sandals just won't make it. Bring a hat, sun screen and water. The island is hot by 10 AM and remains so until dusk.

ACROSS THE LAKE

The third and most exciting of opportunities is a two or three day trip across the lake to **Sibiloi National Park** and a visit to **Koobi Fora** (see page 190 and page 189, respectively). Other than flying to Sibiloi, this is the most comfortable, relaxing way to get there, and crossing Lake Turkana is exhilarating, unless of course you are prone to seasickness. This is not something that can be easily achieved on the spur of the moment: it's not a trip to make in an unreliable boat and in any case you will need to be sure there is a vehicle — with gasoline — at Allia Bay. Plans for the journey must be made in advance: get in touch with **Let's Go Travel** (02) 340331

FAX (02) 336890 E-MAIL info@letsgosafari .com, Box 60342, Nairobi. From Ferguson's Gulf it takes about three hours to make the crossing to **Allia Bay**. Time of departure depends on the weather. At Allia Bay, you are met by a guide with a four-wheel drive, who will take you to the bandas, prepare your meals, ferry you to the archaeological digs, and take you on game drives.

For this trip you will want to bring sturdy shoes, hat, sun screen, wind breaker, and a change or two of clothes.

If you want to visit Lake Turkana while in Kenya, it is difficult for us to recommend one side over the other, as we would each choose a different shore. They are strikingly varied but equally mystifying. A trip to either side is costly in time and/or money, and unfortunately there is no easy way to make a round trip. Surprisingly, few if any boats seem to make the 12-hour crossing from Ferguson's Gulf to Loyangalani where there is, in any case, no reliable transportation south. No journey to Kenya is truly complete until you've been there and there's something captivating about the hot, dusty frontier atmosphere of the northern towns.

The only way back from Ferguson's Gulf is the way you came. The return drive is not so tedious as one would imagine. The boys on the way back tried to come up with a different make of automobile for each ford. Truly a sign that we had been on safari too long! (Another sign of being of safari too long are silly jokes like: "Why does the giraffe have a long neck? Because he can't stand the smell of his own feet.")

Along the return, colors are one by one added to the previously monochrome landscape until you are once again into the verdant greens of the Marich Pass. It probably didn't seem quite so green or cool on your northward journey.

ELGON AND VICTORIA

SAIWA SWAMP NATIONAL PARK

Eighteen kilometers (11 miles) north of Kitale is the 26-sq-km (10-sq-mile) Saiwa Swamp National Park, entry US$15 per adult, US$5 per child, created to protect the rare and

A rocky outcrop on Mount Elgon.

endangered semiaquatic Sitatunga antelope. First classified by Speke, the Sitatunga have highly specialized, splayed, and elongated hooves that allow them to spread their weight over a greater area than a normal hoof would permit. They are thus able to move about the swamp, semi-submerged. They swim well and are reputed to submerge, leaving only their nostrils showing, when threatened.

Several tree blinds have been constructed along the western edge of the swamp to provide viewing. As usual, late afternoon or early morning are the best times for watching these normally shy and increasingly rare creatures. The swamp has also become the home for the white-bearded brazza monkey, and colobus and vervet monkeys, which can be spotted at almost any time of the day. And even if the Sitatunga are being shy, there are plenty of bushbuck to keep your interest.

Bird watchers should enjoy the turacos, cuckoos, kingfishers, hornbills, and crowned cranes. Following the rains, you will get the extra bonus of innumerable butterflies and mountain orchids. And on very rare occasions, when pushing the dusk curfew, you may find a potto.

At any time of the year, the swamp is cool and a wool sweater will be welcome. Also bring film with a fast film (1,000 to 1,600 ISO) rating if you plan to take photos, as there is not much light in the swamp of the Sitatunga. Primitive camping (US$2 per person) near the park entrance is the only accommodation, and running water the only amenity.

MOUNT ELGON

After the heat of Eldoret, Lake Turkana, and Lake Victoria, the massive, cloud-cloaked slopes of Mount Elgon offer a refreshing relief. Mount Elgon is the bulkiest of Africa's mountains, having the largest mass. Only 877 m (2,877 ft) shorter than Mount Kenya, Mount Elgon (Ol Doinyo Ilgoon — "Breast Mountain" in Maa) straddles the Ugandan border. The first European to climb to the top was Frederick Jackson, in 1890.

The highest peak on the rocky crater, Wagagai, at 4,322 m (14,178 ft), is actually in Uganda outside the national park. You may have great trouble getting a guide to take you there, or find yourself on the wrong side of the border without a reentry visa. The Mountain Club of Kenya does not recommend climbing this peak because of the potential border problems, and the occasional presence of hostile, armed Ugandan rebels. Recommended instead are short hikes within the park itself, paying the daily fee of US$10 (adult) or US$5 (child), or freely outside the park limits.

Mount Elgon National Park is a hiking and camping paradise that is seldom visited. Wildlife is plentiful, and there are specified hiking trails to the major caves, along **Elephant Platform**, or to 4,038-m (13,248-ft) **Koitoboss Peak**, the highest of Mount Elgon's peaks in Kenya.

The hiking is especially good because the driving is singularly bad. You will often be denied admission unless you have a four-wheel drive. Indeed, it is doubtful that you could be able to get as far as the gate if you didn't have four-wheel drive. We once met an American family in Kisumu whose rental car could not, even during a dry spell, tackle the steep climb to the **Kitum** or **Elephant Caves**, once one of the major attractions in the park.

Along the eastern slope of Mount Elgon is a series of enormous caverns — **Kitum**, **Mkingeny**, and **Chipmyalil Caves**. During colonial times, they were inhabited by Maasai and thought to be man-made. Descriptions of them by the explorer Joseph Thomson supposedly inspired the English writer, H. Rider Haggard, to site part of his famed novel *She* in the El Goni caves.

It is now, however, the accepted theory that the caves were over the millennia dug by elephants in search of salt. And there is certainly enough elephant dung on their floors to support this theory. When we visited, we wondered how the elephants could have moved some of the gigantic boulders that littered the floor. This mystery was explained by Mike Clifton, the naturalist at The Ark (see THE ABERDARES, page 155). They were deposited there during an earthquake which coincidentally was filmed.

"A film crew had obtained a permit to set up lights in Kitum Cave to film the elephants at night," Mike said. "On one particular night, while elephants were present and film rolling, the cave ceiling began to fall. The footage was spectacular with the giant animals fleeing to avoid the shower of rock."

"However, during the next week, the director had his film confiscated and his research visa revoked. He was accused of having set off explosives in the cave. Luckily, he was able to prove from seismographic data at the university that there had indeed been an earthquake whose shock waves, not explosives, had caused the rock shower. The footage was recovered and used as part of a television documentary on elephants."

If you want to go to **Koitoboss Peak**, check with the rangers at the entrance of Elgon National Park as to the dangers of hiking. If they see no problem, the trail starts at the end of the "drivable" track to the northern boundary of the park, and should take between two to three hours. From the peak, a trail leads to the left across glacial moraines, down into the crater and the Suam warm springs for a relaxing bath. This can be done in a day, but get an early start in order to be out of the park or back to your campsite by the 6:30 PM curfew.

These caves were also the setting for the movie *Quest for Fire*. However without doubt the caves' biggest claim to international fame was as suspected epicenter for the Ebola Virus immortalized in the film *The Hot Zone*. Despite several spacesuited research expeditions by American scientific teams no connection was ever proved. Although in Richard Preston's famous book the link is left as a hanging question, it is far from certain there is in fact any connection. Hard-hit hoteliers blame the international media for yet another scare story. Nonetheless, the caves are eerie, and you'd be wise to bring a flashlight and extra batteries if you wish to explore. Thousands of bats of several species darken the sky as they flock into the dust.

The forests of Mount Elgon are among the most impressive in Kenya, with giant podos (podocarpus), junipers, and Elgon olive trees, the largest variety of olive in East Africa. Some reach heights of 25 m (80 ft). Flowers are abundant in the forest and moorlands at all times of the year, but they are at their peak in June and July when you can also find several varieties of terrestrial and epiphytic orchids.

The park's animals are extensive but well-hidden. They include the Sykes', brazza, and colobus monkeys, olive baboons, civets, genets, the rare golden cat, giant forest hogs,

The giant groundsel *(Senecio)* grow to 10 m (33 ft) on the highest slopes of Mounts Kenya and Elgon and the Aberdares.

bush pigs, duikers, sunis, and bushbuck. Leopards are fairly common but difficult to see, and usually not dangerous. Buffalo are frequent up to at least 3,000 m (10,000 ft), and should be treated with extreme caution. Elephants are rare due to poaching, and the black rhino is gone.

Where to Stay
You can either camp in the park or stay at **Mount Elgon Lodge** ((02) 229751 or (02) 330820 FAX (02) 227815, Box 42013, Nairobi, for US$70 to US$120 for a double, full board. The lodge is two kilometers (just over a mile) before the Chorlin gate. Formerly a colonial estate, the lodge has several elegant spacious rooms with large bay windows in the manor house, and double cottages on grounds with sculptured shrubs and formal glades. Days on Mount Elgon are warm, but, like Mount Kenya and the Aberdares, the nights are chilly, near-freezing at the higher campsites. Even at the lodge, a sweater and/or jacket will be useful, particularly if there are no logs blazing the dining room's massive two-meter (six-foot) fireplace.

Let's Go Travel in Nairobi keeps a list of private estates on Mount Elgon which take visitors on an occasional and usually expensive basis: otherwise there are several grassy campsites in the park (US$2 per person), all with running water keeps a list of **Kapkuru Campground**, 500 m (1,640 ft) from Chorlin gate, is at the lowest elevation and would be the best place to stop unless you have plenty of warm clothes and heavy sleeping bags. If you are planning to camp at Mount Elgon, be sure to buy provisions in Kitale. In our estimation, the best way to see Mount Elgon is to camp and hike.

How to Get There
The difficulty of getting to Mount Elgon National Park and the limited accommodations are probably part of the reason this park is not more popular. As we said before, a four-wheel drive vehicle is recommended year-round. The best access is through the Chorlin gate, 27 km (17 miles) from Kitale, via Endebess Road (watch the signs carefully and ask directions if in doubt). It will take the better part of an hour to cover this distance. For the first 19 km (12 miles) pavement heads

west from Kitale to the village to Enderbess, which is as far as you'll get by *matatu* — or indeed, saloon car. The rest of the distance to Chorlin gate is rough: if hitching don't expect more than a couple of vehicles to pass each day.

KAKAMEGA

Much of the area between Mount Elgon and Lake Victoria is rolling hills, steep escarpments, and narrow valleys. The entire area was once thick tropical rain forest. Kenya's burgeoning population and extensive logging have reduced the original forest to a few scattered remnants, which the government has recently tried to protect by gazetting as forest reserves.

One of the most important of these — well, about the only one that still exists — is the world-famous **Kakamega Forest Reserve**, located just east of the town of the same name. You can reach it easily from Mount Elgon by driving south through **Kitale** and **Webuye**, beyond which the huge, dark-cliffed **Nandi Escarpment** extends on your left.

Conservationists in Kenya are now attempting to change the status of the Kakamega Forest to a national park, but at present it is just a reserve: entry fee is just 100 KSh. Unfortunately this won't pay for any environmental protection measures — well, to be honest not enough visitors make it here anyway — and human encroachment continues apace. The forest, all that remains of the equatorial jungle that once stretched from the Atlantic through the Zaire basin, may not survive for much longer. Kakamega is similar to the equatorial rain forests of West Africa but drier. As a result, much flora and fauna are found in Kakamega Forest that exist nowhere else in Kenya, or probably the world. At least 350 bird species have been identified in the 100 sq km (39 sq miles) that remain of the original forest, including turacos, parrots, trogons, barbets and woodpeckers, honeyguides, greenbuls, and crowned hawk eagles.

Whereas the typical North American or European temperate zone forest may contain an average of eight to ten tree species per hectare, equatorial rain forests like Kakamega often have 100 to 150 different tree species per hectare. This amazing diversity of vegetation supports an equal variety of animals; over 40% of the mammals in the Kakamega Forest live in the trees, and some amphibians, insects, and reptiles never descend to the ground. More than half the mammals inhabiting Kakamega are nocturnal, sleeping during the day in tree hollows or high in the branches.

The proposed Kakamega Forest National Park will provide at least temporary protection to the undamaged part of the forest. This is the portion lying northeast of the town

rest. This means that most of the population settle in areas such as Kakamega and use up its resources.

The flowering plants of Kakamega bloom most colorfully after the long rains, from July to September, when the forest's butterflies are at their peak. From various points in the forest, the hiker can see the grassland, **Nandi Plateau**, escarpments to the east, and the **Kisere Forest** to the north. The major tree species include ebony, podocarpus, teak, mukumari (*Cordia africana*)—favored by bees, and seven species of fig including the "stran-

of Kakamega, including nearly half the watershed of the Isiukhu River. However, even if the park is approved, the pressures on the forest are so overwhelming that it will probably not last long as a viable habitat for the rare species still remaining there.

Kakamega's problems are similar to those threatening all the parks, reserves, and wildlife of Kenya: logging (both authorized and illegal); firewood collection, which kills young trees; cutting of saplings for household and agricultural use; livestock grazing; and game poaching. The root cause of all these is population growth. Kenya not only has the world's fastest birth rate, desertification is growing and further areas are made unsafe by politically motivated tribal un-

gler fig." The latter is a huge, broad-canopied tree found in most hardwood forests in Kenya, from Lake Victoria to the Matthews Range and the coast. It usually propagates when its fruit is eaten by birds or monkeys, whose droppings may be excreted on the branch of another tree species. The seed then grows, sending down long tendrils to the earth for nutrients and water. Over a period of years, these tendrils multiply, thicken, and join, until the fig completely encompasses its host tree, killing it, and growing above and around it, to achieve the great height and wide crown often seen in Kakamega.

The Mount Elgon Lodge ABOVE, once a rancher's idyllic estate. OVERLEAF: Many Maasai still practice polygamy; many may have twenty or more children.

Specially worth noting in Kakamega Forest are the red-tailed, Sykes', and colobus monkeys, giant forest squirrels up to 65 cm (26 inches) in length and flying squirrels which can glide up to 19 m (60 ft) from tree to tree, the ant-eating tree pangolin, the giant fruit bat, the potto, bush babies, the rare leopard and more common wild forest hogs, baboons (near the Buyango Hill road), and the occasional duiker that has escaped poaching.

The forest was once home to the elephant (exterminated by white hunters before the First World War), Cape buffalo, Uganda kob

If bitten, pressure bandages are the only approved method of treatment before medical advice is sought: try to kill the snake for identification. To our knowledge, however, no tourist has expired from snakebite in Kenya for many years.

The Gaboon viper, like its similarly-patterned cousin, the puff adder, which is more common in open country and closer to the coast, is viviparous, bearing its young alive. It may give birth to 80 offspring at a time, all of which, in true snake fashion, are on their own from the moment of birth.

(a small, reddish, thickset antelope with ringed horns), and the Defassa waterbuck, all of which are now gone.

Still present, though the tourist is unlikely to see them, are snakes. They include at least five highly poisonous cobras and mambas, and the delightful Gaboon viper, Africa's biggest poisonous snake, which can grow to over two meters (six feet) and weighs up to 11 kg (25 lbs). Its fangs are over five centimeters (two inches) long. Although its bite is fatal to humans, the Gaboon viper is not usually aggressive unless cornered or annoyed. The tourist who keeps to the trails in Kakamega, and is willing to tread heavily (and carry a big stick), need generally not fear an unscheduled demise by snakebite.

Where to Stay

The **Kakamega Forest Rest House** is famous among ornithologists, naturalists, and just plain tourists for self-help rooms in a rotting wooden building set amid a dense grove of trees (US$2 per person); some space is available for camping and if I had a tent I'd use it here. Space is limited, so it's best to make reservations first with the Kakamega Forest Ranger (no phone), Box 88, Kakamega. In any case, accommodation is basic at best. For urban comforts you'll need to stay in Kakamega town at the **Golf Hotel (** (02) 229751 or (02) 330820 FAX (02) 227815, Box 42013, Nairobi, at US$75 for double with bed and breakfast. It has handsome large rooms overlooking elegant lawns pecked by vultures, a swimming pool, and cheerful staff.

How to Get There

Kakamega town is 50 km (31 miles) north of Kisumu on the main A1 road heading north to Lodwar. By public transportation the most frequent *matatus* run from Webuye and Kisumu.

Finding the forest from the town can appear confusing unless you realize that there are two access points into the forest: both, in their way, worth visiting. Thus equally valid may be missing, however). Drive 13 km (eight miles) through the village of Shinyalu, past the reserve boundary and the Isicheno Forest Station and turn left for the last few hundred meters to the Forest Rest House. By public transportation ask for the daily *matatu* traveling between Kakamega town and Eldoret via Shinyalu village and Kapsabet: ask to be dropped at Isecheno, ten minutes walk from the Forest Rest House. At either forest station, it's possible to hire a guide.

Heading south from Kakamega you may see men pushing bicycles laden with large

directions can send you in opposite directions. With your own vehicle, drive from Kakamega either south toward Kisumu or north toward Webuye. Going north, you pass Lubao and turn right (east) some 16 km (10 miles) from Kakamega, just before the road to Kambiri, at the sign reading "Ministry of Tourism and Wildlife." From there, it's two and a quarter kilometers (nearly one and a half miles) to a forest station set among subsistence farms and a recently clearcut pine forest. If using public transportation, take a *matatu* heading towards Webuye, but you'll have to walk the last stretch from the main road. Going south, you drive 10 km (six miles) toward Shikondi and turn left (east) on to a dirt road at the sign "Forest Rest House," (the sign burlap sacks — these are 90-kg (200-lb) bags of maize kernels being transported all the way to Kisumu. Depending where the man began, this may be a distance of 60 km (37 miles) or more, nearly all of it up and down steep hills. For this he receives, if the maize is good, about as much as tourists pay for a quick meal at a lodge.

KISUMU

Suddenly, you break through the last of the foothills above Kisumu, and **Lake Victoria**, resplendent, blue, and expansive, lies before you. It feels very much the same

OPPOSITE: Foreplay is an intricate part of lion courtship. ABOVE: The Thinker: an olive baboon.

as dropping down to the Mediterranean from the French or Italian Alps or the Costa del Sol, of reaching the Pacific from the northern California Coast Range, or of coming down to the Caspian from the Caucasus. It is a sense of the infinity of both land and sea.

The land is green and everywhere cultivated; the water is flat, reflecting the sky, and free of man except when a small boat cuts across it. Above Kisumu, a white Coptic church is set against the slope as if transported from the Cyclades.

The sprawling city of Kisumu has, like Mombasa, a maritime atmosphere due to its former eminence as a major port on Lake Victoria. The upper part of the city contains many large colonial buildings and residences, set amid more recent shanties and modern structures, on well-shaded wide streets leading down to the port.

At the main traffic roundabout coming into town, you'll find the market and bus station, noisy and teeming with people. Overloaded buses seem to leave every moment for the ends of the earth while black-belching *matatus* are jammed like sardine cans, the squeezed faces of passengers stacked against the dirty windows; other riders hang out the half-shut doors or cling desperately by fingertip to the roof rims and windows, their feet dangling over the speeding pavement.

At this roundabout, you can turn east toward **Kericho** and **Nakuru** or continue south on Jomo Kenyatta Highway into Kisumu itself. To get to the port, turn right after another kilometer (half mile) at the next roundabout, and descend Oginga Odinga Road past the elegant white British Council and Library.

In the days of the East African Community, when Kenya, Tanzania, and Uganda were loosely united in a common market and transportation scheme, the port of Kisumu boomed with shipping to and from Kampala in Uganda, and Musoma and Mwanza in Tanzania. Since 1977, each nation has become responsible for its own transport networks and the port's business has declined. Yet the town itself is busy, and a walk through its jammed, colorful streets, with their traces of Victorian gingerbread

and colonial prosperity, is well worth an hour or two.

It was at Kisumu that the final spike of the "lunatic line to nowhere," the Uganda Railway, was driven on December 19, 1901. It had taken more than five years to build, covered a distance of 920 km (570 miles), cost £5,500,000, and employed a total of 31,983 people, many of whom perished from man-eating lions, accidents, tribal warfare, and disease.

Kisumu was called Port Florence in honor of Florence Preston, a woman of great endurance who accompanied her husband, Ronald, the line's railhead engineer, the entire length of the railway from Mombasa to Lake Victoria. It was she who drove the final spike on that last day.

The town was not considered unduly attractive in its early years. One historian, Charles Miller, described it as the least desirable place to be posted in the British Empire, "a pesthouse, conspicuously vulnerable to malaria, dysentery, blackwater fever and a broad range of other tropical scourges. During construction of the railway, an epidemic of sleeping sickness swept the town and took nearly five hundred African lives. For some years, bubonic plague was endemic in Kisumu."

Those days are long gone. Today, Kisumu, though still packed and hot, is an enjoyable stop, especially if one wishes to take a boat across Lake Victoria or continue on southward to **Ruma National Park**. Although Lake Victoria had long served as a transit and shipping zone for Arab slave traders (the lake's indigenous sailboat is rigged with the same lateen sail as the Arab coastal dhow), it was only after the opening of the Uganda Railway that Kisumu acquired commercial status. It soon became the largest Kenyan community on the lake. Despite the failure of the East African Community, Kisumu now has a thriving fish industry, a sugar refinery, marine workshops, and flour, textile, and cotton mills, threatened only by the rafts of hyacinth that might look pretty but are in imminent danger of stifling all life on the lake.

Worth a visit in Kisumu are the **British Council Library** ((035) 45004, at the top of Oginga Odinga, which has a selection of books and periodicals, the new **Kisumu Museum**, on the Nairobi road east of town, with ethnographic exhibits and more animals than some zoos, and the **Kisumu Park**, with orphan leopard and monkeys pacing in cages and an expanse of unspoiled lakefront, safe-ish for walking as far as the Sunset Hotel, but not, as friendly park wardens are quick to point out, any further.

Where to Stay

Kisumu is an ideal base for exploring Western Kenya. The city has two luxury alter-

with bed and breakfast. Cheapest is the **Western Lodge ((035) 42586, Box 276, Kisumu, on Kendu Lane, at 500 KSh, bed only.

How to Get There

**Kenya Airways ((02) 210771 or (02) 229291 FAX (02) 336252, Box 41010, Nairobi, flies once or twice a day between Kisumu and Nairobi: flight time is one hour, the cost is US$50 one way. Note that in Nairobi, they do not fly from Wilson Airport but use the International Terminal. Their office in Kisumu ((0345) 44055 FAX (0345) 43339 is on Oginga

natives: the **Imperial Hotel ((035) 41470 FAX (035) 40345, Box 1866, Kisumu, located on Jomo Kenyatta Highway near Oginga Odinga Road (3,900 KSh for a double with bed and breakfast), which also offers suites and long-let apartments; and the **Sunset Hotel ((0345) 41100, Box 215, Kisumu (US$72 for a double with bed and breakfast), located just south of the city center, bookable through **ATH ((02) 336858, Box 30471, Nairobi. Get up to the roof for the best view of Lake Victoria and, when the wind's onshore, the vast rafts of hyacinth engulfing the port. Less expensive but still good is the **New Victoria Hotel ((035) 21067, Box 276, Kisumu on Gor Mihia Street: doubles with balconies over-looking the city center and lake cost 900 KSh

Odinga Street. Buses and *matatus* leave morning and evening for the six- to eight-hour journey to Nairobi. Trains leave daily for Nairobi at 6 PM, arriving the next morning at 7 AM, although the service can be suspended for long periods, especially during the rainy seasons. Reservations are essential for first- (2,200 KSh) and second-(1,800 KSh) class travel. Kisumu Railway Station is at the lakeside end of New Station Road, and the booking office is open 8 AM to noon and 2 PM to 4 PM. Lake ferries link small towns and islands along the coast as well as Mwanza in Tanzania from the port.

The hyena plays an essential role as scavenger of the savanna, but will kill his prey when he can.

LAKE VICTORIA

The source of the White Nile, Lake Victoria is 69,490 sq km (26,830 sq miles). It is Africa's largest, and the world's second largest, freshwater lake. Its waters travel some 3,700 km (2,300 miles) to the Mediterranean Sea. If you have the time and the weather's good, a boat trip out on the lake is fun. It's not easy, however, to find the passenger port — turn left about midway off Oginga Odinga Road before you get to the Caltex depot, although this involves lengthy negotiations with both the immigration department, and the skipper of the cargo ferry. The crossing will take 12 hours or more.

If you decide to travel Lake Victoria by boat, try to get a good idea of what the weather would be like the rest of the day. The lake can seem placid, then turn rough suddenly. Most important, remember that the lake is dangerous. Like most slow-moving or stationary fresh water in Kenya, it is a source of bilharzia, a sickness derived from minuscule flukes that live in snails and bore

and cross to a dilapidated freight yard where you may ask employees for directions to the steamer booking office. There, at a very reasonable price, you can buy a round-trip ticket to any one of several lake communities in Kenya.

Kendu Bay, **Kuwur**, **Asembo Bay**, and **Homa Bay** are the main destinations, and often there is no way to return to Kisumu until the next day. Similarly, you can leave on Tuesday for **Homa Bay**, returning Wednesday, or can depart Wednesday and Friday for the port of **Mbita** (on **Rusinga Island**) and **Mfangano Island**, again returning the following day. It's a local boat so fares should vary around the low shilling level. It is possible to get across here to Uganda,

into the skin to multiply. The flukes take a few minutes to burrow through the skin so dry any freshwater splashes promptly.

When the prevailing wind frees the coast of hyacinth, the lake can be very beautiful. It also supplies a major portion of Kenya's protein. In fact, over 90% of Kenya's fish catch is freshwater; despite the country's long coast, only 10% of the catch is from the ocean. Lake Victoria produces much of this freshwater supply, although its resources have lately been reduced by the replacement of the original *tilapia* species, highly favored by the local Luo peoples, with the less-preferred Nile perch.

Kisumu's passenger ferries connect Kenya's major towns and islands on Lake Victoria.

It took four attempts by fishery biologists and the United States Agency for International Development (AID) before the more expensive perch adapted to the lake. The success of this experiment, however, spelled disaster for the resident *tilapia* which was almost wiped out.

In addition to being favored by the local restaurateurs, the *tilapia* is a fascinating fish, raising its young *in its mouth*. The male first clears a nest on the sandy lake bottom and attracts a female who lays her eggs there; he fertilizes them and she then gathers the eggs into her mouth and incubates them there. She is unable to eat during this entire period. After the fry hatch, the mother guards them for the first 10 days or so, gathering them back into her mouth at any sign of danger, and then ejecting them by swimming backward and blowing.

RUSINGA ISLAND

Rusinga offers a visit to the birthplace and mausoleum of Tom Mboya, the brilliant young civil rights activist and pro-Western Luo politician gunned down, apparently by Jomo Kenyatta's assassins, in Nairobi in 1969. Mboya was so beloved in Kenya that he stood in the way of an arranged transfer of power from Kenyatta to Daniel Arap Moi, and was accordingly eliminated. His life, accomplishments, and burial on Rusinga are recounted in Grace Ogot's *The Island of Tears*, required reading for anyone interested in Kenya or women's literature.

"To Kenyans," Ogot says, "Mboya was one of the greatest men who had ever been born by a woman. To the world beyond the seas, he was a symbol of stability, unity and peace. To the Lake Region people he was a warrior and a hero... He appeared to have been blessed by God of the mighty waters, so that he made blades of grass grow where there was nothing before. He had introduced the ferry which could carry people and vehicles... He had given the island adequate schools, good hospitals and roads. He had encouraged the islanders to adopt modern methods of farming. In ordinary conversation, people would say, 'Oh, it is as miraculous as Mboya's ferry,' or 'It is so big, like Mboya's school'..."

Rusinga Island was also the site of a major find in human prehistory, that of a *Proconsul africanus* skull discovered by Dr. Mary Leakey in 1948. An apelike primate estimated to have lived about 25 million years ago, *Proconsul africanus* may have been a direct ancestor of man, and is similar to two other *Proconsuls* considered likely to have led to the development of the chimpanzee and gorilla. **Rusinga Island Club** ((02) 447224 FAX (02) 447268 (US$460 per double for full board including all excursions) is the smart place to stay; otherwise there's a small, name-

less but friendly lodge in Mbita costing a hundredth as much. Rusinga is connected to the mainland by a causeway, and can be reached in an hour by car from Homa Bay, itself two hours' drive from Kisumu: rather quicker than by occasional lake ferries.

MOUNT HOMA

Leaving Kisumu, the Grand Safari takes you southward through the low hills behind the lake, past enchanting Mount Homa, which rises over 600 m (nearly 2,000 ft) above the shore. A hike to the mountain's top is worthwhile for the incomparable view it offers of the hyacinth-bound lake, volcanic plug islands, and the green hills. A local guide is advised. Although the town of Homa Bay suffers from humidity and insects, it offers a good place to stay in the **Homa Bay Hotel** ((02) 229751 or (02) 330820 FAX (02) 227815, Box 42013, Nairobi (US$75 for a double, bed and breakfast). It is also a suitable point from which to start exploration of the relatively unknown Ruma National Park.

RUMA NATIONAL PARK

Formerly known as Lambwe Valley Game Reserve, Ruma has 194 sq km (75 sq miles) of rolling savanna mixed with trees and brush. It is set between the lakeside **Gwasi Hills** and the sheer **Kaniamua Escarpment**. Hot, humid, and boggy during the rains, it is nonetheless one of the best places in Kenya to see several rare species such as the magnificent, scimitar-horned roan antelope, the huge, curve-horned Jackson's hartebeest, and the diminutive, graceful oribi. You may also see Rothschild's giraffes and the occasional leopard and cheetah.

The park's birdlife is spectacular and includes species not likely to be seen elsewhere such as the barefaced go-away bird, the blue-cheeked bee-eater, the Hartlaub's marsh widow-bird, the yellow-fronted tinkerbird, and the African mustached warbler. Despite the battering roads, Ruma is not to be missed.

KISII

From Homa Bay, it's 45 km (28 miles) of poor but passable tarmac to Kisii, pretty, full of energy, and developing rapidly with good architecture and dynamic people. Situated at an altitude of 1,700 m (5,580 ft), Kisii is a welcome relief from the sultry humidity and ubiquitous mosquitoes of Lake Victoria. It is one of the most vital, fastest-growing commercial centers in western Kenya.

Center of the one-and-a-half-million-strong Gusii tribe, Kisii was an area of strife early in this century, when nearly a thousand tribesmen were massacred by the British. Next came massive engagements between the British and Germans during the First World War, with the Gusii forced into service as British troops. Now it seems the most peaceful in Kenya, and its people among the most hospitable.

Sixteen kilometers (10 miles) south of Kisii is the village of **Tabaka**, where most of the world's soapstone comes from. This is the source of racked soapstone candlesticks, animals, vases and bowls which fill countless shelves in all of Kenya's souvenir stalls.

It's hard to believe. The village is friendly and small. The mines are to the east of the village, mountainsides laid bare to the sun and crowds of workers chipping out rocks. Different areas produce soapstone of various colors. The road is filled with workers carrying sacks and bags of stone or staggering under the weight of heavy chunks. Back at the village small, family-run factories carve and polish the rocks on piecework to precise formulae. Craftsmen—mainly women—chisel, polish, and paint, establishing a national art form for the entire country. You won't go short of shopping opportunities: It seems more ethical to sidestep capitalism and shop instead at one of the cooperatives, often set up with the help of foreign aid agencies. One is the **Kisco Co-op**, where profits are shared with the artists: see more at their shop on the route between the quarries to the north and the village. Almost every house in town is devoted to polishing and sanding soapstone carvings, washing the sculptures in water to soften the stone and finally waxing the finished product to give it the characteristic luster. Specialists focus on animal shapes, candlesticks or stylized sculptures, while others polish fruit-bowls, either sent for immediate export or delegated for etching and painting. Once racked in Nairobi shops or at Rift Valley viewpoint stalls, there are so many soapstone sculptures they start to look mundane, but at source the level of skill, craftsmanship and sheer effort is suddenly clear. Prices are low and this is a great place to buy lasting memories.

From Kisii, you can hike up to the **Manga Ridge** (ask directions at the Kisii Hotel), or trek among the green, terraced slopes reminiscent of the Himalaya foothills. You can also drive south to **Tarime** in Tanzania, or take the new macadam road to **Kilkoris**; from Kilkoris, you can cross the savanna on a dirt road to **Lolgorien**, at the foot of the Soit Ololol Escarpment, and suddenly you're back in the land of the Maasai.

Traditional Luo basket fishing on Lake Victoria.

Where to Stay

Kisii is the best base to explore the area, and there is another advantage: you can stay in the **Kisii Hotel (** (0381) 30134, Box 26, Kisii, a quaint hangover from colonial days, with spreading gardens overlooking the fields just below the hilly and potholed center of town. Its a comfortable and friendly place with good food and a bar full of gregarious people most evenings (700 KSh for a double, bed and breakfast).

How to Get There

With your own transportation, there are two routes to Kisii from Kisumu: fastest is to stick to the A1 heading south towards Tanzania. However it is well worth the detour to take the tarmac C19 that runs along the coast of Lake Victoria, and then link back with the A1 by taking the 20 km (14 miles) dirt road to Oyugis. It's a spectacular drive and doesn't take much longer. By public transportation, frequent *matatus* make the three-hour journey to Kisumu. Two bus companies link Kisii with Nairobi three times a day: reserve tickets a day in advance. The trip takes nine hours.

KERICHO

If you were asked the color of tea, you'd probably say brown or black. Once you've seen Kericho, tea will always mean green. For as far as you can see around the town of Kericho, tea plantations carpet the rolling hills. From a distance, the chest-high bushes look soft and cushy. Up close, they are brittle and sharp. Pickers wear oilskin aprons and protective sheaths on their picking fingers.

On any given day, you can usually see a crew (mostly women with male supervisors) working the fields. They move methodically across bright green rows to pick the thumbnail-sized leaves, returning every two weeks to each row. On a good day, one can pick up to 70 kg (150 lb) at 3 KSh per kilogram (1.34 KSh per pound). The baskets can hold between seven and twelve kilograms of tea and it takes about an hour and a half to fill the basket. A Luo woman who picked tea for nine years told us that some days were better than others. "After several hours of picking, your fingers always get sore and eventually

they are covered with calluses. It is hard work, but a relatively secure job with a wage that is determined by how hard you work." The almost daily rainfall in Kericho has made it the tea capital of Kenya. Over the past two years, tea has steadily grown as an industry, surpassing earnings from coffee.

Because most of the inhabitants of the area live and work on the tea plantations, the town of Kericho is mainly a shopping, and not a trading, center. Stores in town cater to the needs of the estate owners and managers as most plantation workers rarely come

to town. Nonetheless, the town is one of the tidiest in Kenya and has a beautifully maintained central square.

The area also offers good trout fishing, particularly during the drier months (November to March). The **Itare** and **Kipteget Rivers**, each about an hour's drive from town, have the best fishing and scenery. They run through the dense rain forest on the western edge of the Mau Escarpment, which has numerous butterflies, birds, and wild orchids. Closer to town is the **Mara River** and a short walk from the Tea Hotel is the **Kimugu River**. The Upper and Lower Saosa Dams also offer good fishing, particularly in the evenings. Arrangements for fishing can be made through the Kericho Tea Hotel.

If you don't have time to visit Kericho, but still want to see a tea plantation, there are several near Nairobi. The **Mitchell's Kiambethu Tea Farm (** (0154) 50756 gives guided tours on prior arrangement, at a cost of 1,100 KSh. They prefer groups to individuals. If you would like some help arranging it, **Let's Go Travel (** (02) 340331 FAX (02) 336890 E-MAIL info@letsgosafari.com, Box 60342, Nairobi are the best people to find a group you can join.

Where to Stay

Before or after visiting the fields, you can stop for a cup of tea or a meal at the **Kericho Tea Hotel (** (0361) 30004 FAX (02) 20576, Box 75, Kericho. The pink, Spanish-style hotel was built in 1952 by the then-owner of the surrounding tea plantations, Brooke Bond. It now belongs to African Tours and Hotels. The hotel has an excellent restaurant and well-maintained rooms (US$84 for a double, bed and breakfast).

Less expensive and in a rather better, riverside setting is the **Kericho Lodge and Fish Resort (** (0381) 20035, Box 25, Kericho at 1,000 KSh for a double with bed and breakfast. The **TAS Lodge** (no phone) on the Moi Highway in Kericho is even cheaper and allows camping in its gardens.

How to Get There

Kericho is an hour and a half by road from Kisumu: travel east along the B1, which continues to Nakuru, Naivasha and Nairobi. From Kisii take the C23 which skirts the Mau Escarpment: a spectacular 115 km (72 miles). By public transportation, frequent *matatus* link Kericho with Kisumu and Nakuru, with plentiful connections on to Nairobi.

MAU ESCARPMENT

From Kericho, it's barely a hop, skip, and a jump through the rolling, terraced hills of the Nyanza district toward the world-famous savanna of the **Maasai Mara**. This might be too much hopping, skipping and jumping after heavy rain: roads into the park from the west can be impassable, but this is certainly the most varied and scenic route. The Mau Escarpment, one of the most beautiful and least-visited natural wonders of

Kenya, is difficult to reach because its roads are atrocious. With four-wheel drive, it's possible to make a day's trip of the **Mau Forest** from Kericho via Nakuru, climbing the west side of the Rift Valley through **Njoro**, and then south to **Mau Narok**. After Mau Narok, the road worsens (impassable in rainy seasons), descending south along the Ngusur River to **Narok**, which is also an access to the **Maasai Mara National Reserve**.

Sixteen kilometers (10 miles) south of Narok, you reach a small settlement and

cross the Ewaso Ngiro River (not the same one which flows through Samburu country). Turn right on a reasonably poor road along the forested lower edge of the Mau Escarpment, and loop round through **Sotik** eventually back to **Kericho**.

Half way along this section, at the hamlet of **Bomet**, you can try the dirt road back up the Mau Escarpment to **Shabaitaragwa**, on the river of the same name, and from there (perhaps) return to Mau Narok, if by some miracle this road has been repaired. The best way to see the magnificent forests of the Mau Escarpment is still on foot.

Raising tea seedlings and picking the mature leaves. Tea has replaced coffee as Kenya's largest export crop.

Across
the South

MAASAI MARA

Before you, at dawn, extends a vast plain of dusty brown. The red sun inches above a jagged, distant ridge. In the stillness of breaking light, the dawn breeze carries the songs of a hundred different birds and, from afar, also the loud roar of a waking lion.

Suddenly, the entire brown plain before you stirs. It begins to move with the surprising quickness of an earthquake, with the thudding of many thousand hooves. In the quick-rising dust, you see that the entire plain was but one herd of wildebeest, aroused now by that distant lion's roar.

With the earth rumbling and roaring, the wildebeest pour past. It seems they will never end. The air grows thick with their dust and loud with their strange cries. Zebra are passing too — fat, striped, whinnying horses, thousands of them, kicking up their heels. Finally, the herds diminish. Here and there, a loner gallops nervously to catch up, glancing back over its shoulder. And you think, "Ah, the lion's coming."

But no, the ground begins to shake again. More wildebeest are thundering towards you, dashing madly about, bleating, tossing their glossy horns. Still more come, then more, till finally they thin out. Exhausted with waiting, you say, "There, that's over!" only to find you've misconstrued. This entire vast dawn shadow moving toward you across the valley is not bush, as you thought, but wildebeest — hundreds of thousands of them!

No words nor photographs can convey the Maasai Mara. It and Tanzania's adjoining and even more vast Serengeti National Park are perhaps the only places left in Africa that retain a sense of the vastness of plains game before the coming of the white man.

The standard rule among Kenya outfitters is to save the Maasai Mara for last, lest everything that follows it seem anticlimactic. But no matter when you go to the Maasai Mara, it will not cease to amaze you. On the Grand Safari, you come to the Maasai after 4,000 km (2,500 miles) of mountains, deserts, and lakes. But no matter how short your time is, do not go to Kenya without visiting the Maasai Mara.

The 1,812 sq km (700 sq mile) Mara is approached either directly from Nairobi via Kijabe and Narok, or, better yet, from Kisumu and Kisii after wandering the Kericho tea district, Ruma National Park, and the coast of Lake Victoria. This allows you to drop down over the **Soit Ololol Escarpment**, with the Mara spread out before you in all its vastness — or so it seems. In reality, even from the Soit Ololol, you see only a fraction of the Mara.

The road from Kisii is macadam as far as **Kilkoris**, after which you turn left and descend, then climb a slope on a dirt track that rapidly worsens, and which on rainy seasons can only be negotiated by a four-wheel drive — if then. All the way to **Lolgorien**, a distance of 31 km (19 miles), the road wanders across the Migori River basin, in and out of mudflats and gullies. At times there's no road at all, just a choice of tracks (try to follow the most recent and heavily used). But once you cross the Migori River bridge, with hippos and crocodiles basking on its black lava banks, the road improves.

At Lolgorien hamlet, which is really just a collection of *manyattas*, turn directly east and climb the long slope of Soit Ololol. We stopped here to give a ride to a girl who'd been picking wild onions in the forest. She smiled and talked rapidly in Maa, but unlike most Maasai, spoke no English or Swahili. As you approach the Mara, the land turns wilder. There is less overgrazing by livestock, and gazelle, impala, and giraffe are more common.

Suddenly, the road breaks out over the edge of the world, and there, spread before you, is the Maasai Mara. It's only 24 km (15 miles) from Lolgorien to the Mara, but it could be two different worlds. As far as you can see are undulating plains, tree-bordered rivers, and towering, far ridges, with mountains here and there thrusting out of the savanna.

As you drive down the steep side of Soit Ololol, your next decision is, which way to go? This depends on where you want to stay. Like many of Kenya's parks and reserves, the Mara has a number of accommodations, depending on your budget and goals. Our advice is to pick a place here on the west end

The distinctive markings of the reticulated giraffes, specially adapted to blend with its habitat.

of the reserve, where the landscape is more open and the weather less arid. It's also true that the in-and-out safaris coming from Nairobi tend to use the east to save an extra hour's driving, so it's sometimes easier to find remote spots in the west.

Generally the lodges organize game drives, so partly the experience might depend on where you're staying. Usually they go out in the early morning and late afternoon, for it's then that the wildlife is supposed to be at its peak. The Mara, however, is full of game all day long. Moreover, some

zebra, and consequently, the greatest numbers of predators. The vast migrations of wildebeest up from the Serengeti in August is one of the Mara's most famous sights. Generally, the wildebeest reside in great numbers in the Mara until mid-November or even until the end of December, depending on the rains.

Also excellent for game watching is **Musiara Swamp** and the downstream area outside the Musiara gate. Here, you'll likely see lions and cheetahs. The entire course of the Mara and Talek Rivers in the reserve is a

animals such as the cheetahs have been sufficiently harassed by vehicles during the game-drive hours that they now may be hunting more in the middle of the day.

The other advantage of early and late game drives is that the weather's cooler. But again, we've found in the five or so times we've been in the Maasai Mara that we never could get enough wildlife, and would be out all day.

Generally, the best place to find game is in the less-arid western half of the reserve, between the **Mara River** and the **Soit Ololol Escarpment**, including the so-called **Mara Triangle**. Here, you'll find the largest herds of wildebeest (in Boer Dutch, literally a "wild beast," also known as gnu) and common

good area for elephants, giraffe, hippos, antelope, crocodiles, buffalo, spotted hyenas, warthogs, black-backed jackals, and even the solitary leopard. The Mosee plains to the east are good for all the herbivores and lions, and the high, steep country in the southeast of the reserve, beautiful and more thickly forested, is excellent habitat for lions, leopards, and giraffe and most other herbivores. Some 53 different bird of prey species have been identified in the Maasai Mara, and 430 other bird species.

Like all wild areas in Kenya, the Mara can be deceptive and dangerous. It's not wise for a tourist to travel alone off the beaten track, nor is the Mara a good choice without a four-wheel drive, except at the height of the dry season. These caveats aside, it remains, with the Serengeti, the most exciting wildlife habitat left on earth.

WHERE TO STAY

If you're going to camp, there are two alternatives just outside the reserve, neither particularly safe; one is north of **Musiara gate**, on the east bank of the Mara River downstream of Mara River Camp, the other on the **Talek River** near Fig Tree Camp. When we asked the rangers at Ololol gate about them, they suggested that a safer option was to camp either at Ololol or at Musiara gate. However, the reliability of camping changes from season to season in the national parks, so if you wish advance information, write the Warden, Maasai Mara National Reserve, Box 60, Narok.

A wiser choice in the Mara is a tented camp or lodge, even though entering the park does entail the daily fee of US$27 per adult and US$10 per child. It all goes to help the wildlife. The advantage of a tented camp is that it's more open, often cooler, and closer to the place itself. Of all the places we looked at, we found **Kichwa Tembo** ((02) 441001/5 FAX (02) 750512, Box 74957, Nairobi, to have the best combination of superb accommodation and reasonable price. Lying in a lovely, shady grove of trees on the edge of the Mara between Ololol and Musiara gates, Kichwa Tembo looks out on the whole of the northwestern Maasai Mara. Most of the large, comfortable tents face the plains; each is protected by its own screen of vegetation yet is not far from the others. There is an excellent pool — quite enjoyable after a hot, dusty day of game driving, very good food, and a large, comfortable bar. Kichwa Tembo never seemed too hot even at noon, and the nights were cool. The name, in Maa, means "Elephant's Head" and the camp is run by Abercrombie & Kent. They charge US$250 for a double with full board.

Also at the northeast end of the reserve, but further outside it, is **Mara River Camp** ((02) 331191 FAX (02) 330698, Box 48019, Nairobi, on the far side of the Mara River, east of Kichwa Tembo, at US$206 for a double with full board. Just inside the Musiara gate, and upstream of the large swamp of the same name, is the famed **Governor's Camp** ((02) 331871 FAX (02) 726427, Box 48217, Nairobi, the former location of a major hunting lodge by the Mara River. Governor's and **Little Governor's** (across the river) have perhaps less of a view than Kichwa Tembo, but boast excellent cuisine and fancy prices. They charge US$440 for a double with full board.

If you like looking down on the world, there could be no better place than **Mara Serena Lodge** ((02) 711077/8 FAX (02) 718103, Box 48690, Nairobi, located on the heights of Limutu Hill above a large, forested bend in the Mara River. Here, the rooms are in the style of individual Maasai bandas (with all modern conveniences). Again, there's a pool, and a marvelous terrace overlooking hippo pools far below in the river, with a telescope mounted at the edge for viewing. The grounds are well-vegetated, with individual tree and bush species identified in English and Latin. The rate is US$138 for a double with full board.

Just outside the Talek gate is **Fig Tree Camp** ((02) 221439 FAX (02) 332170, Box 40683, Nairobi, at US$200 for a double with full board, a lovely tented camp set in a grove of monstrous fig trees on the banks of the Talek River. Further south, there is the original **Keekoruk Lodge** ((02) 540780 FAX (02) 543810, Box 40075, Nairobi, the oldest in the reserve, but completely modernized and very comfortable. It has a swimming pool and good food. The rate is US$174 for a double with full board.

Also available, just inside the Sekenani gate, is **Mara Sarova** ((02) 713333 FAX (02) 718700, Box 72493, Nairobi, at US$200 for a double with full board. It is set on the high bank above a tributary stream of the Olosokon River, but like many of the lodges and camps at the east end of the reserve, it suffers from the drier, hotter weather. Just outside Sekenani gate is the **Sekenani Tented Camp** ((02) 212370 FAX (02) 228875, Box 61542, Nairobi, (US$247 for full board). At the reserve's far southeast end, situated on the higher and cooler Olaimutiek Plateau, is **Mara Sopa Lodge** ((02) 336088 FAX (02) 223843, Box 45155, Nairobi at US$216 for a double with full board.

From the Maasai Mara's Limutu Hill, the plains seem to stretch "beyond the rim of the world."

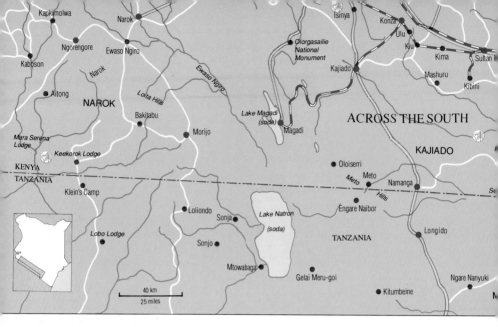

An excellent alternative outside the reserve is **Siana Springs Tented Camp** ((02) 441001 FAX (02) 746826, Box 74957, Nairobi, (US$250 for a double with full board). Located on a large spring surrounded by croton, fig, and acacia trees about 15 km (nine miles) outside Sekenani gate, it offers truly superb food, personalized and comfortable accommodations, and the option of guided daytime hikes in Mara country and nighttime game watching at the Leopard Lookout. Some of Kenya's largest lions live thereabouts, and 275 bird species have been identified in the area. Siana Springs will also arrange a three-day guided walking safari, with night camps in some of the Mara's most exciting game country.

HOW TO GET THERE

Approaching the Maasai Mara from the west is already described above as part of the Grand Safari. However the conventional route is from Nairobi. Leave the city heading towards Naivasha, but once you've dropped down the side of the Great Rift Valley turn left on the B3 for Narok, where the tarmac ends. This small town has seen rather too many tourists to keep the friendly atmosphere of less visited parts of Kenya. It is however the last gasoline you'll see for a while. Continue on the B3 for 17 km (10 miles) to the Ewaso Ngiro River. At this point it is

possible to turn right on the B3 and drive west towards Lemek and the west of the park, but the road can be rough, especially after rain. Only attempt this if you have a good high-clearance four-wheel drive and plenty of confidence. Otherwise keep straight on: the road is reclassified as the C12, the tarmac stops and dirt rules for the next 60 km (37 miles) to the park gate. Newly surfaced roads mean five hours driving can get you into the heart of the Mara.

All the major tour operators run daily safaris on this route and it is also possible to take to the skies: **AirKenya** ((02) 501421/3 FAX (02) 500845, Box 30357, Nairobi, flies twice daily from Wilson Airport, taking just one and a half hours to the airstrip in the east of the reserve for US$158 round trip.

AMBOSELI

It's not just the animals that attract visitors to Amboseli National Park, but also magical Kilimanjaro, the largest mountain in Africa at 5,895 m (19,340 ft). Hemingway immortalized it in his *Snows of Kilimanjaro*, later filmed in Amboseli. When the border was being drawn between German Tanzania and British Kenya, Queen Victoria put a kink in the line to give the mountain, sight unseen, to her cousin, Emperor of Germany. As amusing as this story is, it reflects the callousness of the nineteenth-century partitioning of

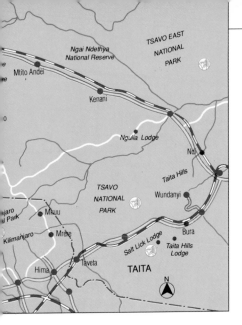

Africa, where all it took was the stroke of a pen to divide one country from another, and brother from brother.

Though Kilimanjaro seems so close from Amboseli's flat open plains, its peak is almost 50 km (31 miles) away as the crow flies, and across the Tanzanian border, making it a major expedition for the Kenyan tourist. On your own, this means an extra visa for Tanzania, a reentry visa for Kenya, road tax in Tanzania (approximately US$60), and US$20 in United States currency per person for entry into the Kilimanjaro National Park. If you find the requirements inconvenient, it may be wiser to return to Tanzania as a separate destination. Compared to Kilimanjaro, Mount Kenya offers easier climbing to a higher altitude, without needing climbing gear, expertise, and pre-planning. If you are dead set on visiting Mount Kilimanjaro, **Let's Go Travel** ((02) 340331 FAX (02) 336890 E-MAIL info@ letsgosafari.com, Box 60342, Nairobi, can arrange a tour and help you with the visas.

For many who visit Amboseli, the mountain can be as elusive as its wildlife, but the early riser is usually rewarded with an unobscured view of Uhuru Peak, the summit, and Mawenzi, 5,151 m (16,900 ft). During the day, clouds usually play hide and seek about one or both peaks. Sometimes they become so thick you are unaware of the mountain's presence. If you have arrived on a cloudy afternoon, look to the south in the

early morning. The mountain will surprise you with its enormity.

Even without Kilimanjaro, Amboseli, just a four-hour drive from Nairobi, has much to offer. It has a unique ecosystem and variety of game. There are five different wildlife habitats — the seasonal lake bed of Lake Amboseli, swamps and marshes with a few sulfur springs, open plains, yellow-barked acacia woodlands, and lava rock thornbush country.

Amboseli is probably the best place to watch elephants in Kenya, and if you'd like to learn more about them, *Elephant Memories* by Cynthia Moss, an American scientist who has studied them in Amboseli since 1972, is the best book available.

In recent years, poaching has driven many elephants into Amboseli, where Moss' research project has followed their lives and where perhaps the presence of many scientists and observers has provided a slight protection. Nonetheless, the poaching continues. *Elephant Memories* chronicles a recent example:

"Torn Ear was just reaching for a small succulent herb that was nestled in amongst the grass when a quick movement to her left caught her eye. She whirled toward the movement and there were two men only 30 yards away. Without hesitation she put her head down and charged toward them. She did not even hear the explosion before the bullet ripped through the light airy bone of her forehead and penetrated deep into her brain. She was dead by the time she fell forward onto her head and tusks and skidded along the ground for several feet from the momentum of her charge. Her son was hit next, first in the shoulder, which made him scream with pain and rage, and then through his side into his heart… The men turned and began to run but let off one volley of shots, missing most of the elephants but catching Tina in the chest with a shot that went into her right lung… it took seven shots in her head and neck and shoulders before Wendy fell and died.

"Teresia took them to the far side of Meshanani, a small hill up on the ridge above the lake. There was some protection here, and Tina could go no farther. The blood pouring from her mouth was bright red and her sides were heaving for breath. The other elephants

crowded around, reaching for her. Her knees started to buckle and she began to go down, but Teresia got on one side of her and Trista on the other and they both leaned in and held her up. Soon, however, she had no strength and she slipped beneath them and fell onto her side. More blood gushed from her mouth and with a shudder she died.

"Teresia and Trista became frantic and knelt down and tried to lift her up. They worked their tusks under her back and under her head. At one point they succeeded in lifting her into a sitting position but her body

Despite the threat of poachers, the elephants of Amboseli are accustomed to tourist vehicles — it is one of Kenya's busiest parks — and will not generally flee if you wish to sit and watch them as they go about their daily routine — showers, dust baths, 16 to 18 hours of grazing, and playful bouts of rock or stick throwing.

You can also expect to see waterbuck, Maasai giraffe, buffalo, Coke's hartebeest, common zebra, eland, gazelle, and impala. Cheetah and lion sightings are almost sure bets.

flopped back down. Her family tried everything to rouse her, kicking and tusking her, and Tallulah even went off and collected a trunkful of grass and tried to stuff it into her mouth…".

Every tourist who visits the game parks of Kenya is helping to protect the elephants by manifesting his or her interest in Africa's wildlife. In addition, we can all help by refusing ever to purchase any item made of ivory, even if it's sold as an "antique," by adding our support to the East African Wildlife Society, the World Wildlife Fund, and other conservation groups, and by joining in international efforts to discourage ivory smuggling which is almost entirely organized by Japan, Taiwan, Hong Kong, and China.

We once found cheetahs by asking a tour driver, who gave explicit directions for finding three who'd been traveling together for days. It was mid-morning, and very hot. The three cheetahs were huddled under a bush no larger than they. Without the driver's help, we never would have found them.

You will probably also want to ask for directions and information. It is an unwritten safari law to pass on wildlife sightings. Don't hesitate to flag down an oncoming car

LEFT: Mount Kilimanjaro's snow-capped peak is just over the border, in Tanzania. ABOVE: Kilimanjaro Lodge in Amboseli. OVERLEAF: Wildebeest congregate on the banks of the Mara River.

or tour van and ask if they have seen any interesting animals. Everyone usually stops and the information passed on can either improve your safari or theirs.

WHERE TO STAY

Among the better lodges in the park are: **Amboseli Serena Lodge** ((02) 710511 FAX (02) 718103, Box 48690, Nairobi (US$166); and **Tortilis Camp** ((02) 748307/27 FAX (0154) 22553 or (02) 740721 E-MAIL chelipeacock @attmail.com WEB SITE www.chelipeacock .com, Box 39806, Nairobi (US$310). Less good than they used to be are **Amboseli Lodge** and **Kilimanjaro Safari Lodge** both ((02) 227136 FAX (02) 219982, Box 30193, Nairobi, and costing US$180 per double with full board. Near the Lemito gate is the slightly dilapidated **Kilimanjaro Buffalo Lodge** ((02) 227136 FAX (02) 219982, Box 72630, Loitokitok, also US$180 per double with full board. Perhaps a better option is **Ol Tukai Lodge** ((02) 540780 FAX (02) 543810, Box 40075, Nairobi, near the Amboseli Lodge and Kilimanjaro Safari Lodge: costs are US$182 for a double with full board.

South of the Serena Lodge is an excellent campground run by the Maasai (600 KSh per person). There are few amenities (usually there is water), but the campsites are flat, dry and well-spaced. The wildlife is so tame that at night you can expect to be visited. Elephants and giraffe often pass through. Most campers leave a large fire burning upon retiring. Because of the nearby marshes, mosquito netting is a must if you want to get any sleep.

At **Namanga**, a pretty town 75 km (47 miles) west of Amboseli on the border with Tanzania, is the **River Hotel** ((02) 330775, Box 4, Namanga, a very scenic array of cottages under shady acacias with a good restaurant for Kenyan cuisine. The rate is 1,500 KSh bed and breakfast for doubles. Camping is also available at 150 KSh per person. Also in Namanga are a couple of cheaper *hotelis*. Since Namanga lies on the direct route south from Nairobi to Amboseli, it can make a nice stop for lunch, or for the night if you're taking your time or started late.

HOW TO GET THERE

From Nairobi, join the lines of heavy traffic heading southeast on the Mombasa Road. It is possible to reach Amboseli by staying on this road to Emali and then branching off on the dirt road to Oloitokitok but this is hard work. Better to turn right 25 km (16 miles) out of Nairobi on the A104 towards Arusha. At Namanga, 165 km (103 miles) south of Nairobi, turn left on the C103 for the final 75 km (47 miles) to Amboseli or dirt road. How long the drive will take depends partly on how recently this last stretch has been graded: four hours is a good run. By public transportation it is easy to get to Namanga but hard thereafter. Hitching will be your only option. **AirKenya** ((02) 501421/3 FAX (02) 500845, Box 30357, Nairobi, flies at 7:30 AM daily from Wilson Airport, taking just one hour to Amboseli.

MAN-EATER COUNTRY

"...the lions had a range of some eight miles on either side of Tsavo to work upon; and as their tactics seemed to be to break into a different camp each night, it was most difficult to forestall them. They almost appeared, too, to have an extraordinary and uncanny faculty of finding out our plans beforehand, so that no matter in how likely or how tempting a spot we lay in wait for them, they invariably avoided that particular place and seized their victim for the night from some other camp. Hunting them by day, moreover, in such a dense wilderness as surrounded us, was an exceedingly tiring and really foolhardy undertaking."

So does Colonel J.H. Patterson describe, in his *The Maneaters of Tsavo*, some of the difficulties he faced when sent by the British Foreign Office in 1898 to direct a section of the Mombasa-Uganda Railway, where the depredations of two ravenous man-eating lions brought work to a standstill. After months of hunting them, during which time they killed numerous workers, Patterson describes being stalked by one lion:

"I again kept as still as I could, though absolutely trembling with excitement; and in a short while I heard the lion begin to creep stealthily towards me. I could barely make out his form as he crouched among the whitish undergrowth… I took careful aim and pulled the trigger. The sound of the shot was at once followed by a most terrific roar, and then I could hear him leaping about in all directions…"

Patterson was finally able to kill another man-eater and capture a brazen third that had entered a railway carriage and killed and carried off one of the line's engineers. There's a photo of him doing just that hidden away in Nairobi's Railway Museum. But man-

TSAVO WEST

As you drive southeast from Amboseli through the rolling savanna of Maasai country, the monstrous mass of Kilimanjaro looms ever higher and higher. When you turn right at the town of **Kimana** and left before **Oloitokitok**, the mountain towers so tall it seems ready to fall upon you. At this point, if you wish, you can drop into Tanzania for a visit (the border post is five kilometers or three miles away), but, as noted

eating lions have remained part of the lore and mystique of Tsavo.

Now the biggest park in Kenya, and at 20,807 sq km (8,000 sq miles) one of the largest in the world, **Tsavo National Park** is an international wildlife and environmental treasure chest. It contains a variety of habitats, geologic/soil types, animals, birds, and plants, and offers excellent camping, lodges and other accommodations.

Divided by the Nairobi-Mombasa road and railway into **Tsavo West** (7,000 sq km or 2,700 sq miles) and **Tsavo East** (more than 13,000 sq km or 5,000 sq miles), the park is a change from nearby Amboseli. Tsavo West is hillier, greener, and much more vegetated than Tsavo East, but each has its advantages.

earlier, you'll have to pay a US$60 vehicle tax to cross the border, and US$20 per person to enter Kilimanjaro National Park.

From the Maasai *manyattas* at Oloitokitok, it's 75 km (47 miles) through volcanic country to Tsavo West's **Chyulu gate.** The road passes over lava beds so new that not a blade of grass has grown. To the north, the most recent cones stand naked and black. One, named Shetani ("devil" in Swahili), is thought to have erupted most recently 200 years ago; a trail of several kilometers winds around the flow (hungry lions have interrupted more than one stroll, so check with the rangers at Kilaguni gate before hiking).

Mother lions are gentle with their cubs and ferocious in their defense.

There is a *very* rough four-wheel drive trail which turns north here up into the **Chyulu Hills** (the steep ridges to your left). These are considered by geologists to be very young mountains, and offer stunning views of Kilimanjaro, the Taita Hills, and the Kenya plains, as well as much wildlife. Check with the rangers at the gate or the nearby park headquarters before venturing too far into them.

Alternatively you can drive south to Tsavo West's southern borders with Tanzania to Lake Jipe. Lake Jipe appears to have been

the Tanzania border 10 minutes south of **Taveta**. Follow the dirt road east of Taveta northward until you see a small hill: this is a crater, with Lake Chala inside it. Descend with care: there are crocodiles in the lake.

The landscape of Tsavo West is everywhere spectacular, with wide valleys, rivers, ridges, and peaks. One of the best views is from **Roaring Rocks** at the north end of Rhino Valley. Follow the sign from the major road junctions east of Kilaguni — it's but a two-minute climb from the turnaround at the end of the road — and suddenly spread out be-

visited by ancient Greek mariners whose belief that it was a source of the Nile was quoted by Ptolemy. Ptolemy's map of Africa, completed in the second century, was used well into the 1500s. Just north of the lake are the extensive sisal plantations begun by the eccentric and brilliant Captain Ewart Grogan, an incredibly wealthy timber exporter who in 1898 walked 7,250 km (4,500 miles) from Capetown to Cairo (supposedly for a fiancée he then decided not to marry), and later posted a mining claim on the city of Nairobi. Amid the sisal is **Grogan's Castle**, the huge, rambling, disorganized mansion which he built in the 1930s.

As pretty as Lake Jipe but less commercialized is the smaller **Lake Chala**. It straddles

low you is an incredible expanse of savanna. From here, you can also see Tsavo River and Tembo Peak crouched massively above it.

The most famous of Tsavo West's sites is **Mzima Springs**, where rainfall collected in the porous volcanic rock springs forth at the rate of 225 million liters (50 million gallons) a day, more than 10 million liters (over two and a half million gallons) an hour, into a pool and stream of crocodiles and hippopotamuses. Here, you can walk along an interpretive trail and even descend to a partially submerged lookout to watch the animals swim by. Schools of fat barbel inspect the tourists from the far side of the glass. Unfortunately, some three-quarters of Mzima's flow has been diverted by pipeline to Mombasa, to serve as the city's water supply. This has reduced its downstream flows and aquatic life. Despite this, the springs remain a miracle of nature, a green outpost of tamarind, wild date, raphia palms, and wild fig amid Tsavo's dry expanse.

An adventurous itinerary from Mzima is to follow the south bank of the **Tsavo River** east on the dirt track, winding in and out of the many luggas draining from the south. This is *definitely* four-wheel drive country, and may be impassable even then. It's best attempted with two vehicles (hopefully one can go for

of most parks are common), stay in your car. *Always* let someone know (a park ranger or lodge personnel) before attempting any backcountry.

Only 20 years ago, Tsavo was host to the largest herds of elephants still left in Africa —with counts of up to 20,000 at a time! People who have seen them speak of elephants covering the entire surface of the land as far as the eye could see. But such a concentration led rapidly to a degradation of Tsavo's carrying capacity. After they had eaten all the grass and shrubs, the elephants tore down

help when the other's incapacitated), and has proved fatal to unprepared tourists in the past. It's well worth the effort, but *not* for the faint of heart, or the inexperienced.

Less dangerous, but also *four-wheel drive only*, is the track along the river's north bank, 35 km (22 miles) from the Ngulia intersection (number 18) to Tsavo gate. The cardinal rule in any backcountry wandering is: *do not leave your vehicle*. If you do, you can become prey to various carnivores, lions in particular, irritate a passing herbivore (buffalo and hippos kill more people in Kenya than lions), or what's most likely, succumb to heat and dehydration. Unless you're positive no one will be looking for you, and that there's no way another vehicle will pass (overflights

the trees to get at the bark and softer top branches. In the process, they altered fundamentally the vegetation of Tsavo West and turned Tsavo East from a forested savanna into desert and plains.

With vegetation depleted, drought followed. The elephants died by the thousands. As they began to recover, the poachers came to finish off those who were left. There are few elephants remaining in Tsavo now, but if the Kenyan government enforces recent proclamations to hunt down poachers (including those with ties *to* the government), it's possible that they may once again be common in Tsavo.

The lava fields of Tsavo West stretch to the distant mountains.

The outlook for the black rhino is bleaker. Thirty years ago, there were up to 9,000 in Tsavo alone; now there are none in Tsavo and probably less than five hundred in Kenya: only by massive international fund-raising efforts are numbers slowly starting to creep upwards.

WHERE TO STAY

If you've brought a tent, Tsavo is a great place to use it: nothing can beat the millions of sharp, bright stars visible in Tsavo's clear night sky. There are good campsites in the gates not far from the Nairobi-Mombasa highway, at **Ziwani**, where there are also self-help bandas, and at **Lake Jipe** on the Tanzania frontier, with its astounding views of Kilimanjaro and Tanzania's Pare Mountains.

There are excellent self-help bandas at **Ngulia** and **Kitani Safari Camps** (4,000 KSh per person, bring your own beverages and food), operated by **Let's Go Travel** ((02) 340331 FAX (02) 336890 E-MAIL info@ letsgosafari.com, Box 60342, Nairobi, but these may be full in peak season. If you want to go whole hog, there are a number of ex-

park, as well as inexpensive self-help bandas. We particularly liked the campsite located just west of the Chyulu gate (US$12 per person, payable at the gate). There are thatched verandahs to place a tent under or next to, fireplaces, running water, showers, and toilets. Keep a fire going during the night to keep the more aggressive of predators at a distance; be sure also to leave nothing in your tent during the day, lest it fall prey to baboons or other primates. Because the poaching problem is less serious at Tsavo West, the rangers are less uptight, and don't usually mind if you drive back to the campsite at 9 PM.

Entry fees to the park are slightly lower: US$23 per adult and US$8 per child. You can also camp at the **Mtito Andei** and **Tsavo**

cellent lodges in Tsavo West, including **Ngulia Safari Lodge** also run by Africa Tours and Hotels, which costs US$216 per double for full board and has a fascinating water hole; the area is famous among ornithologists for its migrating birds from Russia and western Europe. The **Lake Jipe Lodge** ((02) 227623, Box 31097, Nairobi, on the shore of the lake is slightly more expensive and becoming run down. It does offer dhow trips on the lake, and visits to nearby Grogan's Castle. Rate is US$150 per double, full board. Also near Lake Jipe is the **Ziwani Tented Camp** ((02) 716628 FAX (02) 716457 E-MAIL prestigehotels @formnet.com, Box 748888, Nairobi (US$250). Smartest is perhaps **Finch Hattons** ((0302) 22468 FAX (0302) 22473, Box

71, Mtito Andei, where the sherry circulates in a decanter amongst cut-glass and Mozart (US$350 for two, full board).

HOW TO GET THERE

Tsavo West is on the main road between Nairobi and Mombasa. Indeed it is rather nearer Mombasa and the coast. From Nairobi take the A109: how long the journey will take depends on the state of the road. Once the trip used to take six hours but it has been known to take twice as long. The nearest

2,209 m (7,247 ft), that in 1848 the missionary Rebmann saw Kilimanjaro's white spire, the first European to do so.

The hills are home to the friendly Taita people, of whom the explorer Thomson spoke fondly. Their settlements are centered around the bustling hill town of Wundanyi and the terraced slopes between Voi and the Tanzania border. To reach the Taita Hills, leave Tsavo West by the Maktau gate and drive toward Voi. The area between Maktau and the town of Bura was the site in the First World War of intensive fighting between the

gate to Nairobi is at Mtito Andei: from here it is 40 km (25 miles) to Mzima Springs. Tsavo gate is 48 km (30 miles) nearer to Mombasa, and a main access point for visitors from the coast. If traveling by public transportation, get off at Mtito Andei and pray for a lift with another tourist vehicle.

TAITA HILLS

Leaving Tsavo West, you can choose between the **Taita Hills** and **Tsavo East**. The Taita Hills are actually outside the park but offer a varied landscape worth seeing: set against the broad plains, they rise steep and forested, punctuated with crashing creeks and waterfalls. It was from their tallest peak, Vuria, at

British and German troops. The latter, under the command of Colonel Von Lettow-Vorbeck, were trying to cut the Mombasa-Uganda Railway.

If you're in an adventurous mood, or like military history, there's a rough road (often impassable in the rains) leading southeast from the next town, **Mwatate**, across the arid flatlands, called "durststeppe" (thirst plains) by the German troops. This leads to the sheer escarpments of **Kasigau Mountain**, 1,641 m (5,384 ft), where blistering battles were fought between the Germans and British for control of the region's only water sources.

OPPOSITE: The magnificent views of Tsavo West are easily accessed. ABOVE: Zebra, like domestic horses, are playful and generally unafraid to block the road.

At **Bungule**, the town at the foot of Kasigau Mountain, you can, providing your vehicle is in good shape and you have plenty of gas, turn west to reenter Tsavo West by the Kasigau gate. This takes you into some of the finest, and emptiest, terrain in the park, with the possibility of swinging north up to Maktau, or west all the way to Lake Jipe. Check with the people in Bungule first as to road conditions, and if the gate's open. From Bungule, you can also attempt the drive across to **Mackinnon Road** on the Mombasa-Nairobi highway—again, ask first for road conditions.

too, at US$250 per person; reserve through Hilton. The surrounding area is a private game reserve developed by Hilton, which is said to burst with wildlife at times, who also run a satellite tented safari camp in various patches of untouched bush. From here it's a short drive down to Voi on the Mombasa-Nairobi highway. Depending on the road surface, the sweltering coast should be in easy reach, Nairobi just within range, but best to cross the main road for a quick trip — or a lengthy exploration — of marvelous Tsavo East National Park.

WHERE TO STAY

In the Taita Hills, there are two fancy places to stay: **Taita Hills Lodge** (US$308 for a double with full board) and **Salt Lick Lodge** (US$308 for a double with full board), both run by **Hilton Kenya (** (02) 334000 FAX 339462, Box 30624, Nairobi. The former is built in the style of a German outpost, though far more luxurious than Prussian. It is separated by seven kilometers (four miles) from Salt Lick Lodge, which is situated by a water hole, a strange agglomeration of mushroom shapes on pylons. Both have pools and all other amenities imaginable. This is the only place in Kenya apart from the Maasai Mara where it is possible to go ballooning: it's cheaper

HOW TO GET THERE

The Grand Safari approaches Taita Hills from Tsavo West, but this is not the most common way to reach them. Taita Hills are especially popular with visitors to Kenya's coast, as they are near Mombasa and paved all the way. From Mombasa the drive takes just three hours. From Nairobi it will take at least twice as long, even if they have finally repaired the road. The turning to Taita Hills is at Voi, 140 km (87.5 miles) from Mombasa and 300 km (187 miles) from Nairobi, where the A23 forks west towards Mwatate and the two

Looking like an outpost in the desert, Salt Lick Lodge in fact provides a luxurious viewing platform for Kenya's wildlife.

Hilton lodges are 55 km (34 miles) on. This road continues on to Moshi and then Arusha which means it is possible to get here by public transport: change *matatus* at Voi for one heading to Taveta, Kenya's border town with Tanzania.

TSAVO EAST

Tsavo East is vast even by African standards. It is the legendary Kenyan wilderness, with limitless vistas across its gray-brown scrub to impossibly distant table mountains. Of its

this road all the way to the coast city of **Malindi**, following the Grand Safari, but it's worth taking a look at some exciting options along the way.

If you've come from Tsavo West and the Taita Hills, the normal place to enter Tsavo East is by the park headquarters at **Voi gate**. From here, it's a quick drive to several lodges or past the **Kandari Swamp** down the north bank of the Voi River. The swamp had dried up during the recent droughts but was damp when we were last there. Some 34 km (21 miles) from the Voi gate is **Aruba Dam**.

13,000 sq km (5,000 sq miles), nearly two-thirds (the area north of the Galana River) is off-limits to tourists. This is in part because of the continuing war between Somali poachers and Kenyan security forces, and in part to give the country a chance to recover from the damaging droughts of the 1970s. Also because it is rarely visited in any case, closure cuts management costs. Entry fees to the park are US$23 per adult and US$8 per child.

South of the Galana River, there's more than enough to keep any wanderer occupied for months. The easiest place to start is the main road following the south bank of the Galana, with its numerous offshoots up tributary ravines. If you wish, you can take

During the early dry seasons, when there's little water to be found in the area, the dam provides a strong draw for wildlife. Here, you have excellent chances of seeing gazelles, impalas, buffalo, greater kudu, Defassa waterbuck, and associated predators.

From the dam, you can follow roads back up to the Galana River or descend further on the Voi, depending on the season. Although Tsavo East is much drier than Tsavo West, its roads can become boggy in the rains and sandblasted ruts in the dry seasons, so proceed with caution.

No trip to Tsavo East is complete without a visit to imposing **Mudanda Rock**, a flat-topped inselberg of Promethean proportions some 13 km (eight miles) south of Manyani

Across the South

gate. It has a water hole which draws wild-life from miles around, except at the height of the dry seasons. Just south of Mudanda Rock, you can turn northeast down the bank of the seasonal Mbololo River, and in 29 km (18 miles) pick up the **Galana River** road again.

The Galana River is formed by the join-ing of the Tsavo and the Athi River, which descends all the way from Nairobi. It drops from the high plateau country into a nar-row canyon at **Lugard's Falls**, named for the adventurer, soldier, and antislavery ac-

two wandering this largely unvisited park. The **Voi Safari Lodge** ((02) 336858 FAX (02) 218109, Box 30471, Nairobi (US$216 for a double with full board), is justifiably famous for its endless panorama across the dry sa-vannah. Two water holes below the lodge entice a multitude of beasts, and it is an easy drive off the Mombasa-Nairobi highway from the Voi gate. **Tsavo Safari Camp** ((02) 227136 FAX (02) 219982, Box 30139, Nairobi (US$160 for a double with full board), is located 24 km (15 miles) northeast of Mtito Andei gate on the east bank of the Athi River.

tivist Lord Frederick Lugard, who stopped here in 1890 on his way to becoming the proconsul of Uganda. (Surely, the coura-geous Lord Lugard deserves greater com-memoration than this brown, turgid cascade, with its complement of crocodiles basking below!)

From Lugard's Falls, it's an easy half-day drive down the Galana to Sala gate. From there, another three hours down the south bank of the Sabaki River brings you to a whole other world in Malindi.

It offers guided tours into the off-limits zone of Tsavo East. It is necessary here to make a reservation, or the guards at the parking lot won't let you cross the river (by boat) to the lodge on the far bank. Coming into the park along the dirt C103 road from Malindi, one of the first places to stay is **Kulalu Camp**, reservable through **Hemingways** ((0122) 32624 FAX (0122) 32256 WEBSITE www.hemingways.com/, Box 267, Watamu or **Ocean Sports** ((0122) 32008 FAX (0122) 32266, Box 100, Watamu.

Camping in Tsavo East is available at Buchuma and Voi gates, and at Aruba Lodge.

WHERE TO STAY

In Tsavo East, there are excellent places to stay, and it's worthwhile spending a day or

The wild landscapes OPPOSITE of Tsavo East and are home to exotic plants such as this Toothbrush plant ABOVE.

The Coast

THROUGHOUT TIME, KENYA'S COAST AND IN-LAND have had separate but connected histories. This remains somewhat true today. For tourists, there's a great difference between a coastal resort and a game park lodge.

Coastal development has primarily catered to those who wish to relax in the sun, dine well, and be entertained at night. Most Kenyan coastal resorts are like those at Miami Beach or the Caribbean, with the major difference being that they generally cost less. However they also offer the opportunity to explore Kenya, whether the inland world of game and parks or the coastal life of weekend discos and local restaurants.

Typical coastal development is based on large hotels catering for sun 'n' sand visitors. Luckily, there are exceptions: notably the areas of **Watamu Bay**, **Lamu**, and **Shimoni**.

As the coastal resorts have been developed mainly for and by European market, there is a preference for employees speaking Italian, German and English. Unlike the practice in other parts of Kenya, Swahili is the first, and often the only, language spoken at home. Beach boys selling curios, shells, and "guide" services usually address tourists first in Italian or German; when they get an English or Swahili response, many back off and leave you alone (English-speaking tourists are well known for not being interested in their wares). Beach-boys concentrate on the main resort strips north and south of Mombasa: travel further, or stay in any area for length of time, and word gets around and you are rarely bothered.

The Indian Ocean offers some of the best snorkeling and diving in the world. The water, during the dry months, is calm and crystal clear, and the marine life is astounding. Because there are relatively few motorized coastal fishing boats (one deep-sea fisherman estimates that there are less than 300 for the entire 480-km or 300-mile coast and less than 20 north of Kilifi), fish here can reach enormous sizes.

In the **marine parks** at Malindi, Watamu Bay, and Shimoni, the coral reefs grow relatively undisturbed with resident populations of fish so numerous and colorful as to defy description. Outside the parks, however, the coastal coral reefs have been abused, and fishing keeps the shoal size down. At low

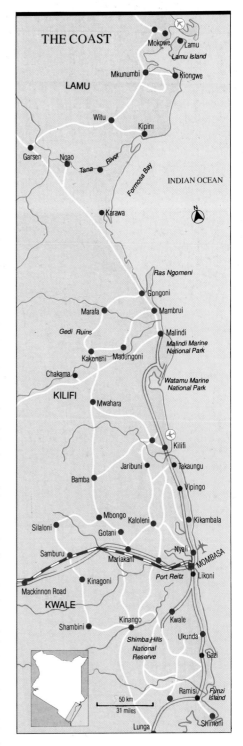

Traditional Arab dhows still ply the coast of Kenya.

tide, you can walk along the beaches and find pools that often contain small fish and a variety of crustaceans. You can also watch the fishermen setting nets from the shore or dhows. In recent years, the spear gun has been introduced. Many a young fisherman, weaned from his canoe dug from a Mango tree by offers of nets from the West, has now progressed onto goggles, snorkel, and gun to earn his livelihood.

Except at river inlets and bays, the ocean bottom slopes gently out to wide fringing and barrier reefs. There are three main reefs,

beaches become shaded, it's often warmer in the water than out, although the coastal breeze is more likely to cool than chill.

Kenya's coastal beaches are of the finest pure white sand. During and after the north-east trade winds, called the *kaskazi* (December to April), they are swept clean by an off-shore current and virtually no debris is present. Unfortunately, a change of direction, precipitation, and current during and after the southeast trade winds or *kusi* (May to November) brings seaweed to shore. This is the coast's low season and bargain hotel

starting with the sheltering onshore reef, often exposed at low tide, and heading out to three kilometers (two miles) offshore, a fertile home to the Ocean's big fish some 30 m (100 ft) below sea level. Occasional small atolls, such as at Shimoni, complete the wide variety of habitat that make Kenya's coast the marine treasure-trove of East Africa. The water near the shore is heated to surprisingly high temperatures. Average monthly temperatures for offshore surface waters vary from 25°C (77°F) in the fall to 29°C (84°F) in the spring; at low tide, it's possible to find shallow pools over 35°C (95°F). Even at high tide, the coastal water is warm and it's possible to swim for hours without getting cold. As the sun sets and

prices can be negotiated, especially in the north around Watamu. The seas run high and there is daily rain. Many of the deep-sea fishermen take their boats out of the water but in any case are unable to ride the reef out to the open sea. Further south, around Diani, Mombasa and Shimoni, the weather is less severe and beach breaks from July onwards are fine.

High season on the coast is December through mid-February. Rain is infrequent, the water is calm, snorkeling is excellent, the fish are numerous, and there is usually enough wind to make windsurfing exciting. Even if you are not interested in sailing, the breeze will be welcome, because without it, the heat and humidity can be exhausting.

The pace of life along the coast is slow. "Coasties" are famously more laid-back than their "upcountry" brothers. For Islamic believers, life is tranquilly easy. Traditionally, there has been an abundance of fish for the taking, providing protein; bananas, coconuts, mangoes, and papayas grow wild, and small garden plots supply plentiful vitamins for a family's sustenance. No wonder it's hard to find labor to work in the tourist industry.

In dress and architecture, the Arab influence, dating from as early as the sixth century, is undeniable, particularly in the ancient

towns of Lamu, Malindi, and Old Mombasa. The elegance of the thirteenth through fifteenth centuries, the height of coastal Kenya's power and affluence, has disappeared, but in the ruins of Gedi and the island of Lamu, you can still capture a glimpse of the past.

Reminders of the period of Portuguese domination during the sixteenth and seventeenth centuries are Mombasa's Fort Jesus and a small chapel and monument in Malindi. This period created much disruption but left little mark on the daily life of the native Kenyans. Although Catholicism endured in the Portuguese colonies of the New World, it never really took hold in Muslim coastal Kenya, and once the Portuguese left, so did their influence.

As in earlier times, the coast today is separated into individual spheres of influence. There is **Mombasa** with its northern resort strips, linking into a nightlife center but with beaches that recede, at low tide, to the distant horizon. To the south are the self-sufficient resorts of **Tiwi** and **Diani**. For the independent traveler the best areas are further afield: north and first place of interest is quietly charming **Kilifi**, then **Watamu Bay** for deep-sea fishing and the offshore Marine Park, nightlife resort of **Malindi** with its Italian restaurants and casinos. A short air hop reaches to Kenya's northern coast, the Swahili island of **Lamu**, and a mangrove coast dotted with exclusive hideaways.

Head south from Mombasa over the Likoni Ferry to Tiwi and Diani Beaches, and further south towards Tanzania to **Shimoni** with the offshore Wasini Island and the Marine Park of Kisite.

The road between Malindi and Shimoni is paved and in relatively good condition: one roadside stop is proudly called the "New Surface" café. This link makes it easy to reach the different marine parks, ruins, coastal forests, wildlife areas, and old towns that line Kenya's shore. The road to Malindi is also good, but from there north to Lamu and Pate becomes a bit of a challenge. Unpaved, and often impassable during the rains, even in good weather it is an endurance test and best circumvented by a short air hop.

MOMBASA

Mombasa is Kenya's second largest city and its only deepwater port. In many ways, it is the country's lifeline to the world. Once a scarcely developed island in a mangrove-lined bay, with dhows in the harbor, today Mombasa is crowded and busy with container berths at Kilindini ("place of deep water") on the west side of the island. The surrounding mainland sprawls with industrial development and suburbs.

There are no bathing beaches on Mombasa Island, so you may not choose to

OPPOSITE: Kenya's coral reefs contain some of the world's densest and brightest populations of tropical fish. ABOVE: An equally bright patchwork of cloth sold in Old Mombasa.

stay here, but the Old Town and Fort Jesus will make one- or two-day trips worthwhile.

Mombasa appears on Ptolemy's map as Tonika, and was probably the most sophisticated and largest of the coastal city-states in Kenya in the early days. It resisted Portuguese domination in the fifteenth and sixteenth centuries and was looted and burned by them on four separate occasions. As a result only a few archaeological remains of its early glory have been found. It is interesting to note that Mombasa's population in 1500 was estimated at 10,000, roughly the

story houses along the main roads. Most of the Old Town dates from this period. In 1906, the government headquarters moved to Nairobi, but Mombasa still remained Kenya's major commercial and industrial center until after the First World War. Though still a major industrial center today, Mombasa has lost its former splendor.

The **Old Town** and **Fort Jesus** are situated at the northeastern tip of Mombasa Island and can best be visited on foot. It is wise to start early, as the town can get steamy in the midday heat.

same as medieval London. Fort Jesus remains a reminder of the eventual Portuguese victory which cost the lives of every native of Mombasa who had not fled the island, and ultimately every Portuguese stationed there.

After the Portuguese came a period of Omani control that was scarcely more peaceful, as the governing Mazuri family and the Sultan were constantly at odds. These differences led directly to reluctant British involvement in Kenya when Mombasa became a protectorate.

From the end of the nineteenth century until 1906, Mombasa boomed. Government buildings were erected and affluent Indian merchants constructed large two- and three-

Old Town

The streets of Mombasa's Old Town are narrow and not designed for automobiles. They are just wide enough for a camel or a donkey with panniers, or for the hand carts (*mkototnei* or *hamaili*) still used in the area today.

Although most of the buildings are no older than the early 1900s, they often stand on older foundations, and show strong Arab influence. The Fort Jesus gift shop sells an excellent historical guide, *The Old Town Mombasa*, which gives a history of the town and details for a self-guided walking tour. With it, you can trace the lines where the Portuguese built a wall to separate the

"Cidade dos Portugusos" (Portuguese City) and the "Cidade dos Moros" (Moorish or Swahili City). But nothing remains of the wall that was said to be one and a half meters (five feet) wide with several towers and three gates.

The Old Town has numerous mosques, each built by different groups of Muslims arriving at various times in Kenya. There are many colorful buildings with intricate grillwork, a few with fretted balconies. The carved wooden doors described by Portuguese chroniclers have long ago disap-

peared, many lost when the Portuguese burned the city, but the stone *baraga* seats are still found flanking the doors of many Old Town houses. Examples of carved doors can be seen in Fort Jesus; the best surviving examples grace homes in Lamu, further north on the coast.

Mombasa also boasts Kenya's first public library, as well as an open-air pavilion, Jubilee Hall, built to commemorate Queen Victoria's diamond jubilee in 1897. There's also Government Square, a hub of colonial activity in the 1890s. Glen's Building was named for a dog called Glen owned by a government official, Sir Ali bin Salim. The dog appears in many photos of Sir bin Salim taken at state functions.

FORT JESUS

Fort Jesus, a national historical monument, is a testimony to the determination of the Portuguese to control the coast of Kenya, and to the tenacity of Mombasa's inhabitants in retaining their identity and culture. Once inside (entry fee is 350 KSh per person), you are isolated from everyday Mombasa, just as the Portuguese were. The fortress is not unlike medieval castles along the Mediterranean.

The fort is very well maintained. Several major buildings and the ramparts looking toward the sea are restored. In one barracks room, drawings of ships, churches, and figures in armor have been uncovered, revealing the longing of many Portuguese sailors for a more familiar home. There are the foundations of a chapel, a storeroom, and dwellings or shops against the inland wall. Fort Jesus is impressive, and although it might lack some of the charm and romance of European fortresses it catches the nervous

OPPOSITE: Old and new blend in Mombasa's skyline. ABOVE: The strong influence of Islam on the coast LEFT results in many mosques. Fort Jesus RIGHT in Mombasa: "Nothing remains but deathless fascination."

isolation of Europe's first settlers, the Portuguese sailors charged with maintaining a precarious toehold on the East African shore, where threats came from both land and sea.

There are several carved doors in the fortress, not original, but hung for display. Also preserved are chambers with carved beams and inlaid inscriptions that were decorated by the Omani after they defeated the Portuguese in the eighteenth century. These rooms are reminiscent of the splendor of the Moorish castles of Spain, a few with traces of poetry similar to that which embellishes the Alhambra.

A museum in the main courtyard houses "treasures" from the wreck of the *Santo Antonio de Tanna*, which sank in Mombasa Harbor in 1697. The museum also has an extensive display of pottery recovered along the coast. Some of these are over 1,000 years old, from as far away as China. The pottery finds are keyed to the ancient settlements and ruins along the coast. This is a good place to begin if you plan to tour the coastal ruins. It also has a small collection of Swahili artifacts from Old Town Mombasa.

The fort has a fine gift shop selling reasonably priced craft items and an excellent selection of books on Mombasa and the coast. Proceeds from the shop help support restoration and maintenance of the site. You can tour the fort by yourself, as it is adequately marked, or you can hire a guide. The guides are very well-informed and can usually give their tour in Swahili, Italian, German, or English.

WHERE TO STAY

Perhaps because Mombasa Island lacks a beach, recent years have seen many of the city center hotels deteriorate if not close down completely. The remaining establishments are good values. **The Royal Court Hotel (** (011) 223 379 FAX (011) 312398, Box 41247, Haile Selassie Road, Mombasa, is centrally-located and charges 3,000 KSh for a double, bed and breakfast, but avoid the single rooms, which are oppressively small. Just across the Nyali Bridge the best value on the entire coast is offered by the newly-built but echoingly empty **Orchid Bay Hotel (** (011) 473238 FAX (011) 471365, with doubles at 3,000 KSh, bed and breakfast. Perhaps prices will go up when it gets better established.

For less expensive rooms, there's the decaying charm of the **New Palm Hotel (** (011) 311756, Nkruma Road that charges, 1,190 KSh for a double room with bed and breakfast. The **YWCA** is on the junction of Kaunda and Kiamba Avenues: good in that it takes both men and women, bad in that it caters mainly for stays of a month or longer.

If you want to stay at the ocean for a week or longer, you might consider renting a house or cottage. Prices range from 750 KSh per day for one bedroom to 10,000 KSh per day for a villa. **Let's Go Travel (** (02) 340331 FAX (02) 336890 E-MAIL info@letsgosafari.com, Box 60342, Nairobi, can make advance reservations, or help with immediate reservations. Reservations are rarely necessary except during December, January, and August. Travel agents in Mombasa usually have listings of houses available up and down the coast. You can also ask residents when you find an area where you'd like to stay. The houses are generally sparsely furnished, but come with cook and housekeeper. Though the cook and housekeeper get a wage from the owner or manager, it's customary to leave 500 KSh for each of them for each week you're there.

Both north and south of Mombasa are numerous coastal resorts. Each hotel at least tries to have its own appeal, and the quality and type of food varies. Most are relatively modern, have standard resort accommodations and quote prices in United States dollars or sterling. To head south along the coast from Mombasa Island means using the Likoni ferry, which makes the southern resorts feel pleasantly isolated from the bustle of city life, and the beaches are better than those an equivalent distance from town to the north. To the north of Mombasa the new Nyali Bridge has brought the beaches of Nyali and Bamburi within easy reach of the city and given the hotels a rather busier feel. The beaches aren't great, but easy access to Mombasa's attractions and entertainment make this a preferred choice for many

visitors. The best hotel is probably the **Nyali Beach Hotel (** (011) 471567 FAX (011) 471987, Box 1874, Mombasa, with prices in the region of US$200 (depending on season) for a double with half board; rather cheaper is the **Traveler's Beach Hotel (** (011) 485121 FAX (011) 485678, Box 87649, Mombasa, with prices in the region of US$140 (depending on season) for a double with half board. Travelers on a budget should head away from the tempting ocean waters and go inland: **Monique Hotel (** (011) 474231, Box 97263, Mombasa, charges 1,000 KSh for a double, bed and breakfast.

OPPOSITE: Even in Fort Jesus the Portuguese were never safe. ABOVE: Mombasa's sun sets to the distant call of countless muezzins.

Most hotel rates in the Mombasa region are negotiable. If you're arriving in the high season and want to reserve in advance, try one of the hotels listed above directly, but you might find better value by asking your travel agent to help: tour operators have often negotiated the keenest rates. Even in December, January and August, you should, in the current climate, be able to pick and choose where you want to stay. Tour operators have often negotiated the best prices: this means that if you're just after a beach vacation it is often cheaper to arrange package rates from

at the local market. Behind is a large, shaded courtyard with traditional furniture and rather smarter style. Whenever you eat at local restaurants wash your hands in the sink provided or in the jug and bowl brought to you: not to do so is considered very rude. And as in all Muslim societies, eating is only with your right hand. Food is served on a base of *ngara*, a flat Ethiopian bread that also serves as knife and fork. Mounds of spiced meats and vegetables are designed to be picked at and shared with costs in the range of 200 KSh per person. The Surya is open for lunch and

home. Charter airlines from Europe and Canada often include several nights at coastal hotels for the price of a round-trip ticket (see TRAVELERS' TIPS, page 289). This option gives you the security of a place to stay on arrival and time to decide how and where you are spending the remainder of your vacation.

WHERE TO EAT

Even if you don't stay in town, Old Town Mombasa is one of the best places in Kenya to experience the local cuisine. An excellent stop for lunch after visiting Fort Jesus is **Surya Restaurant** on Nyeri Street, Mombasa's best Ethiopian restaurant. The wood-paneled front room has plastic tablecloths and is aimed

dinner. A few doors up is Mombasa's best Swahili restaurant, the **Recoda**, but this opens only for dinner. If you're early enough you can sit outside at sidewalk tables and watch the inhabitants go about their evening routine. There is no menu: the waiters will explain what has been prepared for the day, usually mild curry-flavored stews, fish cooked in coconut milk and *pilau* (spiced rice with meat). Desserts include iced, pureed papaya with slices of orange, mango and banana, or chilled, pureed avocado with milk and spices. Prices, once again, in the region of 200 KSh per person. Don't expect a wine list — or even a beer — at these two restaurants but they will provide cutlery if you ask. They're both worth visiting for the excellently prepared and quite unique food and I'm still trying to work out which I prefer.

More conventional meals, with perhaps the best seafood in East Africa, is offered by the **Tamarind Restaurant** ((011) 471747, overlooking Mombasa's Old Port. It's expensive — but well worth it — and there's a top-floor casino to try to recoup the service charge. Reservations are usually needed.

HOW TO GET THERE

By car, the A109 links Kenya's two major cities. Several buses leave Nairobi every day for Mombasa, but the road is in bad repair and a journey that once took as little as six hours now takes up to 20. An overnight train links the two cities and takes 12 hours. Reservations are essential for traveling first or second class: two or three days in advance are generally enough to secure a berth. Without a reservation you'll end up traveling on the benches in third. Reservations can be made in person at Nairobi Station, one and a half kilometers (one mile) from the city center on Station Road, or at Mombasa Station, on Haile Selassie Avenue near the junction with Moi Avenue. Rather less securely, reservations are apparently taken by telephone (Nairobi ((02) 221211, Mombasa ((011) 312221), or perhaps are easiest through a travel agent such as **Let's Go Travel** ((02) 340331 FAX (02) 336890 E-MAIL info@letsgosafari.com, Box 60342, Nairobi. **Kenya Airways** ((02) 210771 or (02) 229291 FAX (02) 336252, Box 41010, Nairobi, and ((011) 221251 FAX (011) 313815, Box 99302, Mombasa, flies five times every day from Nairobi International Airport to Mombasa's Moi International Airport. The fare is US$50 one way and the flights take an hour and a half.

AROUND MOMBASA

JUMBA LA MTWANA NATIONAL MONUMENT

Around Mombasa, there are several sites to lure you from the beach, or to occupy your time if you've overdone the sun. A short drive north along the coastal highway, just past the Mtwapa Bridge, is **Jumba la Mtwana**

National Monument, ruins of a fourteenth-century town. It is much smaller and less intricately planned than Gedi to the north. Situated right on the beach, the town, whose Swahili name means "Mansion of the Slaves," gives one the impression that at its peak Jumba was much more in the mainstream of coastal commerce, with nearby Mtwapa Creek as a safe anchorage. The site is dotted with the giant-trunked baobabs, some of which could have existed when Jumba was inhabited.

The most interesting of the ruins is the mosque by the sea that, according to archaeologists, has a separate room in which women could worship. Near the north-facing wall of the mosque are several tombs, one of which has an interesting inscription, that translated, reads: "Every soul shall taste death. You will simply be paid your wages in full on the Day of Resurrection. He who is removed from the fire and made to enter heaven, it is he who has won the victory. The earthly life is only delusion."

Entrance fee to Jumba is 200 KSh; you can buy a guidebook to the site at the entrance. After visiting the ruins, it's fun to walk the beach, which has a stand of aerial rooted pines, the mangroves of the pine family.

BAMBURI NATURE TRAIL

Closer to town is Bamburi Nature Trail (open daily, 300 KSh per person), the most zoo-like park you'll find in Kenya. There are tamish hippos called Sally, Potti and Cleopatra, aldabra tortoises, crocodiles, a *tilapia* aquaculture project that produces over 30 tons of fish per year, pelicans, crowned cranes, antelope in enclosures, and a family of serval cats. An attached restaurant called Whispering Pines is good for lunch: set amongst the casuarina trees it provides a welcome breath of the bush experience at a cost of about 200 KSh per person. Thursdays to Saturday the restaurant stays open for evening meals.

The nature trail is a rehabilitated quarry owned by the Bamburi Cement Factory, which continues moving its operation north and west as its mining techniques dictate.

OPPOSITE: The coastal mangrove swamps are a dense haven for birdlife. OVERLEAF: Fishermen dry their nets on Kenya's fine white coral sand.

The quarry revegetation began in 1971 with the planting of a hardy casuarina trees from Australia. Now a dense forest of whistling pines has taken hold and the ground below is starting to recover its fertility.

SHIMBA HILLS NATIONAL RESERVE

Even if your primary interest is the beach and the sun, you shouldn't pass up an opportunity to explore at least one of Kenya's game parks and see the animals. Easily accessible from the coastal highway is Shimba Hills National Reserve. Wildlife here is not as abundant as in Amboseli or the Maasai Mara, but you can often see the rare sable antelope. With luck, you can find genets, elephants and civet cats, and occasionally, leopards. Park entry fees US$20 per person per day.

To get the most of a trip to the reserve, consider staying a night. If you're equipped (food, cooking equipment, and mosquito nets), there are the superb **Shimba Hills Self-Service Bandas** (US$10 per person) overlooking a steep, thickly-vegetated ravine where the air is cool and refreshingly dry. The view east is magnificent and the sunrise across the Indian Ocean is beyond description.

Alternatively, a night-viewing lodge built along the same lines as Treetops (see THE ABERDARES, page 152) but with infinitely more style and charm, the **Shimba Hills Lodge** ((02) 540780 FAX (02) 543810, Box 40075, Nairobi. Prices vary by season from US$90 to US$130 for a double, bed and breakfast; children under seven are not permitted. Shimba Hills is a good coastal version, a sturdy and comfortable treehouse in the heart of dense jungle. If Shimba is the only wildlife reserve you will visit, by all means stay at the lodge for a night. Elephants are frequent visitors to the waterhole and bush babies are attracted to the activities. Shimba Hills National Reserve is the only place where you'll find the rare sable antelope, which can be found along with other game on morning or evening game drives.

The lodge overlooks an emerald glade of dense coastal rain forest with giant cycads. In the early morning and late afternoon, you can sometimes see a leopard; giant monitor lizards are numerous. Animals are now well used to whispering visitors to their domain. There have been sightings of elephants at night but these are rare at present.

Nearby — but just outside Shimba Hills National Park — is the brand new **Kwale Elephant Sanctuary**, a community-based project to protect a large population of elephants marooned by encroaching human development. A new lodge gives grandstand views at low prices. Reservations can be made through **Traveler's Beach Hotel** ((011) 485121 FAX 485678, Box 87649, Mombasa.

RABAI

A 45-minute drive west of Mombasa (towards Nairobi, turning north at Mazeras on C-107) is **Rabai**, site of Krapf and Rebmann's mission. It was from here that they left on their separate expeditions which led to the mapping of Mounts Kenya and Kilimanjaro. The ruins of Krapf's house can be seen; Rebmann's is still occupied. The people of Rabai will be glad to show you around.

Krapf departed on several expeditions from this mission at Rabai. He became the first white man to cross the Tsavo River, to explore the Yatta Plateau in what is now Tsavo East National Park, and to locate Mount Kenya. Local tribesmen had described the mountain as taller than Mount Kilimanjaro, which no one had climbed because of "the intense cold and the white matter which rolled down with great noise" — a reference to the snow avalanches that now, with world climate change, no longer occur on Mount Kenya.

THE SOUTH COAST

Heading south from Mombasa means using the Likoni Ferry, which shuttles cars and flooding pedestrians across 400 m (a quarter of a mile) of water to the mainland and the southern strip of the B8 Coast Road. This tends to give the southern resort areas a more timeless, relaxing atmosphere even though, as the crow flies, they are quite close to the city. The beaches tend to be better than those an equivalent distance north of Mombasa, with the ocean — and the fringing coral reef — nearer to land.

Thread straight through the suburb of Likoni, scene of some of the worst disturbances in the the 1997 elections and still with an uneasy atmosphere. This quickly fades. Although some hotels have been built on the shore here — known as Shelley Beach — it's not especially recommended: the sea goes a long way out at low tide and it's prone to seaweed.

TIWI AND DIANI

Better carry on south: after 20 km (12.5 miles) two turnings to the left head off into the

Ten kilometers (six miles) further south at the small town of Ukunda a left turn leads down to the resort of Diani, the most developed stretch of Kenya's coast. Traditional vacation-style resorts line the beach and colobus monkeys swing around the few patches of forest that squeeze between the developments. The classic Diani activities are scuba diving on the fringing reef or game fishing out in deeper waters. For game fishing, **Grand Slam Charters** are endlessly helpful and accommodating, while the best dive operator is **Dive the Crab**. Both are

small, cottagey atmosphere of Tiwi Beach, four kilometers (two and a half miles) from the B8 coast road. Traditionally this area is popular with backpackers who shudder every time they see the new and enormous Traveler's Beach Hotel that has been built on the coast and stay instead in a range of smaller chalet-type developments. Few *matatus* mean that visitors without a car will find most of Tiwi's beach lodges feel quite isolated: access is by taxi or rental car and the pleasures quiet, beach-based ones. One lodge example is the **Tiwi Sea Castles** ((0127) 51220 FAX (0127) 51222, Box 96599, Likoni (2,800 KSh for a double bed and breakfast), ideal for families, where guests stay for weeks — or months.

bookable **Safari Beach Hotel** ((0127) 2726 FAX (0127) 2357, Box 90690, Mombasa. Day-trips from Diani head down to Kenya's deep south for the very best diving: Shimoni, the offshore island of Wasini, and the Marine National Park of Kisite. At a cost of US$80, these excursions include a sail by dhow out to the best snorkeling area and an after-swim feast of crab and seafood which relegates most people comatose: fortunately wicker beds are laid out under trees. Reserve through **Kisite Dhow Tours** ((0127) 2331 FAX (0127) 3154, Box 281, Ukunda.

Generally, guests look to their own resort hotels for a choice of restaurants and night

---

Tiwi Beach is a favorite with backpackers and ideal for a longer stay.

clubs, but it is worth getting out occasionally: **Ali Baba's Restaurant**, set deep underground in limestone caverns, is perhaps the most atmospheric eatery on the East African coast. For evening drinking, Kenyan watering-hole is the **Forty Thieves Bar** where *YMCA* echoes from disco speakers over the sea. For a more Kenyan experience cross the road to the **Bushbaby** night club, or take a *matatu* or drive to the town of Ukunda on the main coast road: for instance, at the (unlicensed) **Happy Moment** café, it's a struggle to spend more than US$2 on a meal.

beachfront hotel was **Nomad** ((0127) 2155 FAX (0127) 2391, Box 1, Ukunda. Perhaps they were too cheap. On my last visit it was closed with no immediate plans to reopen.

How to Get There

Take the Likoni Ferry from Digo Road, Mombasa and follow the A14 coast road which stays near, but not in sight of the ocean, and the beaches are clearly-marked turnings to the left. Tiwi comes first, 20 km (12.5 miles) and two turnings south of Likoni. The Diani turning is 10 km (six miles) further south, at

Where to Stay

Most of the hotels here depend on European tour operators for most of their business: walk-in rates are steep and often it is cheaper to buy a package vacation from home. There are exceptions: most notably a small Seychellois restaurant called **Boko Boko** (/FAX (0127) 2344, at the northern tip of the resort road, opposite the Neptune Village Hotel: they have four en-suite guest rooms available. The rate is 2,000 KSh for an air-conditioned double, bed and breakfast, 1,800 KSh with fan only. Otherwise it's back to luxury: for US$192 per night for a double the sophisticated but welcoming **Safari Beach Hotel** ((0127) 2726 FAX (0127) 2357, Box 90690, Mombasa, is possibly the best. Traditionally the cheapest

the town of Ukunda. Turn left and drive three kilometers (two miles) to a strip of tarmac that runs along the back of the beach developments. Turn right for most of the hotels and restaurants. Drive carefully here: there are ladders to let the colobus monkeys cross the road but they still sometimes use the road and have very little traffic sense.

Diani is easy to get to by public transport: buses and *matatus* leave from the Likoni Ferry throughout the day and take about 30 minutes. Many buses and *matatus* go directly to the beach, although it might be necessary to disembark at Ukunda if your bus is heading to Tanzania. If heading for Tiwi Beach, taxis lurk around the turning and offer the only alternative to a long hot walk to the coast.

SHIMONI

Shimoni is a low-key coastal resort catering primarily to deep-sea fishermen, but it offers excellent snorkeling in Kisite Marine National Park, subterranean caves, and Wasini Island to explore.

Kisite Marine National Park is one of Kenya's three offshore reserves where fishing and collecting shells and coral are strictly forbidden. Because of this, the underwater spectacle is unrivaled. You can snorkel any-

The town of Shimoni takes its name from the Swahili *shimo,* meaning caves, which refers to a series of underground coral grottoes. A path from the Shimoni jetty leads to a ladder entrance. The caves are now inhabited by bats, but legends claim that they were once used for storing slaves or were the secret refuge of the locals against Maasai raids. They evoke thoughts of pirate ships and hidden treasures among the nooks and crannies that some claim extend for 20 km (12 miles). The adventurous should bring a flashlight although the area around the

where off Shimoni or Wasini Island, as the sea is calm and clear. The best viewing, however, is around Kisite Island. There are organized trips from the hotels along Diani Beach or reserve directly with **Kisite Dhow Tours (** (0127) 2331 FAX (0127) 3154 Box 281, Ukunda.

The cost — US$80 per person including transfers — includes a sailing-dhow crossing to the island, snorkeling equipment rental, and a lavish banquet lunch after which most people collapse on rattan beds spread around under shady trees. Alternatively, walk to the small and friendly Wasini Village. The Kisite National Park has probably the best snorkeling in Kenya and qualified divers can also rent scuba equipment.

entrance is well-lit by sunlight filtering through holes like the one through which you descend.

Wasini Island

A short boat ride offshore from Shimoni is Wasini Island, a small scrub-covered atoll. It measures five kilometers by one kilometer (about three and a half miles by two-thirds of a mile) and is home for a few fishermen. There are no cars; it is a bit like living adrift on the sea. You can wander around the island, explore a raised dead coral garden alive with

OPPOSITE: Craftsman sculpts attractive tropical hardwoods for tourists. ABOVE: The interiors of Watamu's homes reflect the coast's diverse architectural heritage.

birds and butterflies instead of fish, swim and snorkel off the beach in front of the village, and discover the ruins of an Arab-African town around which the present village is built. The **Wasini Island Restaurant** caters for snorkeling groups during the day although it closes for the months of May and June.

Where to Stay

The **Shimoni Reef Lodge** ((011) 471771 FAX (011) 473249 WEB SITE www.africa-direct.com/, c/o Reef Hotel, Box 82234,

Mombasa, at US$130 for a double with half board, caters mainly for keen scuba divers, while the **Pemba Channel Fishing Club** ((011) 3132749 FAX (011) 316875, Box 86952, Mombasa, which is a club (in the British sense) for serious deep-sea fishermen. They do, however, open their doors to nonmembers who share their fishing interests.

If you'd prefer to stay on Wasini Island itself it is always possible to stay at **Mpunguti Guest House**, where rooms cost 1,000 KSh per double, bed and breakfast, and it is possible to camp for 200 KSh per person. Negotiate hard with a boatman for a dhow ride across to the island: how much they charge depends on how much money they think you have; 800 KSh would be a reasonable price.

How to Get There

To get to the south coast from Mombasa, drive to the end of the Digo Road and down the ramp to the Likoni Ferry. Two boats shuttle across the water and it's rare to wait more than 20 minutes. Pay at the office before driving on board if in a vehicle: the charge is 25 KSh. Pedestrians travel free. *Matatus* and buses wait on the other side. Kenya Bus Service buses leave every 20 minutes or so. For Shimoni, a couple of buses and *matatus* each day go directly: otherwise take anything heading for Lunga Lunga on the Tanzanian border and get off 32 km (20 miles) early at the Shimoni turning. You'll then have to hitchhike the last stretch.

If driving your own vehicle, the A14 coast road stays near, but not in sight of, the ocean, and the beaches are clearly-marked turn offs to the left. The Shimoni turn is 70 km (44 miles) south of Likoni: then a *murram* road takes you the final 14 km (nine miles) to the tip of the peninsula.

THE NORTH COAST

North of Mombasa and the Nyali, Bamburi, and Kikambala hotel strip, there is little development. Most of the coastal land between Kikambala and Kilifi is the privately owned Vipingo Sisal Estate, one of the largest sisal estates and Kenya's most impressive. The sharp-pointed sisal plants in neatly lined rows cover the landscape in an endless sea of dark sage-green.

Sisal's succulent leaves, which can grow up to one and a half meters (five feet) have sharp spikes at the tips, and when not "in bloom" sisal is easily mistaken for pineapple. (Pineapple are grown at the coast and they are the best we have eaten anywhere, even better than the famed Hawaiian ones.) The bloom of the sisal plant is a three- to six-meter (10- to 18-ft)-tall rigid stalk which bears yellow flowers. A coarse, yellow-white fiber is obtained from a process of crushing and beating the succulent leaves. These dry one- to two-meter (three- to six-foot)-long fibers are then used to make twine and rope for nets, hammocks, and carpets. Sisal was one of Kenya's major exports until lighter synthetic fibers elbowed it out of the world market. Nonetheless, Vipingo is still in operation and a major employer on Kenya's north coast.

The monotony of the sisal rows is broken frequently by huge, light-gray, almost silvery, baobabs. These trees are without leaves for most of the year, bearing leaves only after periods of heavy rain. Most Africans consider the baobab a sacred tree. They can live up to 2,000 years and at Vipingo, when one dies, it is removed.

The baobab looks like a normal tree until it is about four and a half meters (15 ft) tall. Then its trunk begins to swell and continues to swell throughout its life. Some trees reach a diameter of six meters (20 ft) and the trees look somewhat absurd with trunks almost as broad as they are tall.

There are several local legends as to why the baobab looks the way it does. One suggests that the baobab was once the most beautiful tree in Africa, but it was also very proud and boasted too much. As punishment, God turned it upside down, making its beautiful foliage its roots.

Another claims that the first baobab refused to stay planted in one place. It wandered the countryside causing trouble. When God caught it, he planted it upside down as punishment.

The baobab's green nuts can be used to make flour and the leaves and fruit-pulp are a Kenyan cure for fever. Inside its thin bark, the trunk is soft and pithy, storing a great amount of moisture. During periods of drought, elephants rip the baobabs apart and extract the water.

KILIFI

Kilifi is the first town north of Mombasa with any tourist amenities. Originally dependent on trading with traffic waiting for the ferry, a 1991 bridge has left it rather without purpose. But as the locals say, it's a "bit cool." It has several *hotelis* in town, a motel, and two coastal resorts. When the Portuguese arrived on the Kenyan coast, Kilifi was known as Mnarani and was centered on the south bank of Kilifi Creek. Ruins of the town are situated on a high cliff above the creek and include a pillar tomb and mosques. There is little mention of this establishment in Portuguese or Arab writings of the times, and one

theory is that the settlement was solely a slave trading center, not mercantile and agricultural like Mombasa, Malindi, Lamu, and Pate.

On the Mnarani side of Kilifi Creek is the **Mnarani Club** ((0125) 22320 FAX (0125) 22200, Box 1008, Kilifi, run by Clubs International. Rates include all food, water sports, and drinks until 11 PM and are in the region of US$200, although once more, this is cheaper reserved with flights through a package operator. Behind the Agip station on the highway going north is the **Mkwajoni Motel and Restaurant**. It has clean rooms with mosquito nets at 500 KSh per double, bed and breakfast, but be warned: the rooms surround a disco that operates Wednesdays, Fridays and Saturdays. On these nights the similarly priced **Dhows Inn** ((0125) 22028, south of the bridge, is a quieter bet. North of the cashew plantation are grazing lands, a coconut grove or two, and the start of the **Arabuko-Sokoke Forest**, a United Nations Biosphere Reserve.

WATAMU BAY AND WATAMU MARINE NATIONAL PARK

Watamu Bay is the prime destination for this part of the coast, a quiet community sandwiched between two United Nations Biosphere Reserves: the forest inland and the Marine Park offshore. **Watamu Marine National Park** which has superb snorkeling, or "goggling" as it is locally called. As at Shimoni in the south, fishing of any kind is forbidden in the park and the variety of fish, coral, and anemones is phenomenal.

We've snorkeled several times in Watamu Bay. Sometimes, a swimmer may be surrounded by a thousand or more gregarious and colorful fish. Among the common species we've seen are butterfly fish, angelfish, golden trevally, cardinal fish, hawkfish, white-breasted sturgeons, blue-lined snappers, rock cod (groupers), and jewelfish. The rock cod can grow to several hundred kilograms in weight, and hide under coral outcrops; most of the others are very small, from one to ten centimeters (one-half to four inches) in length.

The coast has been built over millions of years by coral growth.

Low tide is the best time for snorkeling because the sea water filters the sunlight, and the red end of the spectrum disappears after the first one to two meters (three to six feet) of depth, depending on water clarity. Thus, at low tide, the reef will appear much more colorful as there is less water covering it.

The local hotels all have boats to take you to the reef and along the coast for 300 KSh to 450 KSh per person, although the park entrance fee is also US$5 per person per day. The park extends the length of the ocean in front of the hotels, and you won't be charged an entrance to swim as long as you're not using a mask and snorkel. If you want fins, ask at the dive centers at **Hemingways**, or **Ocean Sports** (see WHERE TO STAY, below). To protect the reef none of the standard snorkeling operators include fins: they argue you'll see more without them. Some of the largest fish are near shore, hiding under the moored boats in an area known to the early settlers as "The Larder." If you want to go scuba diving, the best operator is **Aqua Ventures** ((0122) 32008 FAX (0122) 32266, next to Ocean Sports.

At the south end of Watamu Bay is another drowned river valley, **Mida Creek**. It is lined with low-lying mangrove swamps and mud flats. A boat tour of Mida Creek is a pleasant way to spend a morning or afternoon and it can be combined with snorkeling stops in the marine park.

We went one Sunday from Ocean Sports, leaving around 9 AM, stopped to snorkel for an hour, and cruised Mida Creek seeing fish eagles, egrets, plovers, and hundreds of song birds (often you can sight osprey and terns). Late April, just before migration, is the best time to watch the birds in Mida Creek. From Mida Creek, we stopped at the reef for another hour of snorkeling before returning to Ocean Sports for their famous Sunday lunch. For 750 KSh, you can choose from the cold seafood buffet, which usually features smoked sailfish, shellfish, a selection of salads and cold cuts, a hot entree usually of curry, fresh fruit, and several desserts.

The more expensive hotels in Watamu run boats daily to the Marine Park and Mida Creek, and have boats that can take you deep-sea fishing. Their catch rate includes — blue

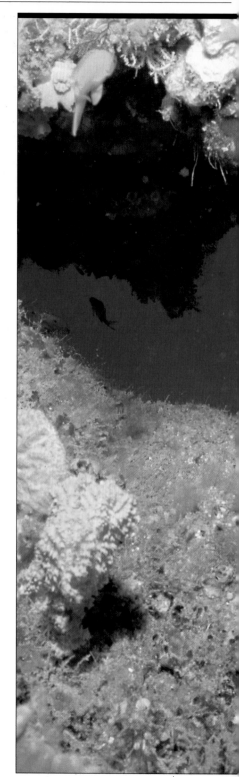

Rainbow reef shelters a myriad of tropical fish.

and black marlin, sailfish, shark, bonito, and tuna. If you like the sport, and don't want to kill the fish, Kenya is at the forefront of East Africa's tag-and-release program. Guests and fish buyers gather each afternoon around 4 PM to watch the weighing in and to bid on the catch. One afternoon, we watched a 27-kg (60-lb) sailfish being transported away on a bicycle, snout resting on the handle bars and tail extending beyond the back wheel. If you're tempted to give game fishing a try, see DEEP-SEA FISHING, page 20 and SPORTING SPREE, page 38.

GEDI NATIONAL MONUMENT

Gedi National Monument is the most extensive of the ruins on the Kenyan Coast. It comprises the remains of a late thirteenth or fourteenth century city that was at its peak in the middle of the fifteenth century, and was abandoned in the early seventeenth century. Its history is somewhat a mystery. No one is certain when it was founded and by whom. Unlike most of the Arab-African towns, it did not have a harbor and was

ARABUKO–SOKOKE FOREST

To fill your time away from the beach in the Watamu Bay area, you will find the Arabuko-Sokoke Forest and Gedi National Monument. The Arabuko-Sokoke Forest is the largest surviving lowland jungle in Kenya. It has stands of hardwoods and rubber trees and the borders of the forest, thanks to United Nation Biosphere listing, seem relatively secure. You can hike along the many dirt tracks and logging roads and will see birds, butterflies, and, if you are lucky, the Zanzibar or Aders' duiker, a 35-cm (14-inch) antelope, or the forest's two unique species, the Scopps Owl and Elephant Shrew.

possibly not a major commercial or political power. Nonetheless, the quantity and quality of porcelain discovered here indicate that its inhabitants were prosperous. The city had a palace that covered about a tenth of a hectare (a quarter of an acre), houses with sunken courtyards, numerous mosques, ornate pilaster tombs, and inner and outer protective walls.

Archaeologists suspect that only a few of the buildings were still occupied in the sixteenth century. By the end of the seventeenth century, Gedi was empty. The writings of the Portuguese from this period shed no light on the history of this mysterious city.

In the seventeenth century, the invading Galla from Somalia either massacred or chased away the inhabitants of all the Arab-

African cities between Juba River in present-day Somalia and Mtwapa, 24 km (15 miles) north of Mombasa. Gedi was probably no exception. In the second half of the nineteenth century, the Galla were in turn attacked by Somalis and Maasai and lost control over the northern coastal area. The site of Gedi was never reoccupied or rebuilt, but a nearby town, also named Gedi, has been built. There is a school, a few shops, and numerous homes and small farms.

A national historic site, Gedi has been partially excavated and the grounds are well

benefits for local farmers living on the border of the Arabuko-Sokoke Forest. At least eight farmers, working from makeshift frames on the edge of the forest, are breeding butterflies for export to Europe. At the heart of this project is a butterfly center by the Gedi Ruins, where the pupae, often more beautiful than any jewel, are packed in cotton-wool for the journey to the West. This has brought US$50,000 to the local economy, in an area that already contains at least 260 butterfly species, fluttering through the dense trees of the forest in vivid bursts of color.

maintained. You can purchase a booklet at the entrance which guides you through the town and along the walls. A tall coastal forest that has grown up around and in the site all but dwarfs this 18-hectare (45-acre) town. It is now home for vervet monkeys who frequently take a dislike to visitors and toss fruits and nuts on the unsuspecting. A small museum displays many of the artifacts uncovered during the excavations between 1939 and 1958.

KIPEPEO BUTTERFLY PROJECT

One of the few good things to result from the Rio Conference on climate change, the Kipepeo Butterfly Project has started to reap

WHERE TO STAY

There are three main resorts in Watamu. **Turtle Bay** ((0122) 32003 FAX (0122) 32268, Box 10, Watamu, is an all-inclusive hotel popular with tourists from England and charges US$168 per double per day, including full board and all drinks until 11 PM, while **Hemingways** ((0122) 32624 FAX (0122) 32256 WEB SITE www.hemingways.com/, Box 267, Watamu, is a luxury hotel catering mainly —but not exclusively—for big-game fishermen, and charges US$265 per double with

OPPOSITE: Watamu Bay Marine Park protects some of the best coral on the coast. ABOVE: Ruins of the thirteenth- to fifteenth-century Arab city of Gedi.

half board. Local Kenyans tend to walk a few meters up the beach for the family-owned **Ocean Sports** ((0122) 32008 FAX (0122) 32266, Box 100, Watamu, which charges 4,800 KSh for a double, half board. They only offer half-board (breakfast, tea, and dinner), but you can buy lunch as a supplement. However, in the heat of the coast, half board will leave you more than full each day. Afternoon tea with fresh homemade scones and jam is a great substitute for lunch. During May and June, admittedly not the best season at the coast, Ocean Sports reduces its rates dra-

beach. By public transport, take a bus or *matatu* heading for Malindi, and get off 24 km (15 miles) early at Gedi village. Further *matatus* will reach Watamu village. Alternatively it is possible to fly to Malindi and take a taxi back to Watamu: the cost to cover the 24 km (15 miles) should not be much more than 1,000 KSh.

MALINDI

Malindi was the city state that in the fourteenth century sent a Kenyan giraffe

matically. Just ask. Meanwhile Hemingways closes completely through May. Travelers on a budget can find cheaper accommodation in Watamu, a 30-minute walk up the beach and across a headland from Watamu Bay. **The Dante Hotel** ((0122) 32083, next to Happy Nights Disco, charges 500 KSh for two, no breakfast, while opposite, **Veronica** ((0122) 32243 includes breakfast for 700 KSh.

HOW TO GET THERE

It takes just over an hour to Watamu from Mombasa. Leave Mombasa on the B8 coast road: after 90 km (56 miles) turn right at Gedi Village. Pass Gedi National Monument and drive four kilometers (three miles) to the

to China, gift of the Sultan of Malindi to the Chinese emperor, which was transported by one of China's most renowned navigators, the Ming Dynasty's Admiral Cheng Ho. The gift probably served a two-fold mission. First, it attempted to prove to the isolationist emperor that the lands beyond China did have something to offer. Secondly, the Sultan wished to establish direct trade with the Chinese fleets that had, since the sixth century, sailed only as far as India or Arabia to purchase slaves and other East African goods. Malindi also welcomed and entertained Vasco da Gama on his visits to the Kenyan coast, but has since lost some of its previous charm to tourism: a rapid boom in Italian development has ended in a bust from which it will take years to recover and silt has affected both its marine park and beaches. The old town is a mishmash of Arab-style buildings, few of which are older than 1900, and boom buildings from the 1930s while to the north are the rather grander hangovers from the 1990s boom.

Most of Malindi's old buildings went to ruin after its ruling family moved to Mombasa in the sixteenth century. When the Portuguese captured Mombasa, they installed Malindi's royal family as titular head of the coastal communities.

Without a ruling family, Malindi's power and prosperity declined. The port no longer attracted merchant vessels and Malindi became a ghost town. Gone are the inlaid doors described by the early Portuguese visitors. Tourism in the past 25 years revitalized the town, and left it hanging. During the peak of the high season (December and January), the town is flushed with tourists, mostly German and Italian, while at other times bars and hotels stand empty.

Located at the mouth of the Sabaki River, Malindi's bay often turns red due to seasonal runoff from upstream overgrazed land. This makes Watamu Bay a better choice for a destination. El Niño floods silted over the reef and built out a bank of brown sand along the town's main beach. It is open to question how long it will take the snorkeling in **Malindi Marine National Park** to recover.

WHERE TO STAY

If Ocean Sports in Watamu is reserved, the next best accommodations in the Malindi-Watamu area is the **Driftwood Beach Club** ((0123) 20155 FAX 214120, Box 63, Malindi, at 4,700 KSh for a double, half board. The atmosphere is much like that of Ocean Sports although it remains to be seen how it will survive a recent change of management which sent staff and customers on strike. In Malindi town there are several small hotels, the best of which, though sandwiched between a bus station and a mosque, is **Ozi's Bed and Breakfast** ((0123) 20218, Seafront Road, Box 60, Malindi, at 700 KSh per double, bed and breakfast, for clean accom-

modation although its position between mosque and bus station might make for a restless night.

HOW TO GET THERE

Malindi is two hours by car from Mombasa along the coast road. It can also be reached by air from Nairobi or Mombasa: the flight from Mombasa offers a spectacular half-hour overview of the fringing coral reef of the shore. **Kenya Airways** ((02) 210771 or (02) 229291 FAX (02) 336252, Box 41010,

Nairobi; and ((011) 221251 FAX (011) 313815, Box 99302, Mombasa; or ((0123) 20237, Box 634, Malindi and **AirKenya** ((02) 501421/3 FAX (02) 500845, Box 30357, Nairobi; ((011) 229777 FAX (011) 224063, Nkrumah Road, Mombasa; or ((0123) 30808 FAX (0123) 21229, Box 548, Malindi, both fly this route. The fare from Malindi to Mombasa with AirKenya is US$28. If you're depending on this flight to catch an international connection, reconfirm often as overbooking is common. Frequent buses and *matatus* link Mombasa with Malindi.

OPPOSITE: A luxury restaurant in Malindi. Malindi and Lamu are the most interesting places to stay on the coast. ABOVE: Lantern-sailed outriggers along the coast.

THE LAMU ARCHIPELAGO

North of Malindi, when the paved road ends, you enter a no-man's-land that Somali bandits (*shiftas*) rule. The landscape is flat with marshy green and arid brown stretches. During the rainy season, the route north is impassable in any vehicle; bus service is often interrupted for weeks. Even in the dry season *shiftas* make the route unsafe. Visitors wanting to go further north to Lamu usually fly from Malindi, Mombasa or Nairobi.

Archaeologists and historians have established that the island has been inhabited since about AD 1200, though the towns of **Lamu** and **Shela** on Lamu Island did not exist until the fourteenth to fifteenth century. The founders of Lamu and Shela were most likely religious refugees from the Arabian or Persians regions of the Caliphate.

These refugees, like those who migrated to Malindi and Mombasa, became the religious, political, and economic force in the area. They assimilated parts of the native population and culture. Lamu and the nearby

There are daily flights from Malindi and Mombasa, and if you are in a hurry you can tour Lamu in a day, flying up in the morning and returning the same night. But that's not really long enough. Lamu is the most exotic site on the Kenyan coast, a mini-Katmandu-by-the-sea.

When you get into the dhow that takes you from the mainland to Lamu (or get on the airplane at Mombasa or Malindi), it is like traveling by time machine. When you set foot on the island, you find yourself in the nineteenth century. There are no automobiles. Electricity has only just arrived. Donkeys and dhows are the only transportation, and the pace of life is accordingly slow.

islands of Manda and Pate were part of the Portuguese Indian Ocean empire. The Portuguese constructed a fort on Pate, but apparently never had a large force on Lamu or Manda. From the number of old buildings still standing, it seems reasonable to assume that the inhabitants did not openly oppose the Portuguese, but maintained their cultural and religious identities without aggravating their rulers. There are reports of the Portuguese executing one of Lamu's sheiks for collaboration with the Turks in the late sixteenth century—a minor punishment when you consider the massive slaughter and pillage the Portuguese inflicted on Mombasa.

Lamu became prosperous in the seventeenth century when Pate's harbor began to silt in. Lamu reached its peak of affluence in the eighteenth century. From the ancient poetry of the region and a few western accounts, historian J. de V. Allen has reconstructed life on the island then:

"Rich men clad in fine silks and turbans moved about surrounded by crowds of retainers, young men who competed, both individually and collectively in personal display, in witty exchanges, in composing poetry and epigrams and also in ceremonial sword-dances. There was a constant buzz of activity, with business being transacted in

husband's suspicions. The art of enjoying harem life is one in which Lamu women have become, over the centuries, very skilled.

"Warfare, when it occurred, was an occasion for impassioned speeches, the wholesale distribution of invulnerability charms, and menacing processions accompanied by the beating of many gongs." (J. de V. Allen, *Lamu Town*.)

Lamu, Pate, and Manda aligned themselves with Oman, and later, Zanzibar when Seyyid Said moved his court there, and thus traded regularly with European and Ameri-

the streets and coffeehouses, workmen and slaves building or refurbishing houses, heavily-laden sailing boats entering or leaving the harbor, and great men coming and going on the eternal safaris which are still so much an integral part of Swahili life.

"Music was provided for the master of the house when he returned home, also massage and baths (both hot and cold) and couches strewn with jasmine. While the women, probably already in seclusion for much of their lives, lived for the weddings and other occasions when they could congregate to dance their own dances and compete with each other in poetry and song, and concentrated meanwhile on enjoying life as much as they could without exciting their

can merchants. There was a period of German occupation in the late nineteenth century, but by then, the islands' prosperity was already in decline. Pate's harbor was completely silted in, Manda never had a good deepwater harbor, and Lamu's could not accommodate the new steamships.

LAMU

Lamu is an amalgam of twelfth- through eighteenth-century buildings in Arab style,

OPPOSITE: Lamu's population LEFT reflects the influence and immigration of northern Arab traders and RIGHT most women go modestly veiled. ABOVE: Sunset falls over a timeless sailing dhow.

with its traditional town plan still intact. Streets are narrow and have the dual purpose of providing shade and producing a slight wind tunnel effect. There are over 20 mosques, the oldest, Pwami, dating from 1370.

Lamu's ornately carved doors, wall niches, and plaster detailing generate the greatest interest, being close to hypnotic in their intricacy. Most of them are distinctly Arabic, but some include universal motifs often found in Celtic, Phoenician and Roman designs.

are festivals for weddings, betrothals, and funerals.

Annually, on the last Thursday in Rabai al-Awal, the week-long festival of **Maulidi** begins (currently in the summer and moving back through the year, according to the lunar calendar). Lamu is then overcrowded as pilgrims come from all over Kenya, Tanzania, Uganda, and Arab countries as well. The island is alive with traditional dance, song, and open-air religious ceremonies.

The **museum** at Lamu is one of the best in Africa. Housed in a classic open-centered

Daily life takes place out of doors; craftsmen work on their doorsteps, businessmen meet on verandas, children play anywhere and everywhere. Although the absence of cars is certainly a factor in this style of life, this has been the rhythm here for centuries. Women still live in relative seclusion, though this is beginning to change. The people of Lamu are social and convivial, most of them sharing common ancestors and history.

Processions occur frequently for various reasons. The most common are the *ziara*, or visits to the graves of religious men. There

building, it has a room depicting a Swahili wedding, displays on coastal maritime culture, ivory and brass *siwas* (ceremonial horns), and exhibits of daily life of the Swahili and the non-Swahili peoples of the nearby mainland. Here, you can buy J. de V. Allen's guide, *Lamu Town*, which gives a detailed history of the area and an excellent description of the historic buildings in the town and the island.

Lamu is the most populous island in the archipelago. The long white beaches are a 40-minute walk from Lamu town (or a 50-Ksh dhow ride), near Shela village. Walk far enough and many will be deserted but don't sunbathe nude or topless as someone will appear and take offense.

ABOVE: Dhows are still used for daily transport on this island without cars. RIGHT: Few coastal artisans still construct dhows by hand, as on Lamu.

The reefs offshore offer good snorkeling, but only from November through February; at other times visibility is a problem. Windsurfing and deep-sea fishing are always available. When the wind is up, you can also body surf — the only place apart from a few dangerous locations further south where this is possible in Kenya.

If you have an extra day (or two) to spend in the area, it is worth visiting **Pate**. There are plenty of dhows providing ferry service; departure times depend on the time and weather. There are no hotels or restaurants

US$180 for a double, full board, is closed annually from April 15 to July 1 but is still the best place to eat and sleep on the island. The small hotels in town are more in keeping with the mood of the city: **Casuarina Guest Lodge** (650 KSh for a suite) is just one example. Don't worry, hoteliers can sense those who need accommodation and will find you: bargaining is expected.

How to Get There

Part of the reason Lamu has retained its special character is that access isn't easy. Not

on the island, but residents meet the ferry boats offering rooms and meals. You can spend only a day, but make sure your dhow or another is going back in the evening. In any case, it is best to bring your own food and water. Around the island (on foot), there are the modern villages of Kizingitini, Bajumwali, and Nyabogi that have a few carved doors, and the ancient towns of Pate, Siyu, and Faza.

Where to Stay

The best tourist class hotel on Lamu is located a 40-minute walk — rather quicker by dhow — from town, but right on the edge of the town's nearest beach: **Peponi Hotel** ((0121) 33154 FAX (0121) 33029 Box 24, Lamu, at

only is the road north of Malindi in poor condition, impassable in the rains, but it is also plagued by *shiftas*. Occasionally convoys of buses and trucks make it through, but the for most visitors access is by air, with flights from Nairobi, Mombasa and Malindi: **AirKenya** ((02) 501421/3 FAX (02) 500845, Box 30357, Nairobi; or ((011) 229777 FAX (011) 224063, Nkrumah Road, Mombasa; or ((0123) 30808 FAX (0123) 21229, Box 548, Malindi; or ((0121) 33445 FAX (0121) 33063, Box 376, Lamu. The fare to fly from Malindi to Lamu is US$65 one way.

OPPOSITE: Lamu's shady, colorful open market. ABOVE: Dhows are a major means of transportation among the islands of the Lamu archipelago.

Travelers'
Tips

GETTING THERE

Your safari to Kenya begins with "getting there." Finding a reasonably priced ticket takes time and a fair amount of persistence.

FROM EUROPE

Your options are greatest from Europe. Prices and restrictions vary. There are direct flights from London, Paris, Amsterdam, Brussels, Copenhagen, Frankfurt, Madrid, Moscow, Athens, Rome, and Zurich on regularly scheduled airlines, British Airways, Air France, Sabena, SAS, Lufthansa, Iberia, Aeroflot, Olympic Airways, Alitalia, and Swissair, respectively. Some are daily, but most are once or twice weekly. Kenya Airways, now a code-share partner with KLM, flies from Paris, London, Amsterdam, Zurich, Athens, Frankfurt, Rome, and Cairo. APEX fares are the most reasonable you can get with these airlines and from the United Kingdom these can cost as little as US$600 round trip, even with scheduled airlines. Some companies will restrict your length of stay and flexibility to change travel dates at this price so check conditions before you part with your money.

For cheaper fares, often on the regularly scheduled flights, you should contact a travel agent who is familiar with the charter and consolidator scene. In the United Kingdom, one of the best is **Flightbookers** ((0171) 7572444 FAX (0171) 7572200 WEB SITE www.flightbookers.net, 177-178 Tottenham Court Road, London W1P OLX, with further branches around the United Kingdom.

FROM THE UNITED STATES AND CANADA

From North America, no flights fly direct, non-stop to Kenya, and a change of plane and airline will be needed, usually in Europe. Depending on departuare point, length of stay and season, the APEX fare will be around US$2,500 to 3,500. KLM's code-share link with Northwest Airlines and Kenya Airways make them amongst the most frequent fliers with a comprehensive range of departures across the United States. Routing through the United Kingdom can give the best rates: operators in London have access to consolidated fares and special rates with safari companies and beach resorts. Student travel companies such as STA or Council Travel offer low fares. Refer to advertisements in the travel sections of *Sunday Times* for more specialists: book by credit card for added security.

FROM AUSTRALASIA

There are no direct flights from Australia or New Zealand to Kenya. A stopover is inevitable. Most direct is via Mauritius using Air Mauritius' weekly flights from Perth: a code-share arrangement with Ansett open this route up to New Zealand and Australian cities. Perth is lucky again with flights to Nairobi and Harare, both of which link up to Nairobi. Kenya's substantial Asian population ensures plenty of flights from India so good linkages exist from various cities in Asia, especially Bombay. Good services are also supplied by Middle Eastern Airlines, including Gulf Air and Emirates. Flying via the United States is not only much longer but also raises the problems already faced by Americans trying to get to Africa, but Kenya can be fitted into round-the-world itineraries. Specialist operators down under include **Africa Travel Centre** ((02) 9267 3048, Level 12, 456 Kent Street, Sydney NSW 2000, and **Africa Travel Centre** ((09) 520 2000, 21 Remuera Road, Box 9365, Newmarket, Auckland.

GETTING HOME

To leave Kenya, traditionally it was necessary to pay an airport exit tax of US$20 (in United States currency *only*). Officially this was meant to be integrated into the cost of the ticket, but if you didn't pay this with your ticket make sure you have US$20 spare when you get to the departure gate: changing money at the airport can be time-consuming and it's not unknown for harassed tourists to be tricked into changing at a very poor rate. The need for all currency transactions to be noted in your currency declaration is no longer generally required.

The first view of Nairobi is from the air as your plane comes in to land.

VISAS

Visas are required for all visitors except citizens of most Commonwealth countries and several other countries with which Kenya has reciprocal agreements, namely Denmark, Ethiopia, Germany, Finland, San Marino, Spain, Sweden, Turkey, and Uruguay. Citizens of Australia, Nigeria and Sri Lanka do need visas. However at time of going to press all United Kingdom and United States citizens need visas at a cost of £35 sterling or US$57 per person. Although any currency will be accepted, credit cards are not. Rush off the plane to beat the worst of the lines. These requirements are subject to change and should be checked with Kenya government offices abroad, airlines, or a travel agency before departure. If visas are required, best get them before leaving home: airport lines can be long and the requirement that the visas must be bought with a hard currency mean that lines move slowly. Standard tourist visas are valid for 30 days and for one entry.

As a rule of thumb, allow six weeks to get your visa from one of the Kenya diplomatic missions listed below, or from the British consulate if Kenya has no diplomatic representation in your country. When such a lead time is not possible, advise the appropriate mission so it can speed your application.
Austria ((01) 633242, Rotenturmstrasse 22, 1010 Vienna.
Australia ((06) 247 4788, 33 Ainslie Avenue, Box 1990, Canberra.
Belgium ((02) 230 3065, avenue Joyeuse Entrée 1-5, Brussels.
Canada ((613) 563 1773, Gillia Building, Suite 600, 415 Laurier Avenue East, West Ottawa, Ontario.
Egypt ((02) 704 455, 20 Boulos Hanna Street, Box 362, Dokki, Cairo.
France ((01) 45 53 35 00, 3, rue Cimarosa, 75116 Paris.
Germany ((0228) 356 041, 53 Bonn-Bad Godesburg 2, Micael Plaza, Villichgasse 23, Bonn.
Italy ((06) 578 1192/808 2718, CP 10755, 0014 Rome.
Japan ((03) 479 4006, No. 20-24 Nishi-Azobu 3-Chome, Minato-Ku, Tokyo.

Netherlands ((070) 350 4215, Konninginnegracht 102, The Hague.
New Zealand — No representation: apply to the Australian consulate.
Sweden ((08) 218 300, Birger Jarlsgatan 37, 2tr 11145, Stockholm.
Uganda ((041) 231 861, 60 Kira Road, Box 5220, Kampala.
United Arab Emirates ((02) 828 022, Box 3854, Abu Dhabi.
United Kingdom ((0171) 636 2371, 45 Portland Place, London W1N 4AS.
United States — Embassy ((202) 387 6101, 2249 R Street NW, Washington, DC 20008; Consulate ((212) 421 4740, 866 United Nations Plaza, Room 486, New York, NY 10017.

TOURS

There is an abundance of tour operators in Kenya, offering a variety of packages. They range from elegant private safaris that claim to recreate *Out of Africa* to camping trips that are more realistically Africa at the turn of the century. Available also are tours for specific interests such as ornithology, gorillas (involves traveling to Zaire or Uganda), and photography. The most abundant are the minibus tours that race you, at six to nine persons per vehicle, along the rattling, potholed dirt tracks from one park or reserve to the next. On a private safari, which is the most expensive of the options, you can select destination, itinerary, and schedule. However, once these details are established, it can be difficult to change them, particularly during the December to February high season, as the safari operator has to reserve hotels, guides, and other logistics. Many private safari operators have their own tented camps and gourmet cooks, and some have access to private game refuges.

Organizing a private safari requires a good rapport between the traveler and operator. And not a little money: expect to spend anything from US$300 to US$1,000 per head, per day. If you take this alternative, try to contact the operator *directly*, to minimize misunderstandings and to get a sense of his or her viewpoint and methods of operation. Discuss your wishes and the particulars involved. Since you'll be investing a sizable amount of money in your trip, take time to ensure it will meet your expectations. Allow several months for correspondence, and don't hesitate to use the telephone, although the Internet provides an increasingly useful source of up-to-date information and fast, cheap communications. Read up on the various sections in this book to decide what areas of Kenya interest you the most.

Among top safari operators are **Cheli & Peacock Ltd.** ((02) 748307/27 FAX (0154) 22553 or (02) 740721 E-MAIL chelipeacock @attmail.com WEB SITE www.chelipeacock .

Of this category, the most reliable are: **Abercrombie & Kent** ((02) 334955 FAX (02) 228700, Box 59749, Nairobi; and **United Touring Company (UTC)** ((02) 331960, Box 42196, Nairobi.

Among younger, more adventurous, and more impecunious travelers, camping safaris are justifiably the most popular. In recent years, with the boom in wandering the outback, a number of new camping safari groups have sprung up like desert roses after the rain, some departing the scene with equal rapidity.

com, Box 39806, Nairobi; **Abercrombie and Kent** ((02) 334955 FAX (02) 228700, Box 59749, Nairobi; **Rafiki Africa Ltd.** ((02) 884238 FAX (02) 710310 E-MAIL safarico@arcc.or.ke WEB SITE kilimanjaro.com/safaris/rafiki, Box 76400, Nairobi.

These companies will provide comfortable, private safaris with knowledgeable guides for groups of any number of people according to their own special requirements.

The bulk of Kenya's tour operators fall into the category of minibus tours. They usually leave Nairobi on regular schedules and offer neither flexibility nor personalized service. Travelers are transported rapidly from park to park with remarkable efficiency and speed, often at very reasonable prices.

For US$35 to US$80 per person per day, depending on the size of group and destination, these operators provide transportation, meals, tents, camp beds, and game drives or walking tours. Usually you are expected to bring your own sleeping bag, although even that can be provided at an extra cost.

Because these groups often take you into inhospitable wilderness, it's wise to rely on someone with experience and reputation. Consistently praised by their clientele are **Gametrackers Ltd.** ((02) 338927 FAX (02) 330903, Box 62042, Nairobi; and **Safari Camp Services** ((02) 228936 FAX (02) 212160, Box 44801, Nairobi.

ABOVE: Champagne breakfast alfresco after a balloon trip.

A range of even cheaper companies direct-sell their safaris on the streets of Nairobi. Three that have been around for a few years at least include **Savuka** ((02) 225108 FAX (02) 215 016, Fourth Floor, Pan-Africa Building, Kenyatta Avenue, Box 20433, Nairobi; **Kenia** ((02) 444572 FAX (02) 217671 WEB SITE www.gorp.com/kenia/, Fourth Floor, Jubilee Insurance Building, Kuanda Street, Box 19730, Nairobi; and **Come to Africa Safaris** ((02) 213186 FAX (02) 216263, Third Floor, Rehema House, Standard Street, Box 8969, Nairobi. But these are just the most established of a rather risky end of the industry. Providing the safari experience at about US$50 a day they don't venture far from the beaten trail, nor offer much in the way of backup, service or information, but for many young travelers they offer the only affordable way to meet Africa's wildlife.

TRAVEL AGENTS

If you're going on your own, you may want to make reservations ahead of time. **Let's Go Travel** ((02) 340331 FAX (02) 336890 E-MAIL info@letsgosafari.com, Box 60342, Nairobi, will do this for you and answer most questions you may have about road and travel condition. In all our wanderings through Kenya, Let's Go Travel has consistently received the highest marks of approbation from its clientele. Efficient and informative without being pushy, they provide useful help to all classes of traveler.

TRANSPORTATION

BUS

Buses of all sizes and shapes, and communal taxis or *matatus* go virtually everywhere in Kenya, except through most national parks and reserves. Prices are minimal, depending on owner and operator, but are usually between 2 KSh to 3 KSh per kilometer. They are always crowded and drivers are more concerned with speed than safety. Schedules are often erratic; drivers will rarely leave without an overfull load. Nonetheless, they will get you to your destination, and can run into some exciting adventures along the way.

TAXIS

In Nairobi and Mombasa, there are taxi services at reasonable prices. The cabs have no meters so always ask the price to your destination before getting in. Bargain or ask a different driver if you think the price too steep.

The minimum tarif is generally 200 KSh: fares from Nairobi city center to the National Museum should be about 300 KSh; and to the International Airport, 800 KSh should be enough but most drivers demand — and usually get — 1,000 KSh.

CAR RENTALS

It's possible to rent both two- and four-wheel drive vehicles in Nairobi and Mombasa; occasionally it's possible also to rent four-wheel drives (with or without drivers) at some hotels and lodges.

If you plan to drive only during the dry season and avoid the Northern Frontier District, Mount Elgon, Tsavo East, Lamu, and all the other areas off the main tourist circuit, you may be able to get by with a two-wheel drive car. However heavy-duty tires are almost essential for occasional potholes in the best roads and the collapsing surfaces of the worst.

To ensure full freedom of travel, and to get into the backcountry (or to get practically *anywhere* during or after the rains), choose a four-wheel drive. Many of the roads in Kenya are so bad in the rainy season even a helicopter could get stuck in them. Still, Kenya's roads are better than those of any other sub-Saharan African country except South Africa.

There are special problems with renting cars in Kenya. First is cost. Bad roads are part of the reason why car rental is expensive, and this factor also means checking over the car for mechanical soundness is very important before driving off on an ambitious safari. There are also traps for the unwary in the small print. First is that cheap rates hide expensive charges per kilometer, often starting to click up your

Buses and *matatus* are Kenya's major form of transportation.

bill from the moment you edge out of the parking space. Rates rarely include CDW (Collision Damage Waiver), TP (Theft Protection) or tax at 17%. Even experienced travelers can be caught by insurance excess: some companies charge clients up to US$10,000 in the case of any accident, and that is when they've paid the CDW excess. Our best recommendation, in terms of vehicle reliability, price, and overall helpfulness, is **Central Rent-a-Car** ((02) 222888 FAX (02) 339666, Standard Street, Box 4939, Nairobi, while other reputable operators — with offices in Nairobi and Mombasa — include **Avis** ((02) 334317 FAX (02) 215421, Box 49795, Nairobi and **Hertz** ((02) 214456 FAX (02) 216871, Box 42196, Nairobi. Central has more than competitive rates on both two- and four-wheel drive vehicles, and their cars are clean, well-maintained, and reliable.

The second question is: what type of vehicle? The best four-wheel drive is probably a Landrover, followed closely by Mitsubishi Pajero and Toyota Landcruiser. Slightly cheaper — to buy or rent — is the Isuzu Trooper. We chose it after test-driving a number of similar vehicles and found we liked it most: it was comfortable yet rugged, roomy and solid but economical on gas. Due to its longer wheelbase, its ride is much smoother than the shorter Suzuki Sierra, which seemed also potentially hazardous and top-heavy. As experienced four-wheel drivers, we know the importance of freewheeling hubs which can be disengaged when two-wheel traction is insufficient.

If there are only two of you, you can try the four-seat model of the Suzuki Sierra (they make a two-seat version with a back bench — this seems quite unstable on the road). The ride of the Sierra is a lot bouncier than the Trooper's, which becomes more and more important as you log more kilometers. If you're not going far, the Sierra may be fine. A compromise would be the Diahatzu Feroza, rather bigger and heavier than the Suzuki but still economical to rent: try Avis.

In any case, no matter what vehicle you choose, be sure it has sufficient seatbelts for each person traveling. Accidents are common in Kenya, and hospitals sometimes far away.

TRAINS

The Mombasa-Uganda Railway, now Kenya Railways, provides nightly service between Mombasa and Nairobi, and Nairobi and Kisumu. The night trip to or from Mombasa to Nairobi is particularly recommended. With a private compartment and an excellent railroad meal, it feels like a bit of the old Orient Express, or the still-marvelous trip on the Trans-Siberian Railway from Moscow to Vladivostok.

To reserve a seat on the train, you generally must make arrangements at the train station in either Nairobi, Mombasa, or Kisumu, where you may be told no first-class tickets are available. If so, buy a second-class one and visit a nearby travel agency, where they may be able to upgrade your ticket to first class for a nominal fee. If this arrangement strikes you as peculiar, try going to a travel agency first. A word of caution: the travel agency may send you to the train station.…

RULES OF THE ROAD

1. DON'T DRIVE ALONE. If you intend to take the Grand Safari, be sure to travel with at least one other person in your car. Several tourists who've rented cars recently for solitary wandering in Kenya have turned up dead.

2. DON'T DRIVE AT NIGHT. Kenyan roads are narrow, often in poor condition, and can be singularly lacking in guard rails, center lines, and other safeguards. Some of the vehicles coming the other way may be without lights or in dreadful mechanical shape ("Brakes? What brakes?"); large trucks often break down (particularly on hills) and are not infrequently left on the road in the dark with no hazard lights or other indication (the normal breakdown alert is to spread branches along the roadside).

3. DON'T GET OUT OF YOUR VEHICLE IN THE PARKS AND RESERVES unless it's allowed at the specific place where you are. Lions have attacked tourists, but buffalo, hippos, crocodiles, and even elephants are more dangerous. Alternatively, take advantage of the many wonderful places where it's safe to walk around. If you have any doubt, check with rangers, lodge personnel, or local folk.

4. DON'T CAMP JUST ANYWHERE. Many of the parks and reserves have reliable campsites at minimal cost, and the rangers can keep you up-to-date on the best places. But camping at non-designated areas can lead to trouble, both from people and animals. Particularly in the Northern Frontier District, be careful where you camp.

5. NEVER LEAVE THINGS IN YOUR TENT, particularly food. Lock them in your car. Baboons will tear a tent apart for a box of cookies; elephants will crush it for a cabbage; as friendly and honest as the Kenyans are, there are still a few who'll rip you off (particularly on the coast or in the cities). Crime in rural areas is minimal but in the cities stay alert: crime rates are approaching American levels.

6. IF YOU'RE A WOMAN, you can expect few male hassles, but keep alert. We've met single women hitching the Northern Frontier who've had nothing but fun, and lots of women driving (two to a car). But, especially in Nairobi and on the coast, take no chances.

7. IF YOU BREAK DOWN in the middle of nowhere, or run into any other kind of trouble, you'll probably be overwhelmed with help. Kenyans are unusually kind and sympathetic, and have a national ethic of peace and assisting others. Their tribal philosophies, often summarized as "African socialism," in most cases require treating a stranger almost as family. But follow your instincts — if somebody makes you uptight, act accordingly. Breaking down at night in any major city represents real danger. Try to avoid any such situation.

USING A TENT

The choice of the right tent is essential. As mentioned before, it should be roomy enough, and closed securely at the bottom and doors, with reliable mosquito screens.

You can rent tents and some camping equipment from **Atul's** ((02) 228064 FAX (02) 225935, Biashara Street, Box 43202, Nairobi.

WHEN TO GO

Being on the equator, the Kenya "season" is anytime, with the winter months (December through February) and the school holidays (July and August) the busiest. During these times, it's advisable to make arrangements ahead of time for safaris and coastal accommodations.

During the rainy seasons (April to June, October to early December), you can frequently get reduced rates on hotels, but many safari outfitters do not operate then due to impassable roads. The animals are still there, the arid regions a little more green than usual, the dangers of sunstroke and sunburn somewhat reduced, and the ocean as refreshing

as ever. Personally, we find off-season travel more relaxing. Accommodations are easier to find and the staff have more time to spend with you individually explaining the countryside and its attractions. May is probably the exception: many hotels and lodges close for refurbishment and roads during rainy seasons are even more dreadful than usual.

WHAT TO WEAR

Year-round, you will need to bring lightweight comfortable clothing, preferable wash-and-wear. Dress is casual throughout the country. For footwear, again the key is comfort. Canvas or running shoes are ideal, and only the more adventurous travelers, those attempting the peaks of Mounts Kenya or Elgon, or those taking a camel safari or a walking tour of the parks or reserves, will need hiking boots. Locally-made boots and shoes are good and inexpensive, but it's better to come with broken-in, supple shoes.

Checking the "Lunatic Line" in Tsavo.

Sandals are only suitable for town and beach wear, and not suitable for walking in the bush.

Whether your plans include an overnight in the mountain lodges or not, bring a warm sweater and light waterproof jacket. A good combination is a polar fleece pullover and a windbreaker or K-way. In the bush, long pants are preferable to shorts, and shirts with long sleeves that can be rolled down to protect you against the sun and insects are recommended. Your clothes will get covered with the ever-present red dust of Kenya, so make sure they are all washable. Laundry is done almost every night in safari camps and lodges, or you can wash it out yourself and it's usually dry by morning. Of course, don't forget a swimsuit!

WHAT TO BRING

If you have made arrangements for a safari, your outfitter will provide you with a list of things to bring. Follow their advice, as they are professionals with years of experience in making Kenya vacations comfortable. Don't forget to pack a flashlight, spare batteries, and binoculars. Sunscreen and a hat are necessities for everyone. You may want to wait and buy your hat in Nairobi, where there is a wide choice, and if time permits you can get an entire safari outfit made-to-measure.

PHOTOGRAPHY

Since the hunting ban in 1977, most legal "shooting" of wildlife has been done with cameras. Print film is readily available throughout the country, especially in Nairobi, but slide film isn't. Processing can be quick but the quality variable.

A 35-mm camera, with a telephoto lens of at least 300 mm is ideal, and films of varying speeds are recommended: 400 ISO for dusk, sunrise, and dense vegetation; 64 and 200 ISO for midday on the savanna, and 1,000 ISO or higher for night shooting in lodges like The Ark and Treetops (see THE ABERDARES, page 154). If you are using a APS (advanced photo system) camera, be warned that film supply and film processing may not be readily available in some places.

But don't weigh yourself down with a lot of bulky and new equipment. If photography will be a major part of your Kenyan vacation, ask the advice of a professional at your local camera store. Then decide which combination of camera, lenses, and film fits your style of shooting best. It might be better to use familiar equipment even if it's a fixed lens or compact camera, than to waste precious time trying to operate an unfamiliar camera. The animals won't wait for you to change lenses and focus. You will miss not only the shot, but also the enjoyment of observing the animals.

On the other hand, a lion or giraffe who seems close at hand will end up shrunken and distant in a normal 50-mm SLR or compact camera slide or print — so if you have the means and a bit of experience, a telephoto lens (at least 200 mm) is a real advantage. The most important thing, however, is to have fun: if you're too hung up on getting a picture of whatever strange beast stands before you, you'll miss the opportunity of seeing him (or her) in a relaxed, enjoyable fashion.

Be sure to keep your film as cool and dry as possible; never expose film canisters or camera to prolonged heat or direct sunlight, as on the dashboard or rear ledge of your car. The best time to take pictures is early morning or late afternoon — the light's best and the animals more abundant. Always pay attention to your light meter reading. If your subject's in the shade, get your reading from him, not from a sunlit area.

Always ask before you take pictures of anyone. Some are afraid of cameras; there is a widespread feeling in Kenya that being photographed robs one of soul or a future life — and perhaps they're right! Others are willing to take the chance for a posing fee. Always agree on the fee before you shoot. Usually, a few shillings will do, but occasionally you'll encounter someone, typically a Maasai, who'll demand outrageous fees. Negotiate or walk away.

ANIMAL WATCHING

For the wildlife observer, a pair of binoculars and the Collins *A Field Guide to the Natural Parks of East Africa*, *A Field Guide to the Birds of East Africa*, and *A Field Guide to the Butter-*

flies of Africa all by J. A. Williams are essential. At all the parks and reserves, wardens are more than happy to explain what species you can expect to see, where and when to find them, and the "rules of the game."

In general, the "rules of the game" are speed limits of 30 kph (19 mph), confinement to vehicles except in specifically designated areas, and, of course, no shooting except with a camera. Travel after dark and before dawn (6:30 PM to 6 AM) is strictly forbidden and enforced. There may be variations from one park or reserve to another, so it's best to check

other valuables may well be listed in your passport so it can be checked off when you depart.

The import of fruit, plants, seeds, or animals is prohibited. Your dog or cat may accompany you, for which you must submit a health certificate to the same office as for your visa to obtain an entry permit. However, dogs are not allowed in national parks and reserves.

If you have any ivory articles (jewelry), make sure you can prove in which country the ivory was purchased by means of a re-

the regulations each time you pay an entrance fee. No matter how cute, friendly, docile, cuddly, or harmless animals may seem, they are all wild and are potentially dangerous. Young animals invariably have parents who can kill you for disturbing their offspring.

CUSTOMS ALLOWANCES

Travelers over 16 years of age may import duty-free 200 cigarettes or 50 cigars of 250 grams (eight and three quarter ounces) of tobacco, one liter of alcoholic beverage and a quarter-liter of perfume. Personal effects, including unexposed film, cameras, and accessories, may be temporarily imported duty-free, but laptop computers and

ceipt, or else it will probably be confiscated. Avoid any hassles and leave ivory objects at home.

Firearms and ammunition require a permit issued by the Central Firearms Bureau, Box 30263, Nairobi. In view of the recent crackdown on poachers, these permits are difficult to acquire.

Export of ivory, rhinoceros horns, game skins, game trophies, and all other anatomical relics of wildlife is strictly forbidden, as is export of live animals, birds, and reptiles except by licensed dealers.

Shoe shine boys in Nairobi.

CURRENCY

The unit of currency is the Kenya shilling (KSh), divided into 100 cents. Notes are in denominations of 500, 200, 100, 50, 20, and 10 KSh. The blue 20 KSh note is sometimes called a "Kenya pound" and is a useful tip for services both small and large. Coins are 5, 10, and 50 cents and 1 KSh. US$1 is worth 60 KSh at the time of going to press.

Any amount of foreign cash or travelers checks may be brought into the country, but the full amount must be noted on a currency declaration form on arrival because you cannot export more foreign currency than you brought. Your foreign currency should be exchanged only at an authorized dealer — banks or licensed exchange facilities at hotels. Your currency declaration form may be required to change unused Kenyan currency back when you leave. Even with proof, this can be difficult to do. Plan ahead and use most of your shillings before departure. The small black market demand for hard currencies doesn't justify the risks of changing money on the streets. Banks are open from 9 AM to 3 PM, Monday to Friday and most from 9 AM to 11 AM on Saturdays. All transactions in banks, whether empty or full, seem to take 20 minutes and involve plenty of forms. Licensed exchange bureaus and hotel cashiers generally stay open longer, give a marginally worse exchange rate, but act quickly. ATM machines give the best rate of all with cash advances on Visa and Mastercard if you have a PIN number. They are found in all major towns but sometimes run out of money or break down: look for branches of Barclays. Machines are sited throughout Nairobi as well as Nyeri, Meru, Kitale, Nakuru, Diani, Kisumu, Kisii, Embu, Thika, Nyahururu, Kakamega, Naivasha, Limuru, Mombasa, Bungoma, Nanyuki, Eldoret, Kericho and Malindi. Travelers checks are useful for carrying substantial amounts in relative safety.

Banks at the Mombasa and Nairobi airports are supposedly open 24 hours.

Young elephants usually stay with their mothers for seven to 10 years or more, females often forming a two- or three-generational matriarchal clan.

Your Visa, American Express, and Diners Club cards will be accepted by many hotels and shops. Credit cards can also be used for cash advances within the limits of your credit card contract.

Many national parks, hotels and services catering to the tourist market quote their prices in United States dollars. Those that quote in Kenya shillings are looking more to a resident market and are invariably cheaper. The service is more offhand and the feel more African. Those quoting in dollars are slicker and sometimes lack the

out. If you're susceptible to stomach upsets, it's wise to treat all water supplies, and to ask before drinking the water in lodges and hotels. Peel your fresh fruits and vegetables, or wash them with potable water. Avoid uncooked foods from sidewalk stands. Even with these precautions, you may get a mild attack of dysentery or the "runs." If you are struck with a serious case of dysentery, the best medication is available in pharmacies under the name of Gabboral, which has replaced Flagyl, but most doctors think that wiping out

Kenyan feeling. We have kept this distinction by quoting prices as the service providers quote them.

HEALTH

It's strongly recommended that you talk with your own physician when planning a Kenyan vacation. At present, the only certificate required is for yellow fever for travelers from endemic areas. However it is recommended that visitors take anti-malaria medication for ten days before, during, and for three weeks after their trips.

It is generally stated that tapwater in Nairobi and other cities is potable, although our experience does not always bear this

the stomach's natural gut flora with high doses of antibiotic is the worst thing to do with an upset stomach. Personally I find the old Caribbean favorite of a teaspoonful of Angostura Bitters mixed with five times as much Coca-Cola invariably settles things down. There are numerous pharmacies with well-qualified staffs to help in the event you do become ill, but they may not have familiar brand names. If you use medication regularly, bring it with you.

OPPOSITE: The world's fastest land animal, the cheetah, runs down his prey in short sprints.
ABOVE: Until recently Kenya's anti-poaching unit was equipped with ancient Enfield rifles.

Nairobi and Mombasa have modern, well-equipped hospitals, capable of dealing with any emergency, but even smaller towns usually have reliable clinics. Health insurance is strongly recommended: get it before you leave home and make sure it covers you for travel in Africa. If you're planning to spend a lot of time in the bush, it would be wise to make sure evacuation by Flying Doctor is covered.

AIDS is in Kenya, is heterosexual and widespread. Avoid blood transfusions if possible; if you need an injection, make sure it's a new needle, or bring your own, and in the event of needing a blood transfusion, try to contact your embassy: often they have lists of healthy donors.

Make sure your tetanus vaccination is up to date to avoid this inoculation in the event of a bad cut. In general, avoid any inoculation. Do not swim in fresh water. As in most of Africa, still fresh water is infested with bilharzia, a parasite that enters the body and causes a general deterioration in health. Treatment is usually effective and fairly straightforward but there can be complications. Note that flowing water is generally clear of bilharzia, so whitewater rafting is fine, but still water is dangerous, ruling out swimming in Lake Victoria. Take local advice before taking any quick dip.

Remember that Kenya straddles the equator and the sun is directly overhead for longer periods of time than most of us are used to. Sunstroke and sunburn are dangers. If you're sensitive to the sun, consult your doctor or pharmacist about the best sunscreen to use. Even if you have never burned, use sunscreen during your first days of exposure and avoid prolonged exposure during the middle of the day. For children, a T-shirt while swimming is always a good precaution. This is highly recommended also when snorkeling, because time passes quickly and reflection from the ocean surface magnifies the effect of the sun.

Bring a sun hat or invest in one on arrival, and use it. Sunstroke's nausea and dizziness can ruin several days of your visit.

The altitude at Nairobi and the Highlands can also cause discomfort to some travelers in the form of drowsiness and passing dizziness. Such mild symptoms usually pass in a couple of days once you've become acclimated to the thinner air, but travelers attempting to climb Kenya's mountains should take the risk seriously and take time to acclimatize. Altitude sickness can kill. Headaches or trouble breathing mean it is time to lose altitude fast, even if someone has to carry you, until the symptoms disappear. Then spend a day acclimatizing before continuing your climb.

COMMUNICATIONS

POST

Mail service from Kenya is good, taking three to six days to reach Europe or the United States. And the stamps are beautiful! Postcards cost 33 KSh to Europe and 42 KSh to North America. Main post offices in Nairobi are open from 8 AM to 6 PM, others from 8:30 AM to noon, and 2 PM to 4 PM; some upcountry post offices are open only in the morning. More expensive hotels and lodges sell stamps for postcards and letters.

TELEPHONES

With the Kenya telephone service, you can direct-dial domestic and international numbers but in general the telephone system is expensive and inefficient. Telephones are provided in some hotel rooms, but be aware that hotels can and do add hefty surcharges to an already large bill. Often charges are made — and high ones — for calls even if they don't go through, so even unsuccessful attempts to send faxes can result in an expensive bill. Thus, it is more practical to make your international calls from the post office.

TELEGRAMS, TELEX AND INTERNET

Telegrams can be sent by phone through the operator. Telex and fax facilities are available at many post offices or private businesses, providing direct dialing to most major international cities on a 24-hour basis. Internet bureaus are just starting to become available in the business centers of the larger hotels and small offices in Nairobi: costs are usually 100 KSh to 150 KSh to send or receive emails. The Internet in Kenya is so new and exciting to the locals it is always a pleasure to use their facilities. In Nairobi, the Intercontinental on City Hall Way offers Internet access from its business center, while Unique Communications on Koinange Street, opposite Marshalls Peugeot, has a phone-fax-cybernet café bureau on the first floor. In Westlands, Internet access is available from the business center of the Mayfair Court Hotel on Parklands Road or in the Westlands Mall, where there's a friendly bureau called La Belle Maison, surprisingly located in the corner of a furniture shop in the basement. New outlets are opening all the time, but access speeds are slow so don't expect recreational surfing.

ELECTRICITY

Electricity is 220–240 volt, 50 cycles, using three-prong plugs as found in the United Kingdom. Some of these are round-pin, and it is useful to carry adapters for many kinds of outlets; they can be purchased at most hardware stores in Nairobi. The larger hotels will have adapters, as well as separate outlets, for 110–120 volt razors. In the parks and reserves, electricity is generally provided by generators, which operate only during specific hours each day. In coming to Kenya, the key is to simplify. Don't rely on electrical appliances like curling irons, hairdryers, etc.

TIME

Local time is three hours ahead of Greenwich Mean Time; Kenya does not have daylight savings time. During winter, it is two hours ahead of continental Europe (only one hour during summer) and eight hours ahead of New York (seven hours in summer).

SECURITY

Opportunistic crime is increasingly common, especially in the cities. In rural areas the temptation can overwhelm — and penalties are harsh if they are caught. It is unfair to tempt — often very poor — locals by leaving out goods they could not possibly buy. Never leave cameras, handbags, and other valuables unattended or visible in your locked vehicle, even in the bush. Most hotels and lodges have safes where you can leave your valuables. Make use of these services rather than leaving money, passports, or traveler's checks in your room. In Nairobi, Mombasa and other cities, don't wear jewelry on the streets or walk after dark — especially past bush areas where muggers can lurk. Strangely, street crime is worst on weekends, when you're dealing with students: they're much brighter than the down-and-outs (known as "Parking Boys") whose ambitions usually end with snatching necklaces and watches. In taxis, don't rest your arm on the window if you're wearing an expensive watch: it may well be torn free. Car-jacking is an increasing problem in Nairobi, but only in certain suburbs. Stick to the main roads and try to avoid driving at night and you should be safe.

SWAHILI

Swahili is the *lingua franca* of Kenya, and English the language of business and commerce. English is taught in schools all over the country, so you can usually make yourself understood everywhere.

Nonetheless, whenever you travel, it is always appreciated when you attempt the native language. Swahili is one of the easiest languages to learn. The pronunciation is entirely phonetic, and the grammar need not worry a beginner. For the vowels, A is pronounced as in *father*, E as the *a* in *day*, I as the *e* in *see*, O as in *go*, and U as the *o* in *do*. The consonants are generally pronounced as in English. If people ask — and they will — if you speak Swahili, *"kidogo sana"* — meaning very little — is less abrupt than "no."

SOME BASIC SWAHILI EXPRESSIONS
AND VOCABULARY

Politeness and Introductions
hello   *jambo*
good-bye   *kwaheri*
good morning   *habari ya asubuhi*
good afternoon   *habari ya mehana*
good evening   *habari ya jioni*
how are you?   *habari?*

I am well (I am very well) *mzui (mzui sana)*
please *tafadhali*
thank you (very much) *asante (sana)*
what is your name? *jina lako mani*
my name is… *jina langu ni…*
excuse me *samahani*
I am sorry *pole*
yes *ndiyo*
no *hapana*

Places and People

hotel (or occasionally just foodhut) *hoteli*
room *chumba*
bed *kitanda*
police *polici*
hospital *hospitali*
street *barabara*
airport *uwanja wa ndege*
river *mto*
mountain *mulima*
where? *wapi?*
where is the hotel? *hoteli iko wapi?*
what? *nini?*
Mr. *bwana*
Mrs. *bibi*
Miss *bi*
who? *nani?*
I, me *mimi*
you (singular) *wewe*
he, she *yeye*
we *sisi*
you (plural) *ninyi*
they *wao*
man *mwamamume*
woman *mwanamke*
child *mtoto*
father *baba*
mother *mama*
son *mwana*
daughter *binti*
husband *mume*
wife *mke*
friend *rafiki*

Food

food *chakula*
coffee *kahawa*
tea *chai*
beer *tembo* or *pombe*; *Tusker*, the name of the leading brand, is usually good enough.
ice *barafu*

meat *nyama*
chicken *kuku*
fish *samaki*
bread *mkate*
rice *wali*
butter *siagi*
sugar *sukari*
vegetables *mbogo*
fruit *matunda*
water *maji*
milk *mazima*
salt *chumvi*
pepper *pilipili*
dessert *tamutamu*
beans and maize *githeri*
peas, vegetables and maize *irio*
steamed bananas *matoke*
flour and eggs *mkate mayui*
cooked green vegetables *mrere*
roasted cassava with chilies and lemon *muhogo ya kuchoma*
roasted meat *nyama ya kuchoma*
boiled spinach *sukuma wiki*
maize meal *ugali*
Kenyan sandwich *samosa*

Counting

half *nusu*
one *moja*
two *mbili*
three *tatu*
four *ine*
five *tano*
six *sita*
seven *saba*
eight *nane*
nine *tisa*
ten *kumi*
eleven *kumi na moja*
twelve *kumi na mbili*
twenty *ishirini*
twenty-one *ishirini na moja*
thirty *thelathini*
forty *arobaini*
fifty *hamsini*
sixty *sitini*
seventy *sabani*
eighty *themanini*
ninety *tisini*
hundred *mia*
one hundred *mia moja*
two hundred *mia mbili*
thousand *elfu*

Adjectives and Adverbs

good *mzuri*
bad *mbaya*
cold *baridi*
hot *moto*
now *sasa*
quickly *haraka*
slowly *pole-pole*
big *kubwa*
small *kidogo*
more, another *ingine*
much, more *mwingi*
that *yule*
this *huyu*
sweet *tamu*
cheap *rahisi*
expensive *ghali*

Directions

right *kulia*
left *kushoto*
turn (right) *geuka (kulia)*
go straight *enda moja kwa moja*
where are you going? *una kwenda wapi?*

Time

now *sasa*
today *leo*
tomorrow *kesho*
yesterday *yana*
morning *asubuhi*
afternoon *alarsiri*
evening *jioni*
nighttime *usiku*
daytime *mehana*
day *siku*
week *wiki*
month *mwezi*
year *mwaka*
Sunday *Jumapili*
Monday *Jamatatu*
Tuesday *Jumanne*
Wednesday *Jumatano*
Thursday *Alhamisi*
Friday *I jumaa*
Saturday *Jumamosi*

Shopping

money *fedha*
cent *senti*
how much? *ngapi?*
how much does this cost? *inagharimu pesa ngapi?*

that's expensive *wawezakupunguz*
shop *duka*
cigarettes *sigareti*
newspaper *gazeti*
clothes *nguo*
shoes *viatu*

KENYA INTERNET SITES

Kato — Kenya Association of Tour Operators http://www.gorp.com/kato/
Frogs of Kakamega http://www.calacademy.org/research/herpetology/frogs/kfrogs.html
Kenya Meteorology Society http://www.meteo.go.ke/
Kenya Web: comprehensive and good but with far too many graphics http://www.kenyaweb.com/
The best bit of the site is their newspaper review with roundups of the stories that Kenyans are reading about, as they happen: http://www.kenyaweb.com/news/newspapers.html
Links: Good set of links to Kenyan sites http://www.sas.upenn.edu/African_Studies/Country_Specific/Kenya.html
Africaonline's effort is excellent. http://www.africaonline.co.ke/AfricaOnline/covertravel.html
Introduce kids to Kenya by logging on to http://www.africaonline.co.ke/AfricaOnline/coverkids.html
Diving Links: Interested in diving? Check out the links http://www.3routes.com/scuba/africa/keny/index.html
Melinda Atwood's account of moving to Kenya. Published only online. http://www.bwanazulia.com/book/index.html
Special interest tours for women but not straying far from the beaten trail with this American organization. http://www.mm.com/womanpower/
East African Wildlife Society http://www.cheetah.demon.nl/eawls.html.

Recommended Reading

Non-Fiction

ADAMSON, JOY. *The Peoples of Kenya*. New York: Harcourt, Brace, & World, Inc., 1976. (Also by Joy Adamson: *Born Free, Living Free*, and *Queen of Sheba*.)

BARTLETT, JEN AND DES. *Nature's Paradise*. Boston: Houghton Mifflin, Co., 1967.

COOK, DAVID, and DAVID RUBADIRI, ed. *Poems from East Africa*. Nairobi: Heinemann Kenya Ltd., 1971.

DINESEN, ISAK. *Out of Africa* (various editions).

GRZIMEK, BERNHARD. *Among Animals of Africa*. Translated by J. Maxwell Brownjohn. New York: Stein and Day, 1970. (Also by Grzimek, *Rhinos Belong to Everybody* and *No Room for Wild Animals*.)

HALTENORTH, THEODOR and HELMUT DILLER. *A Field Guide to the Mammals of Africa*. London: Collins, 1986.

HILLABY, JOHN. *Journey to the Jade Sea*. New York: Simon and Schuster, 1965.

KRAPF, J. LEWIS. 1869 (Ludwig Krapf). *Travels, Researches and Missionary Labours, during an eighteen years' residence in Eastern Africa*. London: Cass, 1968.

LUMLEY, FREDERICK, ed. *Kenya — An Anthology, the Land, its Art, and its People*. London: Studio Vista, 1976.

MARNHAM, PATRICK. *Fantastic Invasion*. Middlesex: Penguin Books Ltd., 1987.

MEREDITH, MARTIN. *The First Dance of Freedom — Black Africa in the Post-war Era*. New York: Harper and Row, 1984.

MILLER, CHARLES. *The Lunatic Express*. London: Elm Tree Books, 1971.

MOSS, CYNTHIA. *Elephant Memories*. London: Elm Tree Books, 1988.

NAIPAUL, SHIVA. *North of South*. London, New York: Penguin Books, 1980.

NGUGI WA THIONG'O. *Detained — A Writer's Prison Diary*. Nairobi: Heinemann Kenya Ltd., 1981.

THOMPSON, JOSEPH. *Through Maasailand*. London: Royal Geographical Society, 1885.

WILLIAMS, JOHN. *A Field Guide to the Birds of East Africa*. London: Collins, 1983.

WILLIAMS, JOHN. *A Field Guide to the Butterflies of Africa*. London: Collins, 1981.

WILLIAMS, JOHN. *A Field Guide to the National Parks of East Africa*. London: Collins, 1983.

Fiction

BEST, NICHOLAS. *Happy Valley: The Story of the English in Kenya*. London: Secher and Warburg, 1979.

HUXLEY, ELSPETH. *The Flame Trees of Thika*. New York: William Morrow and Company, 1959 (Also by Elspeth Huxley: *The Mottled Lizard*).

MOOREHEAD, ALAN. *No Room in the Ark*. Middlesex: Penguin Books Ltd., 1962.

MUDE DAE MUDE. *The Hills are Falling*. Nairobi: Transafrica, 1979.

MWANGI, MEJA. *The Cockroach Dance*. Nairobi: Longman Kenya, 1979.

NGUGI WA THIONG'O. *A Grain of Wheat*. Nairobi: Heinemann Kenya Ltd., 1968.

NGUGI WA THIONG'O. *Petals of Blood*. Nairobi: Heinemann Kenya Ltd., 1977

OGOT, GRACE. *The Promised Land*. Nairobi: East African Publishing House, 1966.

PIERCE, JACQUELINE. *Leopard in a Cage*. Nairobi: East African Publishing House, 1976.

WATENE, KENNETH. *Sunset on the Manyatta*. Nairobi: East African Publishing House, 1974.

Quick Reference A–Z Guide to Places and Topics of Interest with Listed Accommodation, Restaurants and Useful Telephone Numbers

Photography credits

STORM STANLEY PHOTO AGENCY — Karl Ammann: pages 17 *top*, 18, 66 *bottom*, 89, 190.
Allan Binks: pages 17 *bottom*, 33, 35, 37, 40 *top*, 40 *right*, 43, 46, 51, 53, 57, 58 *bottom*, 67 *both*, 71, 75, 77, 161, 177, 203, 205, 263, 280 *right*, 281, 304. **Rick Edwards:** ARPS: pages 22, 31, 34, 47, 66 *top*, 80, 139–141, 157, 208, 247. **Nicolas Granier:** pages 41 *left*, 69 *top*, 156, 252. **Douglas Granier:** pages 16, 25. **Thierry Greener:** pages 63 *top*, 107, 133, 138. **Frants Harmann:** pages 12 *bottom*, 26, 65, 73 *bottom*, 117, 124, 253, 262. **Storm Stanley:** pages 38, 40 *bottom*, 44, 54, 61, 63 *bottom*, 69 *bottom*, 160, 248, 282, **Ian Vincent:** pages 49, 241. **Duncan Willetts:** Camerapix: pages 13, 21, 39, 59, 68, 70, 73 *top*, 79, 131, 153, 240, 276.

JACK BARKER: Pages 19, 27, 28 *top and bottom*, 29 *top and bottom*, 58 *top*, 60, 260, 261 *left*, 269.
NIK WHEELER: Front and back covers, pages 4, 5 *left and right*, 7 *left*, 81, 91, 115, 155, 169, 171, 174–175, 180, 209, 220–221, 222, 225, 232–233, 233, 242–243, 277, 283, 284, 291, 301.
PEGGY AND MICHAEL BOND: Pages 3, 92–93, 179, 186–187. All other pictures:
CAMERAPIX — Mohamed Amin and Duncan Willetts.